A
Resurrection
Gospel

The Glorious Simplicity of
Biblical Eschatology

by

Joseph R. Holder

Sovereign Grace Publications
Shallotte, North Carolina

A RESURRECTION GOSPEL: The Glorious Simplicity of Biblical Eschatology
Published by Sovereign Grace Publications
Post Office Box 1150
Shallotte, NC 28459
www.sovgrace.net
sovgracepublications@gmail.com

ISBN 978-1-929635-27-6

Scripture quotations are from the *King James Version (1900)*, unless otherwise noted.

Printed in the United States of America

CONTENTS

1. Jesus and the Resurrection   1
2. Loving the Truth vs Loving a Lie   7
3. A Living Redeemer & a Literal Resurrection   11
4. Gathered to His People   17
5. Not Left   23
6. The Death of Death in Jesus' Victory   29
7. The Death of Death in Jesus' Death   35
8. "Looking" Alters Living   41
9. Resurrection: Intimately Personal   47
10. Object Lesson on the Resurrection: Lazarus   53
11. Jesus Refutes the Sadducees   59
12. Between Now and Then?   67
13. Jesus' Resurrection: Literal and Physical   73
14. Jesus' Resurrection: Literal and Physical (*Continued*)   79
15. A General Resurrection, Not a Multi-Staged Event   85
16. An Instructive Analogy: A Shepherd at Work   91
17. How Long?   97
18. God's Effectual Drawing   103
19. Resurrection: God's Example for His Glory   109
20. Resurrection and the Lord's Return   117
21. Lazarus Alive!   123
22. He is Alive. What Now?   129
23. A Strange Prophet—A True Prophecy   135
24. God's Answer for a Troubled Heart   143
25. How Many and How Glorious?   149
26. The Foundation of Christian Joy   155
27. What Lies Ahead?   161
28. He Shall Return as He Went   167
29. Jesus' Resurrection: Foundation of Truth & Conduct   173
30. Jesus' Resurrection: Fulfillment of Prophecy   181
31. Jesus' Resurrection: Begotten from Death   187
32. Our Resurrection: For Just & Unjust   197
33. Bodily Resurrection: Jesus First   203
34. Resurrection Ethics   209

35. Heirs with Christ   215

36. The "Creature" & His Hope   221

37. Saved by Hope: Focusing on Unseen Reality   227

38. All Things Work Together for Good?   235

39. Till He Come   243

40. *First of All* – The Gospel's Top Priority   249

41. Beliefs Have Consequences   255

42. He Arose! He Lives! Literally.   263

43. Redemptions Final Scene   269

44. Baptized for Whom?   277

45. What Jeopardy?   283

46. Christian Ethics Based on the Resurrection   289

47. How are the Dead Raised Up?   295

48. Only One "It"   301

Index of Scriptures Examined   307

1
Jesus and the Resurrection

Then certain philosophers of the Epicureans, and of the Stoicks, encountered him. And some said, What will this babbler say? other some, He seemeth to be a setter forth of strange gods: because he preached unto them Jesus, and the resurrection. (Acts 17:18)

The Book of Acts is the only inspired history available of the New Testament Church. All subsequent histories, though they may contain invaluable information regarding the existence and faith of a people, are of human origin. Most historians, however sincere and well-informed, write with a purpose. Their objective is seldom merely to report objective facts; they intend to prove something or to make some point through their writing. Acts bears strong internal evidence of being an authentic historical work. If someone contrived to write a history of the first generations of Christianity to convince unbelievers, he would carefully exaggerate the accomplishments of the apostles, and he would as carefully omit any record of their problems and failures. Not so our Book of Acts. It faithfully records the events that occurred, including major problems and failures. Acts 17, as one example, from the human perspective of convincing unbelievers and converting them to faith in Christ, records a failure on Paul's part. Instead of believing his preaching, they ridiculed and rejected him and his message. Only a few people believed his preaching; Verse 34 makes this point and names two of the people who believed. Paul's preaching on Mars Hill was no Day of Pentecost event for Paul.

And when they heard of the resurrection of the dead, some mocked: and others said, We will hear thee again of this matter. (Acts 17:32)

Jesus prepared the disciples for the reality that they would face. They should not expect everyone who heard them preach "Jesus, and the resurrection" to believe. Everyone didn't believe Jesus when He preached His own gospel "...as never man spake like this man" (John 7:46). The Parable of the Sower and the Seed describes three classes of people who hear the gospel who fail to bring forth fruit. We shouldn't expect a one-in-four reaction to our preaching, but the parable fully reminds us that all who hear will not believe. And all four groups do hear (John 8:43; Matthew 13:16).

Consider the people to whom Paul preached on this occasion. He observed a city (Athens) "...wholly given to idolatry" (Acts 17:16b). Specifically, among those who heard him preach on this occasion were philosophers of two diverse worldviews, Epicureans and Stoics (Acts 17:18). Epicureans held that pleasure as they defined pleasure in terms of "...tranquility and freedom from pain, disquieting passions, and fears, especially the fear of death,"[1] was the chief goal of man. They believed that the gods took no interest in any human activity. The stoics were arrogant in their attitudes toward others. They emphasized self-sufficiency and rationalism. They were also fatalistic. Perhaps other schools of Greek philosophy were present, but Luke records these.

If Paul had subscribed to the "seeker sensitive" politically correct gospel of our world, he would have carefully avoided any reference to Jesus' sufferings and crucifixion, death, and resurrection. Such ideas to the philosophical Greek mind were utter foolishness (1 Corinthians 1:22-25). But notice the emphasis that Luke gives to Paul's preaching, as witnessed in our study passage. "...he preached unto them Jesus, and the resurrection." Notice also verse 32, quoted above.

Paul obviously had more than a passing knowledge of Greek philosophy. In his sermon that day, he quoted from two ancient Greek philosopher-poets, Epimenides (*ca* 600 BC) and Aratus (*ca* 315-240 BC). Despite the original writing of Epimenides being written to Zeus, "Ode to Zeus," Paul interpreted the words to refer to

---

[1] Tom Constable, *Tom Constable's Expository Notes on the Bible* (Galaxie Software, 2003), Ac 17:18.

God, the one and only true God, "For we are also his offspring" (Acts 17:28b).

If Paul knew so much about Greek philosophy, why did he ignore those beliefs and so steadfastly preach a message that they would likely ridicule? The answer is simple. He was faithfully dedicated to preaching the truth of the gospel, not a politically correct message. If we omit "Jesus, and the resurrection," we have no gospel to preach! (1 Corinthians 15:13-19)

Most Bible historians agree that John wrote his contributions to the New Testament much later than any of the other writers of New Testament letters, perhaps in the last decade of the first century. His "General epistles," 1st, 2nd, and 3rd John, all fiercely expose and refute docetic Gnosticism, a first century philosophy that apparently attempted to slip into the church and transform the content of the gospel. It denied that Jesus had a physical body. Instead, it taught that he merely had a "Spirit body" that could give the appearance of a real body. Other Gnostic beliefs of the age taught that Jesus was a mere man, albeit the best of men. They taught that the "Christ," deity, descended onto Jesus the man at His baptism, and that it departed from Him prior to His crucifixion. If John witnessed these heinous errors attempting to compromise the gospel, we can fully appreciate why he wrote these letters as he did. In fact, the presence of these errors also serves to explain why John's gospel is so different from the other three. Gnosticism was never the true message of the gospel; it was a false gospel from the beginning.

Any supposed gospel that denies that Jesus was fully God and fully man fails the most crucial test of gospel truth and earns John's emphatic charge of being "antichrist."

And every spirit that confesseth not that Jesus Christ is come in the flesh is not of God: and this is that spirit of antichrist, whereof ye have heard that it should come; and even now already is it in the world. (1 John 4:3)

For many deceivers are entered into the world, who confess not that Jesus Christ is come in the flesh. This is a deceiver and an antichrist. (2 John 1:7)

No one can deny the literal fact that Jesus "…is come in the flesh" and make a credible claim to believe the truth of the gospel. And, given Paul's theme when preaching to Greek philosophers, "Jesus, and the resurrection," no one can deny His literal, bodily resurrection and lay any credible claim to New Testament truth.

Paul obviously understood the Greek philosophy that ridiculed his preaching quite well, but he refused to compromise the central truth of the gospel for anyone or any group of people.

For the Jews require a sign, and the Greeks seek after wisdom: But we preach Christ crucified, unto the Jews a stumblingblock, and unto the Greeks foolishness; But unto them which are called, both Jews and Greeks, Christ the power of God, and the wisdom of God. (1 Corinthians 1:22-24)

We see more of these two cultures in the New Testament than any other with the possible exception of Roman culture. Paul fully knew that neither of these cultures held any friendship to his gospel. Jews who demanded a sign for everything supernatural would stumble at his preaching. Greeks who prided themselves in their self-proclaimed wisdom would ridicule—call foolish—the idea of a man claiming to be God, but who was so weak that his countrymen arrested and tortured Him before demanding the Romans to crucify Him. The idea that He would literally and bodily arise from the dead was for them beyond foolish. They, no less than the resurrection denying Sadducees, failed to respect the two things that affirm the truth of resurrection: 1) the Scriptures, and 2) the power of God (Matthew 22:23-32; Mark 12:18-27; Luke 20:27-38).

Whether it be a first century Sadducee, a first century Greek student of philosophy, or a twenty-first century critic, those who reject the Bible doctrine of the resurrection fail to respect these same two witnesses to a literal bodily resurrection, both of Jesus' body and of "...the just and the unjust" (Acts 24:15). Jesus confronted and refuted the Sadducees, first century Jews who denied life after death and a literal bodily resurrection. He gave us ample reason to believe this truth, amazing as it is to our minds. He in no way taught this truth in a way that might have suggested that He intended any kind of symbolic meaning to His words.

All the New Testament Scriptures that teach the doctrine of the resurrection, both Jesus' and ours, are framed in literal form to demand a literal fulfillment of the Lord's promise. Jesus didn't come in a "Spirit body" that had no literal flesh and blood. He came in a real, literal human body. He ate, drank, slept, and even became tired in that real human body. And, yes, when the Jews arrested Him that night, they inflicted real torture onto His human body. And the next day when they demanded that the Romans crucify Him, it was a literal human body that they crucified. It was a real human body that Joseph and Nicodemus prepared and buried in Joseph's empty tomb. And, praise be to God, it was a real human body that came back to life and walked out of that tomb three days later. And, some forty days later, it was that real, literal human body that ascended into heaven in a cloud of glory (Acts 1:9-11). It was a real Jesus who appeared to Paul (Acts 9) and to John (Revelation 1).

Apart from Jesus' personal, literal, bodily resurrection, we have no hope of being raised (1 Corinthians 15:12-19). For Paul, inspired by the Holy Spirit, if Jesus didn't literally arise, everything that we believe about God, Jesus, and the gospel becomes an empty fantasy. That is just how central this truth is to the gospel that we believe.

If the doctrine of "Jesus, and the resurrection" is so central to the New Testament gospel, how did saints in the Old Testament view this doctrine? Did they embrace a hope of its truth for them? Do other New Testament writers share Paul's emphasis on this doctrine? In coming chapters, God willing, we shall explore this theme.

2
Loving the Truth vs. Loving a Lie

Remember ye not, that, when I was yet with you, I told you these things?
And now ye know what withholdeth that he might be revealed in his time.
For the mystery of iniquity doth already work: only he who now letteth will
let, until he be taken out of the way. And then shall that Wicked be
revealed, whom the Lord shall consume with the spirit of his mouth, and
shall destroy with the brightness of his coming: Even him, whose coming is
after the working of Satan with all power and signs and lying wonders,
And with all deceivableness of unrighteousness in them that perish;
because they received not the love of the truth, that they might be saved.
And for this cause God shall send them strong delusion, that they should
believe a lie: That they all might be damned who believed not the truth, but
had pleasure in unrighteousness. (2 Thessalonians 2:5–12)

While this late arriving deceiver is not Satan, he is obviously tightly aligned with Satan. His "…coming is after the working of Satan." One of Satan's most successful tactics is to convince naïve Christians that he looks pretty much like the comic character, dressed in a solid red, skin-tight suit, complete with horns and a long tail with a sharp point on the end, spear in hand. And these naïve souls will think in terms of that image and convince themselves that they've never seen that fellow in their entire lifetime, so why be upset or bothered by him. Perhaps he doesn't really exist at all since we've never seen him in this form.

…with all power and signs and lying wonders. If you choose to ignore the first two marks of this beast, power and signs, do not miss the third, *"lying wonders."* Satan and all of his efforts and designs can only succeed if he convinces people to believe his lie, and he can throw in some powerful "wonders" along the way to lead the unsuspecting to believe that his ideas are actually coming from God, not from him. (Proverbs 14:12; 16:18, 25; 1 Timothy 3:6) Through

several of the plagues that Moses brought upon Egypt, the Egyptian magicians duplicated the plague and thereby tried to dismiss Moses as merely another phony magician, not a prophet of the one true and living God. Our culture champions the rugged individualistic spirit in man. Wisely understood and applied, this attitude can be good. However, it also contains a fatal flaw. Satan and his minions love to cultivate this attitude to the point of disconnect. Make a single believer think that he is a better Christian, knows more about the Bible than anyone else knows, is stronger in his faith than anyone else. Give him a mega-dose of the true "Rambo" spirit. And just like the fictional movie character, Rambo, this unsuspecting believer will isolate himself from other believers and go his own way in his often very sincere desire to oppose evil and to fight for what he rather blindly perceives to be true, right, and good. Once isolated, little does this poor soul know that Satan can pick him off at will, most often by further cultivating the ego that drives his pride-filled "I'm better, stronger, and know more than any other believer" attitude. How much does Scripture warn us against pride? Do you think the repeated and powerful warnings in Scripture might suggest that this attitude is one of Satan's favorite strategies, one that has proven incredibly successful for him over untold centuries? Why abandon a successful strategy? When believers leave Hollywood and its version of Rambo, they face the shattering reality; isolate yourself from other believers, and you are an easy target for Satan. Unlike the Hollywood Rambo, you will not end up as a hero, but as a crushed and disillusioned casualty.

...*with all deceivableness of unrighteousness in them that perish.* If something that is unrighteous is deceitful, how might the deceiver himself paint it in the minds of the deceived? Would he not follow precisely the pattern that he so successfully used in the Garden of Eden? Convince the naïve believer that it is actually a very righteous thing. So twist the most heinous of sins as to lead people to think of it in terms of how good it is. How many examples of this very tactic could we name from our present culture? The thought is honestly frightening.

...in them that perish. Scripture often uses "perish" to refer to the people who shall spend eternity separated from God, but all appearances of the word do not convey this meaning. For example, the first prodigal son spoke these words from his "Pigpen, "I perish with hunger." (Luke 15:17) Was this man actually saying that he was entering eternal hell with hunger? No, he was no doubt sufficiently hungry to feel intense discomfort. In this context, it is likely that "them that perish" does refer to people who are outside the family and grace of God. The description of their future that follows distinctly points in that direction.

...because they received not the love of the truth, that they might be saved. Take note. These words do not shift the blame from these wicked and willingly deceived people to God. Paul identifies a clear problem in the character of these people that prompts them to despise truth, not seek it or love it. They prefer Satan's lie to God's truth. Nothing in this context implies that God is responsible for the condition that Paul describes in these people. They did something, or did not do something, that they were capable of doing, and their failure, not God's arbitrary and diabolical action, prompted their present state of judgment.

And for this cause God shall send them strong delusion, that they should believe a lie. This is not the language of a cosmic puppeteer who is busy pulling the strings and manipulating wicked people for his supposed glory or greater good. It is the Bible language of divine and righteous judgment against sin and sinners. Compare this passage with Romans 1 where two times Paul says that "God gave them up...." God only "gave them up" to a lower pit of depravity after they knowingly, consciously, and willingly chose to ignore God and His righteous warnings in their present condition. In our study passage, God doesn't first send strong delusion to deceive these people. He sends the strong delusion only after they have refused the knowledge they had and chose sin over righteousness, Satan's lie over God's truth, and the man of sin over God. Giving them up is an act of judgment against committed sins, not a cosmic setup, put in motion to orchestrate their future conduct or state.

That they all might be damned who believed not the truth, but had pleasure in unrighteousness. The problem with these people is not simply that they did not believe the truth. The greater condemnation is well deserved because they "...had pleasure in unrighteousness." This description points to a state of total moral and spiritual depravity. Give one of these people two options, one righteous and the other sin. Every time he will not only choose the sin, but he will choose it with great pleasure. This is his choice, not God's manipulation.

The state of believing and of preferring a lie to the truth is a rather intimate trait of Satan and those who are wholly under his control.

Why do ye not understand my speech? even because ye cannot hear my word. Ye are of your father the devil, and the lusts of your father ye will do. He was a murderer from the beginning, and abode not in the truth, because there is no truth in him. When he speaketh a lie, he speaketh of his own: for he is a liar, and the father of it. And because I tell you the truth, ye believe me not. (John 8:43-45)

3
A Living Redeemer & a
Literal Resurrection

Oh that my words were now written! Oh that they were printed in a book!
That they were graven with an iron pen and lead in the rock for ever! For I
know that my redeemer liveth, And that he shall stand at the latter day
upon the earth: And though after my skin worms destroy this body, Yet in
my flesh shall I see God: Whom I shall see for myself, And mine eyes shall
behold, and not another; Though my reins be consumed within me. (Job
19:23–27)

We tend to take common blessings for granted, and likely our,
as I believe, inspired and divinely preserved Bible may stand
near the head of the list of neglected, taken-for-granted blessings in
our lives. Think. What if you faced the Job-ordeal without a Bible
to help you understand it? Job lived in such a time. Notice his
longing.

> *Oh that my words were now written! Oh that they were printed in*
> *a book! That they were graven with an iron pen and lead In the*
> *rock for ever!*

If the Job-experience had been written in Job's time, he could
have read it and found far more reliable comfort than any of his
"Miserable comforter" friends gave him. I fear that many children
of grace spend too little time with their Bible because they read on
its pages things that they prefer not to confront and deal with in their
lives. They live in a fairy tale world of fantasy. Pretend the Bible
doesn't condemn your ideas and conduct, and you can continue to
practice those things with the self-deluded idea that you are doing no
wrong. I suggest that their own conscience, along with the energy
that they invest in their delusion, speaks volumes to the fact that

they know more about the wrongness of what they do than they are willing to confess. God refuses to join anyone's private delusions. What He teaches as right and wrong, sin and righteousness, is fixed *and revealed in Scripture.* He measures our thoughts and actions by that fixed principle of His righteousness, and He commands us, not to retire to our private fantasy, but to repent and live in His world in active fellowship with Him and His commandments. And should we choose to claim ignorance, Scripture and His law, written in our hearts, witness against our claim.

Despite no Bible, no preacher, and perhaps no prophet, Job reflects specific knowledge that we often think can only come through exposure to the gospel. No doubt, the gospel is loaded with rich graces and knowledge of God and of His truth. However, we should never discount the power of God to teach His children many principles of His grace abounding to us. (Titus 2:12-14; spend some time in this passage. Learn what Paul specifically names as things that the grace of God teaches us. Paul didn't write that the grace of God plus a preacher teach these things, did he? We should never discount or diminish God's power in grace to teach His beloved children of His goodness and grace) The contemporary notion that no one can possibly have such knowledge apart from a preacher does great damage to Scripture's testimony regarding God's grace teaching, including what it teaches, and God's Law written in the hearts and minds of those who experience the new birth at His loving and sovereign hand.

For I know that my redeemer liveth, And that he shall stand at the latter day upon the earth....

Through Moses' Law, we learn of the debt that sin imposes and of God's rich provision for redemption. However, if Job lived at a time prior to the Law or in a culture that did not know that Law, how did he come to know about a Redeemer and his need for redemption by that Redeemer?

For that matter, how did Job comprehend that this world as we know it would come to an end? Thus, we see his reference to the "…latter day upon the earth."

And though after my skin worms destroy this body, yet in my flesh shall I see God.

I can't recall how many times I have heard preachers misquote this verse. Job did not write about "…skin worms destroying this body." He wrote about worms who went "…after my skin." The details are closer to reality than we would like, but the specific details leave every reader without excuse. No one can deny that Job was writing about his literal body and what would happen to it at his death, but he also wrote about what he expected to happen to that same body at the resurrection. Thus, when Job writes, "***Yet in my flesh*** shall I see God," no honest reader can possibly deny that Job expected his literal, physical body to be raised, that he would see God in and with that literal physical body.

Whom I shall see for myself, and mine eyes shall behold, and not another.

Job makes two major points in this brief comment. He viewed the resurrection as something incredibly personal, "Whom I shall see for myself." It was not some general event, but an event that he would personally experience. Further, Job expected that his eyes, not mythical spiritual eyes, or fabricated eyes from another body, supposedly given to him after death, but "…mine eyes" would see Him. It would not be other eyes that see Him, but Job's eyes.

Though my reins be consumed within me.

As he lived in this world, Job would die. His emotions and conscious thoughts in the here and now would cease. But Job would not cease, consciously or factually. Job would live on and, after the resurrection he would see his Redeemer with his own eyes.

Who is this Redeemer of whom Job writes? In other sections of Job, we see Him in similar supportive, intercessory roles.

Neither is there any daysman betwixt us, That might lay his hand upon us both. (Job 9:33)

Job longs for the daysman, the intercessor, the umpire, who is uniquely capable of touching Job's case and God's, so that He might serve as an effective and worthy mediator. In the ninth chapter, Job doesn't see Him, but in the nineteenth chapter, he does see Him and rejoice in Him.

Also now, behold, my witness is in heaven, And my record is on high. (Job 16:19)

Not only does Job come to see his "daysman," his umpire, but now he understands that this holy One is also his personal witness, One who intervenes in heaven and bears record on Job's behalf before God.

Who is this Redeemer of whom Job writes? The word "redeemer" in the Old Testament is a rich, instructive word.

The primary meaning of this root is to do the part of a kinsman and thus to redeem his kin from difficulty or danger. The root is used in four basic situations covering the things a good and true man would do for his kinsman. First, it is used in the Pentateuchal legislation to refer to the repurchase of a field which was sold in time of need (Lev 25:25ff.), or the freeing of an Israelite slave who sold himself in time of poverty (Lev 25:48ff.). Such purchase and restitution was the duty of the next of kin. Secondly, but associated with this usage was the "redemption" of property or non-sacrificial animals dedicated to the Lord, or the redemption of the firstborn of unclean animals (Lev 27:11ff.). The idea was that a man could give an equivalent to the Lord in exchange, but the redemption price was to be a bit extra to avoid dishonest exchanges. In these cases, the redeemer was not a relative, but the owner of the property. Thirdly, the root is used to refer to the next of kin who is the "avenger of blood" (RSV "revenger") for a murdered man. Finally, there is the very common usage prominent in the Psalms and prophets that God is Israel's Redeemer who will stand up for his people and vindicate them. There may be a hint of the Father's near kinship or ownership in the use of this word. A redemption price is not usually cited, though the idea of judgment on Israel's oppressors as a ransom is included in Isa 43:1–3. God, as it were, redeems his sons from a bondage worse than slavery. [1]

We need not stretch the point or the word to understand that Job's grasp of his Redeemer's identity is not at all different from other Old Testament references to the ultimate Redeemer, or to the New Testament reference to Jesus as our Redeemer.

As the Mosaic redeemer was to be a near kinsman who stepped up to help his near relative who was indebted beyond his ability to pay, so Job and other Biblical saints understand that God has provided them a "Near kinsman Redeemer" who loves them above all others, and who, in loving, familial care, shall step up to pay their debt and thereby deliver them from the consequences of non-payment that they faced apart from His intervention. Further, as in the Mosaic code, this Redeemer is a near kinsman. He is a close relative! In fact, He is your older Brother in grace.

Is it too much a stretch to think that Job or other Old Testament saints entertained such clear thoughts of their Redeemer? I say no. Peter agrees (1 Peter 1:9-12). Not only did they possess the Spirit of God dwelling in them, but "...the "...Spirit of Christ" was in them and signifying, teaching, witnessing to them of Him and of His coming work. A basic provision of God's "new covenant" stipulates, "...I will put my law in their inward parts, and write it in their hearts...And they shall teach no more every man his neighbour, and every man his brother, saying, Know the LORD: for they shall all know me, from the least of them unto the greatest of them, saith the LORD: for I will forgive their iniquity, and I will remember their sin

---

[1] R. Laird Harris, "300 לאג‎," ed. R. Laird Harris, Gleason L. Archer Jr., and Bruce K. Waltke, *Theological Wordbook of the Old Testament* (Chicago: Moody Press, 1999), 144.

no more" (Jeremiah 31:33-34). In Scripture, we should never overlook; God is the primary teacher of His people (Isaiah 54:3; John 6:45).

4
Gathered to his People

Then Abraham gave up the ghost, and died in a good old age, an old man, and full of years; and was gathered to his people. And his sons Isaac and Ishmael buried him in the cave of Machpelah, in the field of Ephron the son of Zohar the Hittite, which is before Mamre. (Genesis 25:8-9)

In Scripture, God repeatedly and simply reveals the important truths for us to learn and to know with conviction. Few topics receive such careful and detailed treatment in Scripture as the experience of death and what lies beyond it. We find ample Biblical evidence of this teaching in many powerful New Testament passages, but we also find similar evidence in the Old Testament.

"...and was gathered to his people." The verses quoted document several separate, distinct events.

1. Abraham gave up the ghost. He died.
2. He "...died in a good old age, an old man, and full of years." He lived a long, full life. His life was not cut short. Some commentaries attribute a sense of completion and well-being to the term "full of years." The suggestion is that Abraham did not die with a heavy heart full of regrets or unfinished business.
3. He was "...gathered to his people." This event is listed as distinct from Abraham's death or his burial in the cave with Sarah sometime after his death.
4. His sons buried him in the cave of Machpelah where he had earlier buried Sarah.

We find three additional passages in the Old Testament that use similar language. Genesis 15:15 contains God's comforting reminder to Abraham that his life would end as it did.

And thou shalt go to thy fathers in peace; thou shalt be buried in a good old age. (Genesis 15:15)

Notice the similar term, "...shalt go to thy fathers in peace." What a rich comfort, to live our life with the Lord's personal word of promise and grace to us that, in the end at death, we shall surely go to our fathers in peace. Genesis 35:29 repeats the same expression regarding Isaac, "...was gathered unto his people." And in the next generation, we read the same description of Jacob's death, Genesis 49:33.

There are times when most believers must deal with trials in life that leave them feeling alone and isolated, even from their natural family. Who are our real "people"?

Dimly, vaguely, veiledly, but unmistakably, as it seems to me, is here expressed at least a premonition and feeling after the thought of an immortal self in Abraham that was not there in what "his sons Isaac, Ishmael laid in the cave at Macpelah," but was somewhere else and was for ever. That is the first thing hinted at here — the continuance of the personal being after death. Is there anything more? I think there is. Now, remember, Abraham's whole life was shaped by that commandment, "Get thee out from thy father's house, and from thy kindred, and from thy country." He never dwelt with his kindred; all his days he was a pilgrim and sojourner, a stranger in a strange land. But now he is gathered to his people. The life of isolation is over, the true social life is begun. He is no longer separated from those around him, or flung amidst those that are uncongenial to him. "He is gathered to his people"; he dwells with his own tribe; he is at home; he is in the city.[1]

As this and any number of similar commentary quotes reminds us of Scripture's truth, the Lord has prepared us for a special place beyond this world, and He has designed that special place for us.

---

[1] *Biblical Illustrator.* Copied from SwordSearcher, electronic Bible study.

While Scripture does on occasion give general descriptions of that glory world, we never see it clearly. For that matter, I suggest that human language and intellect cannot fully grasp what God has in store for His children in that place. Hebrews 11:9-10, 13-16 punctuates the life of Old Testament people of faith with a reminder of this world that lies still ahead of us. In those verses, as well as in the implications of the term "...gathered unto *his people*," we sense a distinct awareness of other people, indeed, our people, as an essential part of that world to come.

For he looked for a city which hath foundations, whose builder and maker is God. (Hebrews 11:10)

By general chronological estimates, Abraham lived around two thousand years before Christ and the first century AD. Yet the text speaks of Abraham's pursuit as if it were today, "...which hath foundations." The present tense verb reminds us that the city that Abraham sought was more than a place in the land that God promised to give to his heirs in coming generations. The city existed at the time that Paul wrote the Book of Hebrews. It is a city that has foundations. It is stable and permanent. That city exists today no less than in Abraham's or in Paul's day. We look for it and long for it just as Abraham and other Old Testament patriarchs of faith did.

These all died in faith, not having received the promises, but having seen them afar off, and were persuaded of them, and embraced them, and confessed that they were strangers and pilgrims on the earth. For they that say such things declare plainly that they seek a country. And truly, if they had been mindful of that country from whence they came out, they might have had opportunity to have returned. But now they desire a better country, that is, an heavenly: wherefore God is not ashamed to be called their God: for he hath prepared for them a city. (Hebrews 11:13-16)

In these verses, the "Pilgrim" mindset expands to include all of those Old Testament saints. Despite living in different ages and cultures, they shared one common trait. By their lifestyle and attitude toward life, they acknowledged that this world is not their home. Accordingly, God reminds us that He fully knows this mindset and encourages it. He is "...not ashamed to be called their God: for he hath prepared for them a city." If heaven and its certain joys were not true, the pilgrim mindset of believers would be a cruel fantasy. If God has actually prepared such a city for His people, and if that city exceeds our expectations, we conclude with Paul that God in no way leaves us to fall into discouragement or doubt. "...he hath prepared for them a city." Indeed, as you read these words, think—think with faith and joyful expectation—"He has prepared *for me* a city."

The concept of a "city" conveys the idea of a place fully populated. Abraham the sojourner—along with you and me in our sojourning mindset—expected something that God affirms is real. A city involves a whole lifestyle. It flavors every aspect of the life of those who live in it. It involves some degree of social interaction with other citizens of the city. We may easily fall into idolatry regarding these points, so we should embrace them with respect for Scripture's descriptions and limits.

Let me give you an example. In my youth, I was friends with an older man, a godly, faithful man who was raised by his aunt. This aunt was a loving and kind woman who taught her nephew by godly example. With good reason, the man loved her dearly. On one occasion after the aunt's death, my friend was talking with me and others about his believe that earthly relationships would be precisely carried over into heaven. In tears of love at the memory of his aunt, the man spoke words that shocked me, "If I thought that I'd get to heaven and not know her, I wouldn't want to be there." Clearly, the man had no Biblical support for his idea, especially his greater priority toward his loving aunt than for the Lord Himself. Terms such as those we here study make the point sufficiently plain that heaven shall be for us a "Social" place, a place where there is some element of knowledge and interaction with other redeemed people.

Abraham was gathered to "...his people." God has prepared "...for them a city." However, Scripture equally reminds us that heaven shall be, first and foremost, a place where God is fully glorified and praised for loving grace and sure redemption. (Revelation 5:9-14; 1 Corinthians 15:28)

There is a glaring problem with my friend's view of heaven. If we know people in heaven as we knew them during our lives, we must accept that we shall not only know those loving, godly saints in our lives, but we shall know those "Unpleasant" people from our lives who may also be there. We can't have the idea one way and ignore the other. I believe Scripture clearly teaches personal individuality of each person in heaven, but in a new glorified relationship, not a perpetuation of our flawed earth relationships.

Abraham's "people" were not buried in the cave at Machpelah with Sarah. Our study verses set Abraham's burial apart as a later event distinct from his being "...gathered to his people." Immediately upon his death, Abraham was "...gathered to his people." However, sometime later Abraham's sons took his body to the cave and buried him with Sarah. From Scripture's testimony, at that time, only Abraham and Sarah were buried in the cave. Yet prior to Abraham's burial, we have Scripture's testimony. Abraham was "...gathered to his people." The man who had lived more years as a pilgrim than as a native at home was no longer a pilgrim. He was home at last. His days of wandering and looking for a city with foundations were ended.

Into the harbor of heav'n now we glide,
We're homeward bound, homeward bound;
Softly we drift on its bright silver tide,
We're homeward bound, homeward bound;
Glory to God! All our sorrows are o'er,
We stand secure on the glorified shore;
Glory to God, we will shout ever more,
We're home at last, home at last.
Author Unknown

5
Not Left

For thou wilt not leave my soul in hell; neither wilt thou suffer thine Holy
One to see corruption. (Psalm 16:10)

We read many Old Testament lessons that give us comfort in their reading and meditation, but, in the case of this verse, we have the added benefit that New Testament writers cited the verse and gave us the Lord's interpretation of it, so we need not question or ponder its meaning.

Sadly, we read more commentary on the word "hell" that grows out of paganism than out of Scripture. How many commentaries are content to imply that the word refers to some mystical underworld place where the spirits of those who die reside till the Second Coming, an idea that New Testament Scripture consistently rejects and refutes? Twice the New Testament specifically refers to the place where our spirits go at death as "paradise," not hell (Luke 23:43; in Jesus' own words, and 2 Corinthians 12:4). Occasionally Scripture uses the word to refer to the grave where our bodies lie till the Second Coming, the interpretation given to our study verse by two inspired New Testament writers. We read non-inspired books and hang on every word, often buying their private interpretations, but, in this case, we have two inspired "commentaries" in the persons of Peter and Paul. I'll take their interpretation over any uninspired notion. Let's examine the lesson with the value of New Testament explanations and see what it really means.

First, take note of the verse. David, the inspired writer, rejoices that his soul would not remain in this place. He adds a prophetic note that his "Holy One," two words that our wise King James translators chose to capitalize, an indication that the words form a name or title, most likely of God Himself in the Person of the Lord

Jesus Christ. His joy is not that he would avoid this place, but that he would not be left there long enough to decay.

What interpretation do New Testament writers, inspired writers, give us to this verse? In Acts 2:22-36, a major segment of Peter's Day of Pentecost sermon, Peter anchors his point regarding Jesus' literal, physical, bodily resurrection on this passage. Rather than citing one verse, Peter quotes several verses from Psalm 16. His primary point relates to verse 10, our study verse.

How did Peter interpret this lesson? We cannot read these verses and reach any conclusion other than that they are a prophecy of Jesus' literal bodily resurrection. While David could indeed rejoice that his body would not remain in the grave, as Peter reasons, his body did remain in the grave long enough to see corruption, decay. But Jesus' body only remained in the grave for three days, and then He arose. His body that was crucified, buried, and arose, alive and was forever then immune from death and its associated corruption. Peter reasons that this passage was intended as a prophecy of Jesus' bodily resurrection. He reminds his audience that David's tomb, housing his body, was known by those present, but the object of David's prophecy, the Lord Jesus Christ, arose from His grave, from death, three days after his death and burial, seeing no corruption and thus fulfilling the prophecy.

While the New Testament uses the word "soul" in a fairly specific way, the word is used in the Old Testament in a more generic sense. Often in the Old Testament, the word is used for a living person, or that person's body. The Hebrew word translated "soul" in our study passage is defined as follows:

> *nephesh* (659b); from an unused word; a soul, living being, life, self, person, desire, passion, appetite, emotion:—any(1), anyone(2), anyone*(1), appetite(7), being(1), beings(3), body(1), breath(1), corpse(2), creature(6), creatures(3), dead(1), dead person(2), deadly(1), death(1), defenseless*(1), desire(12), desire*(2), discontented*(1), endure*(1), feelings(1), fierce*(2), greedy*(1), heart(5), heart's(2), herself(12), Himself(4), himself(19), human(1), human being(1), hunger(1), life(146),

life*(1), lifeblood*(2), lives(34), living creature(1), longing*(1), man(4), man's(1), men*(2), mind(2), Myself(3), myself(2), number(1), ones(1), others(1), ourselves(3), own(1), passion*(1), people(2), people*(1), perfume*(1), person(68), person*(1), persons(19), slave(1), some(1), soul(238), soul's(1), souls(12), strength(1), themselves(6), thirst(1), throat(2), will(1), wish(1), wishes(1), yourself(11), yourselves(13).[1]

We see the wide variation in meaning that appears in the Old Testament in this definition, including Peter's inspired explanation that this prophecy refers to Jesus' body. Actually, given Peter's inspired explanation in Acts 2, especially verses 31-36, we have no need of a definition. Peter quite clearly gave us the precise meaning intended by the Holy Spirit in his explanation. We need little or no explanation of Peter's words. They are clear.

However, New Testament testimony to this lesson adds yet another clear and consistent witness to the truth of Peter's inspired interpretation of our study passage.

Wherefore he saith also in another psalm, Thou shalt not suffer thine Holy One to see corruption. For David, after he had served his own generation by the will of God, fell on sleep, and was laid unto his fathers, and saw corruption: But he, whom God raised again, saw no corruption. (Acts 13:35-37)

In this passage, Paul adds his voice to Peter's and gives us the same precise explanation as Peter in Acts 2. Words could not more clearly identify the prophecy's reference to Jesus' literal body. David died, was buried, remained in the tomb, and his body decayed, saw corruption. Jesus was crucified, buried, and three short days later He arose, bodily, alive. His body saw no corruption. His body is not today in a tomb or otherwise dead and corrupted. He arose in that same body in which He lived, but He arose in glory, and He further accented that glory when He ascended (Acts 1:9-11).

---

[1] Robert L. Thomas, *New American Standard Hebrew-Aramaic and Greek Dictionaries* : Updated Edition (Anaheim: Foundation Publications, Inc., 1998).

That same alive, not corrupted by lingering death, body shall descend at the Second Coming to raise the bodies of His beloved children, glorifying them so that they shall be like His body, all the corruption that destroyed their physical bodies then itself destroyed by His resurrection power.

The New Testament consistently builds our own hope of resurrection on the historical, literal fact of Jesus' resurrection. If you deny His literal, bodily resurrection, you have no grounds for hoping that your own body shall ever be raised and purged from the corruption of death and the grave.

> *Now if Christ be preached that he rose from the dead, how say some among you that there is no resurrection of the dead? But if there be no resurrection of the dead, then is Christ not risen: And if Christ be not risen, then is our preaching vain, and your faith is also vain. Yea, and we are found false witnesses of God; because we have testified of God that he raised up Christ: whom he raised not up, if so be that the dead rise not. For if the dead rise not, then is not Christ raised: And if Christ be not raised, your faith is vain; ye are yet in your sins. Then they also which are fallen asleep in Christ are perished. If in this life only we have hope in Christ, we are of all men most miserable. But now is Christ risen from the dead, and become the firstfruits of them that slept. (1 Corinthians 15:12-20)*

We can't get from our frail and temporary humanity to His glorified and incorruptible immortality other than through His own resurrection.

In the opening verses to this chapter, Paul clearly defines the resurrection as referring to Jesus' literal human body. The body in which He lived during the incarnation, the body in which He suffered, was scourged, crucified, and died, is the same body in which He arose from the dead, appeared to the disciples for forty days, and then ascended bodily—but now a glorified literal body—back to the Father.

Interestingly, Scripture records the translation of two Old Testament patriarchs, Enoch and Elijah, a distinct indication of their bodies being translated directly into glory rather than experiencing death as we know it. Because Moses appeared with Jesus on the Mount of Transfiguration, and because of Jude 1:9, some Bible commentaries hold that Moses was also raised at some point after his burial by God. Was the dispute between Michael and Satan over raising Moses' body or some other event? I don't know. I know what the verse states, and its objective is not to deal with resurrection, but with God's authority, a principle by which we may claim greater authority over Satan and his minions than we might claim personally.

Notice Scripture's inspired and defined objective for Biblical predestination.

Having predestinated us unto the adoption of children by Jesus Christ to himself, according to the good pleasure of his will, To the praise of the glory of his grace, wherein he hath made us accepted in the beloved. (Ephesians 1:5-6)

For whom he did foreknow, he also did predestinate to be conformed to the image of his Son, that he might be the firstborn among many brethren. (Romans 8:29)

We should carefully distinguish Romans 8:29 the conforming into Christ's image in 2 Corinthians 3:18. In that context, our being conformed to the image of Christ, albeit distinctly by the ministry of the Holy Spirit, is contingent on our removing the veil of unbelief that first century Jews consciously used to cover their minds, consciously hiding the truth of Jesus from their minds. We must look steadfastly at Him in the mirror of gospel truth if we hope to experience the Holy Spirit's transforming power in our personal lives. This contingency of personal conduct and faith in us separates this passage from Romans 8:29 where all of the transformation is performed by God alone.

Biblical predestination is not fatalistic at all in that it does not govern what people do, but where God's elect shall arrive in the end at the Second Coming. It uniquely relates to the final outcome or destination of God's beloved and chosen family. If you do not object to being resurrected in His bodily image, you do not in fact object to predestination.

6
The Death of Death in Jesus' Victory

He will swallow up death in victory; And the Lord GOD will wipe away tears from off all faces; And the rebuke of his people shall he take away from off all the earth: For the LORD hath spoken it. (Isaiah 25:8)

Occasionally as we read Old Testament prophecies, we wonder. Is the prophecy fulfilled in a near event in the history of God's Old Testament people, or is it fulfilled in the person and work of the Lord Jesus Christ? In other prophecies, we discover that New Testament teaching answers the question for us, as with this verse.

So when this corruptible shall have put on incorruption, and this mortal shall have put on immortality, then shall be brought to pass the saying that is written, Death is swallowed up in victory. (1 Corinthians 15:54)

We live our lives, beginning to end, under the shadow of death. Young or old, it is never far from us. And, should we momentarily forget it, something happens to remind us, often vividly, of its dreadful presence. David gives voice to this point.

Yea, though I walk through the valley of the shadow of death, I will fear no evil: for thou art with me; thy rod and thy staff they comfort me. (Psalms 23:4)

The idea of death having a shadow richly instructs us. Through much of the daylight hours, the sun is close to the horizon, either in the morning or the afternoon. During these times, anything that casts a shadow makes the point of the verse. The shadow is larger than the actual image.

Often as we live, death seems ominous, far larger than its reality. Even in the face of death's shadow, David takes his comfort in the Lord, his Shepherd. "I will fear no evil." Notice the mention of both a rod and a staff. Shepherds in David's time typically carried two sticks or poles, one a large cudgel to beat down wild animals, and one the shepherd's staff with which the shepherd gently nudged sheep to stay in the fold. David finds comfort in both. He knows his Shepherd's fierce protection and His gentle grace.

David continues his point in this priceless psalm.

Surely goodness and mercy shall follow me all the days of my life: and I will dwell in the house of the LORD for ever. (Psalms 23:6)

Most of the psalm emphasizes our Shepherd's care of His sheep in the here and now; green pastures, still waters, quiet and safe places to rest. But the final verse adds to that point. David rejoices that the Lord's goodness and mercy shall follow him "…all the days of my life." The verse continues, "…and I will dwell in the house of the LORD for ever." In this point, David stretches our minds and hope beyond the days of this life. He hopes to dwell in the Lord's house, not for a long lifetime, but "for ever."

In this clause, David embraces eternity with the Lord no less than Paul embraced it in 1 Corinthians 15. When we leave Psalm 23 as an encouragement for this life only, we miss the most powerful point of the psalm. Our Lord's "Shepherding" care of His sheep transcends even death.

If we did not have Paul's inspired explanation (1 Corinthians 15:54), we might quibble over Isaiah's point that the Lord "…will wipe away tears from off all faces." We may view this thought from at least two perspectives: 1) The Lord's people weep over their sorrows through their pilgrimage, but the Lord never forgets them; He intervenes and wipes away their tears with the comforts of His loving grace; 2) At the Second Coming and resurrection, the Lord shall raise us in His image, thus eliminating any basis for tears that accompanied our steps during our time in this life.

As I ponder my life experience, witness the experience of faithful men and women, and, more importantly, as I read Scripture, I see tears in the eyes of the most devoted and godly of believers, "Serving the Lord with all humility of mind, and with many tears, and temptations, which befell me by the lying in wait of the Jews" (Acts 20:19). Our most joyful day in our pilgrimage is clouded by tears in the background. However, Scripture's consistent description of the Lord's return and raising His people from their graves leaves no ground for a single tear of grief or sorrow. By eliminating the reason for tears, the Lord in effect wipes our tears away, even before we shed them. Tears may go with us to the moment of death, but there they stop! He wipes them away, eliminates them, from that point forward forever.

"He will swallow up death in victory." How is it that the Lord swallows death? The analogy is unique; it captures our attention. The point is not that He treats death as food, but that he consumes it, destroys it—eliminates it!

The analogy adds a military flavor, "...in victory." Imagine two mortal enemies facing each other on the battlefield. Each side brings out its strongest artillery and hurls it against the opposition. Eventually one or the other side gains the upper hand and claims the victory. Isaiah reports Jesus' victory long before He came and engaged His—and our—adversary in battle.

One of—perhaps the very first—Scripture's earliest prophecies of Jesus' coming and victory appears near the beginning of Scripture.

And I will put enmity between thee and the woman, and between thy seed and her seed; it shall bruise thy head, and thou shalt bruise his heel. (Genesis 3:15)

Interesting, God spoke these words to the serpent, the arch enemy himself. By his interference in the Garden of Eden with Adam and Eve, the serpent intended opposition against God, likely hoping to utterly derail God's noble intent for them.

A study of the Hebrew word translated "good" in the first chapter of Genesis urges more than something that is merely useful. The word includes a sense of moral good. If God's intent in the natural creation was to promote His moral character, the serpent in his opposition went after God's last and greatest creation, man, likely intending thereby to bring down everything good that God intended in the creation.

While the scenario plays itself out between the woman and the serpent, and their representative "seed," the outcome of the hostilities of the ages has a certain end. As the serpent bruises the heel of the woman's "seed," the woman's seed shall bruise the serpent's head. Notice; the woman's "seed" doesn't merely go after the serpent's seed. He goes after the serpent personally, and he bruises the serpent's head. In comparison, a bruise to the heel is quite painful. Have you ever experienced plantar fasciitis? With every step, even the slightest weight on the foot is intensely painful. However, notice the contrast in the lesson. The pain of the heel is significant, but it is certainly not fatal. But the woman's seed, the Lord Jesus Christ, delivers a fatal blow to the serpent's head. Crush his head, and he dies.

This passage early on reminds us that Jesus and Satan are engaged in mortal conflict, but it also assures us that the outcome is certain. Jesus gains the final and ultimate victory. "He will swallow up death in **victory**." To "swallow up" something is to utterly consume or destroy it. Consider this New Testament passage.

> *Forasmuch then as the children are partakers of flesh and blood, he also himself likewise took part of the same; that through death he might destroy him that had the power of death, that is, the devil; And deliver them who through fear of death were all their lifetime subject to bondage.* (Hebrews 2:14-15)

No concept of a "spirit body" or phantom image can live up to this passage. Jesus came in literal flesh and blood just as fully—and literally—as you and I. And He came with a purpose, that, through dying, He mighty destroy death and the diabolical one who traffics in the power of death.

But far more to the point, He came to deliver His children who live their lives in the fear of death. Only Jesus can confront and neutralize our fear of death. And, if we respectfully consider these two verses, He delivers us from the fear of death by dying Himself, and rising from the dead. Our sole hope of resurrection rests in Him and His resurrection, a primary point that Paul makes in 1 Corinthians 15, as well as in this passage. Take away Jesus' literal, bodily resurrection, and you cannot escape your fear of death. "...because I live, ye shall live also." (John 14:19b)

If Jesus has in fact swallowed up death in victory, we might ask, at what price? The contemporary view of end times over-symbolizes various Scriptures to paint a gory, bloody image of vast numbers of children of God dying in that final battle. However, if we follow Scripture, we discover an edifying fact. Based on Revelation 19:14, the armies that follow Jesus in this final battle wear linen clothes. Linen is the wardrobe of priests in Scripture, not soldiers. Further examination of the Scriptures dealing with that final battle describes the bloodshed as coming from Jesus' enemies, not His saints. The redeemed, dressed in linen priestly clothes, are present to witness Jesus' victory. He alone engages the battle. Not only does He in the end win the battle, but He "...swallows up death in victory." The victory is decisive and complete. In fact, He alone won the battle by His own death and resurrection. The adversary is vanquished, and Jesus conquers with all of His beloved children safely sheltered in His care.

I love the words of Isaac Watts on this topic.

> His own soft hand shall wipe the tear
> From ev'ry weeping eye
> And pains and groans, and griefs and tears
> And death itself shall die.
>
> - Isaac Watts

We never experience deliverance from our fear of death apart from our Lord and His abiding—His timeless—care over His own. What comfort! We face death constantly in this life. At the Lord's return, we shall witness the death of death as we experience the final, full, and glorious deliverance that our Lord secured for us through His death, resurrection, and glorious ascension. Even so, come quickly, Lord Jesus!

7

The Death of Death in Jesus' Death

Thy dead men shall live, together with my dead body shall they arise.
Awake and sing, ye that dwell in dust: For thy dew is as the dew of herbs,
And the earth shall cast out the dead. (Isaiah 26:19)

The truth of resurrection that Isaiah surfaced in Chapter 25 he now repeats with greater personal emphasis. Not only does our Lord swallow up death in victory, but He claims that victory by the certain promise of personal, individual resurrection for each—and all—of His beloved, chosen people. While the Scriptures teach a general resurrection (Daniel 12:2; John 5:28-29; Acts 24:15), the prophet here singles out God's people for special comfort in this reminder of a personal, individual, literal bodily resurrection to come.

Thy dead men shall live. We should read this simple clause with amazement. Only God could direct a prophet to state such a profound truth so clearly and so simply. This is the way it is. This is a fact that God has promised His people from the beginning. Job put the point in the form of a question, "If a man die, shall he live again?" (Job 14:14). Job comforts himself that he will remember this truth "...all the days of my appointed time...till my change come."

Together with my dead body shall they arise. Many ancient non-Christian religions held to various beliefs that included some form of life after death, but the Judeo-Christian idea of God becoming a man, living, dying, and rising again stands alone. This sentence reads more like a New Testament quote from Jesus' mouth. We cannot isolate the Biblical doctrine of the resurrection from Jesus' resurrection. Further, we cannot accept the truth of this prophecy and hold any view that rejects Jesus' literal, physical human body, a body that lived, suffered, and died, but also a body that arose from death, witnessed His literal resurrection for forty days, and then ascended to glory. How can anyone reject Jesus' literal "incarnation," His coming in a literal, physical, human body? John warns us that those who dare to deny this truth are antichrist.

Hereby know ye the Spirit of God: Every spirit that confesseth that Jesus Christ is come in the flesh is of God: And every spirit that confesseth not that Jesus Christ is come in the flesh is not of God: and this is that spirit of antichrist, whereof ye have heard that it should come; and even now already is it in the world. Ye are of God, little children, and have overcome them: because greater is he that is in you, than he that is in the world. (1 John 4:2-4)

For many deceivers are entered into the world, who confess not that Jesus Christ is come in the flesh. This is a deceiver and an antichrist. (2 John 1:7)

According to John, "antichrist" is not a demonic personality that shall appear near the end with supernatural and sinister powers. Antichrist was a label that John, inspired by the Holy Spirit to write truth and only truth, attached to false teachers in his day who dared to deny that Jesus came and lived in a literal, physical, human body. John expands the point; anyone who embraces this errant idea at any time is no less antichrist than the people in his lifetime of whom he writes.

Together with my dead body.... As a point of precise accuracy, this passage teaches the truth of Jesus' personal, bodily resurrection, as well as our own literal, physical, bodily resurrection. This truth echoes Paul's words.

But if there be no resurrection of the dead, then is Christ not risen: And if Christ be not risen, then is our preaching vain, and your faith is also vain. Yea, and we are found false witnesses of God; because we have testified of God that he raised up Christ: whom he raised not up, if so be that the dead rise not. For if the dead rise not, then is not Christ raised: And if Christ be not raised, your faith is vain; ye are yet in your sins. (1 Corinthians 15:13-17)

When Isaiah wrote the words "...together with my dead body..." he linked our personal resurrection with Jesus' literal bodily resurrection. Take great comfort in these words. When Jesus arose from the dead and left that borrowed tomb, the event guaranteed our own resurrection so surely that the prophet associates our resurrection with that event, "together with my dead body...."

The language of this passage adds to the clarity and the certainty of a literal, physical, bodily resurrection. Words could not make the point more clearly, "together with my dead body...." If Jesus didn't have a literal body, how could He speak these prophetic words?

Sadly often, preachers and Bible teachers affirm the truth of resurrection, but fail to link that truth to the believer's life in the here and now. Scripture abounds with this truth and uses our certain literal resurrection to urge us to live today like "a child of the King."

And you, being dead in your sins and the uncircumcision of your flesh, hath he quickened together with him, having forgiven you all trespasses. (Colossians 2:13)

If ye then be risen with Christ, seek those things which are above, where Christ sitteth on the right hand of God. Set your affection on things above, not on things on the earth. For ye are dead, and your life is hid with Christ in God. (Colossians 3:1-3)

I include Colossians 2:13, for this verse links the forgiveness of our sins and our new birth with Jesus' death and resurrection, "...quickened together with him." Notice the similarity of language. Isaiah 26:19, *"Together with my dead body shall they arise."* Colossians 2:13, *"hath he quickened together with him."* If we are joined with Jesus in His death, we cannot be separated from Him in His resurrection! And that is the point made in Isaiah's words, *"...together with my dead body shall they arise."*

We cannot question that Paul wrote these words in simple, understandable language. Our hope of heaven cannot stand apart from the literal resurrection of Jesus. And our belief in His literal, physical, bodily resurrection appears in Scripture as the bedrock foundation for our hope of a literal, physical, bodily resurrection at the Second Coming. Take this truth from Christian faith, and you have nothing left.

Why preach the resurrection? What difference does it make in the here and now? Evidently, Paul and other New Testament writers understood what we sometimes neglect. *"If ye then be risen with Christ...."* Paul's teaching that believers should live a transformed life that sets them apart from unbelievers around them is all based on the foundational truth of the resurrection. To be precise, he based this teaching on our indissoluble union with the Lord Jesus Christ, including His death and His resurrection.

Earlier I mentioned the deficiency of this teaching in many contemporary Christian pulpits. In one subculture of Christianity, you hear a near obsessive and speculative framework of ideas that secularize the Christian faith regarding the Second Coming in the "Left Behind" imaginative, but unbiblical teaching. In other subcultures, this errant teaching has effectively intimidated believers, even preachers, into ignoring Biblical teaching and leaving a gigantic void of teaching. This subculture almost wholly ignores any teaching at all regarding the Second Coming.

If the tight logical and Scriptural link exists between the Second Coming and our ethical conduct, what might we expect to see in those Christian subcultures where either significant error is taught obsessively or where the whole subject is ignored? We would logically expect to see an erosion of moral consistency in the conduct of those believers? And what, in fact, do we see in the greater Christian culture of our day? Barna and a number of other Christian groups have conducted a survey's, asking extensive questions about respondents' moral outlook. With sad consistency, these surveys report that there is no significant difference between the moral perspective and conduct of Christians and non-Christians. This idea should alarm the serious Bible student/believer.

More to the point, we need to seek any insights we can find in Scripture to reverse this rudderless ship. The answer is not in more sermons against lying and stealing or a higher respect for marriage as an institution that God established and defined. Those teachings should be intertwined in all sound Biblical teaching. However, merely teaching people that these things are wrong will not transform them. The answer lies in a return to the clear teachings of Scripture on the Second Coming and our literal, bodily resurrection! Isn't that Paul's point when he writes, "If ye then be risen with Christ..."?

In several instances in the New Testament, the word translated "conversation" in our King James Bible was translated from a word that refers to one's citizenship in first century Greek language.

...to conduct oneself with proper reference to one's obligations in relationship to others, as part of some community[1]
...to behave as a citizen. Any public measure, administration of the state, the condition or life of a citizen. In the NT, the state itself, community, commonwealth, used metaphorically of Christians in reference to their spiritual community and their status as citizens of heaven (Phil. 3:20).[2]

The principle idea of the word identifies behavior that is compatible with one's citizenship, the country of origin or home. If we truly are a stranger here, and if heaven is our home, we owe our citizenship through this pilgrimage the ethical debt of living like citizens of heaven. And the link that compels this ethical conduct is the resurrection.

---

[1] Johannes P. Louw and Eugene Albert Nida, *Greek-English Lexicon of the New Testament: Based on Semantic Domains* (New York: United Bible Societies, 1996), 507.
NT (New Testament)
[2] Spiros Zodhiates, *The Complete Word Study Dictionary: New Testament* (Chattanooga, TN: AMG Publishers, 2000).

.

.

8
"Looking" Alters Living

Seeing then that all these things shall be dissolved, what manner of persons ought ye to be in all holy conversation and godliness, Looking for and hasting unto the coming of the day of God, wherein the heavens being on fire shall be dissolved, and the elements shall melt with fervent heat? (2 Peter 3:11–12)

All too often when preachers preach on the Second Coming, they focus on the "Sweet Bye and Bye" at the expense of the very challenging "Here and Now." This disjointed and dysfunctional attitude appears among believers who hold to more Biblical ideas of eschatology (i.e. the doctrine of final things, such as the Second Coming) as well as among believers of the popular Dispensational ideas.

In my years of work in a profession, I had occasion to observe a significant number of believers in dispensational eschatology. Many of them loudly professed their faith, but they showed little or no Christian ethic in their business dealings. Regardless of one's view of end times, Scripture is quite clear in its demand that every person who so much as names the name of Christ should "...depart from iniquity" (2 Timothy 2:19).

When our daughters (now in their forties) were in high school, they would occasionally mention students whom they called "Jezoids." These students vacillated regularly between being almost fanatic Christians and being drug addicts. They showed no consistency whatever in their attitudes and conduct. I have observed similarly disjointed conduct among adults in the business world. In fairness, I have also encountered similar hypocrisy among professing Christians who hold to more historical Biblical views of the Second Coming. Rather than blame the disconnect between conduct and a specific view of eschatology, I suspect that the problem lies in a more intimate flaw in these people. Regardless their broad eschatological views, failure to maintain a vigilant eye of faith on the Lord and His return, the professed believers who fail to show their faith by their works fail to keep their faith's view fixed on Jesus.

Our study verses confront and reject this inconsistent and immoral lifestyle. If we believe in the Lord's return, the passage commands us to show our faith in our returning and victorious Lord by the way we live and the way we treat other people.

> *But and if that evil servant shall say in his heart, My lord delayeth his coming; And shall begin to smite his fellow servants, and to eat and drink with the drunken; The lord of that servant shall come in a day when he looketh not for him, and in an hour that he is not aware of, And shall cut him asunder, and appoint him his portion with the hypocrites: there shall be weeping and gnashing of teeth.* (Matthew 24:48-51)

This wicked servant depicts Jesus' description of the believer who does not maintain a fixed faith-view of Jesus and His return. What is this servant's first sinful act that follows his wrong-headed thinking, "My lord delayeth his coming"? His first sin is to beat his fellow-servants. Thankfully, very few professing believers choose to physically attack those with whom they disagree. However, it is sadly commonplace for many who profess faith in Christ to use their words as a club, abusively beating and attacking anyone who dares to disagree with their private ideas or interpretations of Scripture.

....what manner of persons ought ye to be in all holy conversation and godliness. In Scripture, the word "holy" does not imply sinless perfection. It rather identifies something or someone wholly devoted to God and God's use (2 Timothy 2:20-22). This passage reminds us that God chooses the vessels that He uses with discretion and righteous judgment. He will not use a "vessel," in the passage, a person, for His sacred use who has failed to purge himself from profane and vain babbling and endless wrangling that always increases to greater ungodliness and strife (2 Timothy 2:16, 23).

God chooses to use the believer who consciously and consistently avoids such spiritual "profanity" in His "great house."

When a believer in a church compromises his faith by such ungodly conduct toward other believers, quietly observe this person for a time. Slowly but ever so surely the Lord will nudge this person to the sidelines and begin to use the peaceful and gracious believer for His glory in His church. Will we ever learn? I suggest that the consistent command in Scripture that links repentance with baptism includes repentance from far more ungodly conduct than black immoral sins. It also commands repentance from these destructive and self-serving spiritual attitudes and conduct. When a professing believer refuses to repent of these unethical and unbiblical attitudes and behaviors, the Lord will turn away from him/her, and He will use those believers whom He describes in this passage as...

...a vessel unto honor, sanctified, and meet for the master's use, and prepared unto every good work. (2 Timothy 2:21)

In our study passage, "holy conversation" implies our interaction with other believers. Often in the New Testament "conversation" in the King James Bible is translated from a Greek word that identifies one's whole lifestyle, not just the words that he/she may choose in dialogue with other believers. The point of the two words commands a "devoted to God lifestyle," not just a devoted to God vocabulary. Regardless what a person believes about God and eternal issues, our humanity makes it frighteningly easy for any believer to rationalize attitudes and conduct that abuse other believers instead of loving them for Jesus' sake. A strong and Bible oriented belief in Biblical grace imposes an ethical obligation to practice similar grace toward other believers that the Lord has shown toward us.

Let your speech be always with grace, seasoned with salt, that ye may know how ye ought to answer every man. (Colossians 4:6)

In Jesus' words, cited above, how much grace did the unbelieving servant show to his fellow-servants whom he beat? It is immaterial whether someone beats you with his fist or with harsh words. The "beating" is equally condemned by Scripture. Often words are used by such people to inflict far more lasting hurt than they could possibly inflict with their fist.

Every believer in Christ who truly longs to live to and for the Lord's honor needs to constantly keep grace in mind as the filter and controlling factor in their words, attitudes, and actions toward other believers. You are a "grace believer." Are you also a "grace speaker," a "grace worker" toward your brothers and sisters in Christ? Did you ever think how dreadfully inconsistent and how dishonoring your life is to the Lord if you say that you believe strongly in God's grace, but you constantly treat other believers as if they and you are under the Law and you are God's appointed judge and jury of those other believers? "Holy conversation" specifically deals with our interaction with other believers—and non-believers for that matter.

...and godliness. This word turns our focus from interaction with other believers inward to how we live in relation to the Lord and His commandments. In another passage, Paul uses two similar terms, "...work of faith, and labor of love" (1 Thessalonians 1:3). Here "work of faith" addresses our God-ward conduct, and "labor of love" our interactions with other believers.

Why does one's belief in the Second Coming impact how we live? Think. If you believe that you shall spend eternity praising God for your redemption alongside all His other redeemed children, you remind yourself that both you and that brother or sister whom you look down on or verbally abuse will be there side by side with you, both equally there by merciful grace and not by your works. If you know that you and that person will be so changed at the Second Coming that you will rejoice beyond anything you can now imagine, the thought urges you to treat that person with more respect and grace now. Further, the awareness that Jesus died for your sins, including your sin of offense against even one of the least of the Lord's little ones (Matthew 18:6-11), should convict you as powerfully to avoid such offense against His "little ones" as faithfully as you strive to avoid carnal sins of the flesh. If there is any significant difference, a sin against one of the Lord's little ones may well be more heinous in the Lord's nostrils than a sin of the flesh.

A steady fixed focus on the Second Coming and that glory to come is the strongest possible deterrent to personal sin, as well as relational sins. In 1 Corinthians 6:14, Paul injects a clear affirmation of both Jesus' resurrection and ours into one of the most focused lessons in the New Testament against sexual sin. If we try to ignore the present moral power of a right belief in the Second Coming, we will gloss over this verse and miss Paul's powerful point. If you believe that your physical body shall go to the grave and never be raised again to praise God, you may easily become careless about how you use your body. However, if you believe that the Lord shall literally raise and glorify your physical body to join your spirit and soul in praising Him for eternity to come, you will be more careful about how you use that body now. And that moral truth explains Paul's injection of resurrection truth into his teaching against moral, sexual sin.

Looking for and hasting unto the coming of the day of God. The Biblically informed and faithful believer keeps the Lord's return fresh in his heart at all times. Friend, the "day of God" is coming. We can bear faithful witness to our belief in that coming day's reality only to the extent that we impose its "resurrection ethic" on every aspect of our conduct, especially on how we treat our brothers and sisters in Christ.

...hasting unto the coming of the day of God. Nothing that we do can alter the date of the Lord's return. However, by keeping that day fresh in our minds, we live and make every decision, govern every word, and frame every relationship with other believers in the mindset of eagerly awaiting that day. If the people who know you best were to judge your belief in the Second Coming only by your words (both what you say and how you say it) and deeds, would they conclude that you truly do believe in that day, or would they see your behavior as a sad contradiction to your belief in that day? Do your words and deeds shine forth your belief in that day?

9
Resurrection: Intimately Personal

But God will redeem my soul from the power of the grave: For he shall receive me. Selah. (Psalm 49:15)

Often the little teaching that occurs on the resurrection in contemporary Christian culture deals with ideas that miss the personal, intimate teaching of Scripture. David rejoices that God "...will redeem *my soul* from the power of the grave." In the Old Testament, "soul" is used in a variety of ways. Here and in Psalm 16:10, interpreted by New Testament inspired writers (Acts 2:25-31; 13:35-37), soul refers to the body, or perhaps the living animated body that loses its "animation" in death. But these passages remind us that the grave is not the final chapter in the journey of our physical body. It shall not be left there.

In the New Testament sense of the word, our "soul" is not our body, nor does it go to the grave at death. Thank the Lord for these two references in Acts that give us an inspired interpretation of Psalm 16:10, thereby helping us more clearly understand similar passages such as the one we here study. This passage further supports the point made in our last study, that redemption is not complete till the resurrection of our physical body, including its transformation that as fully removes sin and sin's impact and influences from it as God removed sin from the soul/spirit in the new birth.

For he shall receive me. David assigns the reason that God shall redeem his soul from the power of the grave, death. While New Testament teaching affirms a general resurrection of both the elect and the wicked, all in the same hour, not separated by an extended period of time (John 5:28-29; Acts 24:15), it also emphasizes the same personal intimacy that David here claims (Philippians 1:21-24; while Paul here refers more to the intimacy of His being with Christ in personal and joyful fellowship, that close fellowship cannot be ignored or denied relative to the subsequent resurrection). Every act of God in the process of our final deliverance from sin and sin's impact to our being raised at the Second Coming in His glorified image focuses on this personal intimacy that gives David such comfort and joy. We read of the death of godly people in Scripture, people such as Stephen (Acts 7:55-60), but do we embrace the powerful and comforting lessons that these experiences give to us? When faced with a cruel and painful death, Stephen manifests a focus that ignored his pain and rejoiced at seeing and soon being with his Savior, "I see...." "Lord Jesus, receive my spirit" (Acts 7:56, 59).

From election to resurrection, all of God's saving grace is applied personally and intimately to each of His beloved children, almost as if you were the only one being redeemed. But, praise be to our gracious and loving Savior, He is able to treat every single one of His children with the same grace. When you and I face that final moment, by His loving grace, we can say the same words that David wrote and feel the same unspeakable comfort that he felt when he wrote, "For he shall receive me."

Our generation has witnessed an interesting acknowledgement within mainstream Christian thinking of the Bible doctrine of election. However, the contemporary "twist" on the doctrine ignores and contradicts the teaching of Scripture that makes God's love and grace so intimately up close and personal to each child of grace. The modern idea works to depersonalize God's saving work. According to this teaching, God elected Jesus and Jesus only. If you make your decision and comply with the various requirements imposed by the various partnership salvation ideas, you effectively put yourself into Jesus; since God elected Jesus, and since you have put yourself in Jesus, you are supposedly now one of God's elect. How does this idea match up to Scripture? Simply stated, it doesn't.

Who hath saved us, and called us with an holy calling, not according to our works, but according to his own purpose and grace, which was given us in Christ Jesus before the world begun. (2 Timothy 1:9)

Notice Paul's emphatic point. All of this saving work is "...not according to our works, but according to his own purpose and grace." We didn't bring ourselves into contact with this purpose and grace by our decision or by anything that we did. God **gave it to us** "...in Christ Jesus before the world began."

We may reasonably discuss what the Reformers meant by their term "justification by faith." However, the more appropriate discussion should be about terms used in Scripture and what the Holy Spirit intended those terms to mean. The contemporary school of theology that teaches the idea of our putting ourselves into Jesus, who is God's exclusive elect, thereby making ourselves one of God's elect, also imposes an errant idea onto our faith and our belief of the gospel. Supposedly, requiring that a person believe the gospel is not to be classified as "salvation by works." You believe in salvation by works, according to this thinking, only if you require water baptism, and/or a certain minimum level of good works for eternal salvation. The major question to be answered typically remains unanswered and unaddressed. Is our belief a "work" or not?

Then said they unto him, What shall we do, that we might work the works of God? Jesus answered and said unto them, This is the work of God, that ye believe on him whom he hath sent. (John 6:28-29)

If we accept the simple truth that these two verses teach, we cannot accept the contemporary idea that our belief is not a work. Simply stated, **Jesus said it is a work.** It is the work of God, what God commands and teaches His children to do, but, in the end, Jesus did say that believing "...on him whom he hath sent" is a work, didn't He? So do we believe the modern interpreters, or do we believe Jesus? No contest for me; I believe Jesus. How could He have made the point simpler? "This is the **work** of God, that ye believe on him whom he hath sent."

This illogical hybrid belief half-way between Arminian and Calvinist ideas has far less Bible support than its advocates suggest. Jesus' words in John 6:29 contradict and therefore reject the idea. Think further. In Matthew 25:31-46, Jesus used the analogy of a shepherd separating the sheep from the goats in his flock to depict the Second Coming. Pay special attention to the way the saved reacted to the news, "Come, ye blessed of my Father, inherit the kingdom prepared for you from the foundation of the world." When Jesus tells them that they had ministered to Him, what was their response? Did they tell Him that they vividly recalled the date, hour, and place when they first heard the gospel and believed it? Did they tell Him that they still remembered their moment of believing and accepting Him? If God required them to exercise cognitive faith and actively believe in Him and in the gospel to be born again, surely at that epochal day, they would recall such an important event. Surely, Jesus would also mention that event to them. How did they react?

> *Then shall the righteous answer him, saying, Lord, when saw we thee an hungred, and fed thee? or thirsty, and gave thee drink? When saw we thee a stranger, and took thee in? or naked, and clothed thee? Or when saw we thee sick, or in prison, and came unto thee? (Matthew 25:37-39)*

Not only did they not remind the Lord of their "hour of decision," but they reacted to the good news with a touch of surprise, if not bewilderment, "When saw we thee…?"

Think about their response. If the saved at that day respond with surprise at their glorious inheritance, when did they forget about their decisions and all their good and faithful works? That they responded with "When saw we thee…?" instead of proudly rehearsing their decision offers a powerful commentary. According to the common decision-based teaching of our day, only those who consciously hear and believe the gospel, and, to some usually unstipulated degree, obey it shall be invited to spend eternity with the Lord. **Why then does Jesus depict those whom He saved as being surprised at the good news?** Could it possibly be that all of their good decisions and belief in the gospel actually didn't play into their inheritance, either as the cause or the instrument of their inheritance? I suggest that is precisely the case. Thank the Lord, we shall inherit that glorious place and state of eternal, living fellowship with the Lord because of what He did for us and in us, not because of what we did or said, mental or in actions. We shall praise Him throughout eternity, not celebrate our decisions.

For he shall receive me. In these words, David captures the amazing mystery of the ages. Despite the corruption of our physical bodies while we lived in this world, He shall raise us wholly purified from all of that corruption. The same body that sinned against Him and His righteous Law shall be so gloriously changed that it shall praise Him perfectly!

> *For ye are dead, and your life is hid with Christ in God. When Christ, who is our life, shall appear, then shall ye also appear with him in glory.* (Colossians 3:3-4)

In the first two verses of Colossians 3, Paul teaches the Colossians—and us—to respect and to regard our risen state with Christ right now, to seek our God and heavenly things. He builds his point on the premise that, just as Jesus arose from the dead in a glorified body, so also we shall arise in the same body in which we lived, but it shall be wholly transformed. Paul describes as much of this change as we can grasp—if we can fully understand his points. Our corruption is made incorruptible, our dishonor is raised in glory, our weakness is raised in power, our natural body is raised a spiritual body (1 Corinthians 15:42-44).

For he shall receive me. Yes, He shall receive you, you individually and personally. His "Come, inherit the kingdom..." shall be spoken to you, declaring for all eternity that you are His and He is yours. What a day that will be!

10
Object Lesson on the Resurrection: Lazarus

Then they took away the stone from the place where the dead was laid.
And Jesus lifted up his eyes, and said, Father, I thank thee that thou hast
heard me. And I knew that thou hearest me always: but because of the
people which stand by I said it, that they may believe that thou hast sent
me. And when he thus had spoken, he cried with a loud voice, Lazarus,
come forth. (John 11:41–43)

Scripture nicely punctuates its clear teaching of Biblical principles with lessons that apply those principles to the personal lives of individual people. It seems that God intends to remind us that His truth is not an impersonal philosophical idea that never really touches where we live and breathe.

In our study passage, the New Testament devotes a rather lengthy chapter, fifty seven verses, to the experience of Lazarus and his two sisters. In such a focused account of Jesus' time in this world as we see in John's gospel, this much "ink" deserves our interest and attention. The issue on the line is not a matter of casual interest or importance for us. Our study of Scripture should advance through two essential steps, interpretation and application. Our interpretation of this lesson embraces that the narrative gives us an account of a real event in the lives of those involved. Where do we go to learn the right application of this truth to our lives today?

The narrative begins in the first verse of the chapter. In the first two verses, we learn that Lazarus is sick, and that this family has a close and loving history with Jesus. They are not strangers who have heard of His miracles. They are close friends and believers in Him and in His purpose in incarnation, in becoming flesh and living as a man in this world. Verse five emphasizes the point; Jesus loved these three people. Jesus' love in Scripture is never the superficial or casual kind of friendship that might shift with the slightest offense.

His love is a reliable and permanent fixture in the lives of all His children.

At the time of the illness, Jesus and the disciples are some distance away from the Jerusalem suburb where Lazarus and his two sisters live, probably at least a two-day walk, the normal method of travel at the time. From the time that Lazarus becomes ill, the sisters send word to Jesus, Jesus delays going back to Jerusalem for two days. By the time Jesus and the disciples reach the community where Lazarus and his sisters lived, Lazarus has died and been buried for four days. From the human perspective, whatever He might have done had He been present earlier, Jesus is too late to make a difference. His intentional delay is puzzling at best for Mary and Martha. But God is not subservient to time. He created it (Genesis 1:1; "In the beginning...."), and He is Lord over it. Given the details of this lesson, no one can credibly ignore or deny that Lazarus physically, literally died, and the family buried his dead body in a sealed grave. Jesus' reference to Lazarus sleeping (verse 12) refers to his physical death, not to his soul. Scripture never teaches the idea of "soul sleep."

Mary and Martha's accurate faith in Jesus should serve as powerful encouragement to us. They have known Jesus for some time. They have been with Him. He has spent time in their home. However, they accurately understand that He is their Messiah, God come in a human body. Martha's plea when she learns that Jesus has arrived is therefore understandable.

Then said Martha unto Jesus, Lord, if thou hadst been here, my brother had not died. But I know, that even now, whatsoever thou wilt ask of God, God will give it thee. (John 11:21–22)

She has not given up on the possibility of a miracle. Jesus can still raise Lazarus from the dead. Think about her faith. When we read about her complaining to Jesus while Mary ignored household duties and sat at Jesus' feet, we are far too prone to criticize her. Don't be too hard on Martha. Every church needs a few faithful Martha types. Just imagine what the table would look like if your church had only Mary type women in it. You might have great fellowship, but you'd go home hungry. A healthy church needs both kinds of godly women.

Jesus saith unto her, Thy brother shall rise again. Martha saith unto him, I know that he shall rise again in the resurrection at the last day. Jesus said unto her, I am the resurrection, and the life: he that believeth in me, though he were dead, yet shall he live. (John 11:23–25)

Jesus doesn't tell Martha that He shall bring about the resurrection; He tells her that He *is* the resurrection and the life. Further, we learn from Martha that she believed in a literal, bodily resurrection. In this context, how could we conclude any other idea? And Jesus in no way corrected her belief; he thereby affirms her faith.

Given the focus in this whole chapter on Lazarus' literal, physical death, Jesus' point is clear. He speaks of His being the resurrection, the antidote to Lazarus' physical, bodily death. Despite Lazarus being dead, His spirit was alive, even as Jesus spoke the words to Martha, "...though he were dead, yet shall he live." Any effort to interpret this lesson as referring to anything other than to the resurrection of a literal physical body is inexcusable.

Despite their strong faith, Mary and Martha also wrestled with the reality of their brother, now dead four days and buried. Open the grave? By this time, Lazarus' body would be well into its cycle of decomposition. Why rub salt in the wound by opening the grave and smelling the solemn reminder? Ah, but Jesus has something better in mind for His beloved friends.

Then they took away the stone from the place where the dead was laid. And Jesus lifted up his eyes, and said, Father, I thank thee that thou hast heard me. And I knew that thou hearest me always: but because of the people which stand by I said it, that they may believe that thou hast sent me. And when he thus had spoken, he cried with a loud voice, Lazarus, come forth. (John 11:41–43)

Jesus knew that the Father always heard His prayers. He prayed to the Father in full confidence of the Father's presence and answer. Do not overlook a key point. In the midst of grief at Lazarus' death, the one record of Jesus weeping during His incarnation, Jesus begins His prayer to the Father with thanksgiving.

I fear that our prayers are too often a laundry list of wants, especially when we pray in the heat of distress. In our eager despair for Jesus' help, we should never forget to thank Him for the abounding blessings that He showers into our lives constantly. However black the clouds of trial and disappointment in this world—and those clouds can be ominous—the Lord's presence and blessings abound. Jesus didn't pray because He needed to vocalize His request for the Father to respond. He prayed audibly for the benefit of those who stood by.

Lazarus, come forth. The sentence seems so simple, only three words. They are structured to a living man who has the ability to hear and to respond to instructions. We could easily overlook the obvious, that Jesus spoke these words to a man who died several days ago and has been in the tomb for now four whole days. But in the time that Jesus spent before the tomb, He had already brought Lazarus back from death. Now that resurrected man needed to get up and exit the tomb. He no longer needed that space.

It is admittedly difficult for us to grasp the reality of this chapter. A real man, a friend to Jesus, and brother to his sisters, actually died and was buried. Jesus spoke to him, and he arose from the grave.

To help us grasp the reality of this experience, consider this example. Eugene Peterson offers a scenario. Imagine that you have been by the bedside of a dear friend through an extended illness. Perhaps you were present when he breathed his last breath and slipped away into death. You help the family prepare for the memorial service. You attend that service and even witness your friend's burial. A few days later, you are trying to put your life back together and get back to normal. You go shopping for groceries. As you walk through the parking lot with your basket full of groceries, you look across the parking lot and see a familiar figure. You do a double take. That image looks disruptively like your just died friend.

But you know it can't be. He is dead. You can't get that image out of your mind. You put your groceries in the car. The man is still there. You can't resist. You lock your car and walk over to where the man is standing. When you get to the other side of the parking lot and look at this man face to face, you are speechless. *It is your friend! He's alive!* You engage him in conversation. He knows all the details of your relationship together, including intimate and private knowledge that no one else knows. There can be no doubt. You are looking at your friend, now resurrected from the dead. For those first disciples, this experience captures their amazement and surprise at Jesus' resurrection and His many personal appearances to them.

If these disciples had thought about their time with Jesus and His clear and repeated words to them, they should have expected nothing else. They had heard the words, but the full reality was more than they could wrap their minds around. Till they say Him, and He spoke to them. Then they could not deny. Even doubting Thomas reached the point of knowing. His resurrection was real.

Martha saith unto him, I know that he shall rise again in the resurrection at the last day. (John 11:24)

The words are clear enough. However, in the context of Lazarus' death and resurrection, we cannot doubt their literal meaning. The "...resurrection at the last day" shall not be a "spiritual" resurrection of some mystical sort. It shall be a resurrection that, true to the accepted meaning of the word, involves the reviving of our physical bodies that died and were buried.

Our bodily resurrection at the Second Coming shall be just as real and just as literal as Lazarus' resurrection. Ah, but there is one difference. Lazarus was resurrected to return for a season to live with his sisters and friends in this life. Our resurrection shall be to glory, endless glory with our Lord and Savior.

11
Jesus Refutes the Sadducees

The same day came to him the Sadducees, which say that there is no resurrection, and asked him, Saying, Master, Moses said, If a man die, having no children, his brother shall marry his wife, and raise up seed unto his brother. Now there were with us seven brethren: and the first, when he had married a wife, deceased, and, having no issue, left his wife unto his brother: Likewise the second also, and the third, unto the seventh. And last of all the woman died also. Therefore in the resurrection whose wife shall she be of the seven? for they all had her. Jesus answered and said unto them, Ye do err, not knowing the scriptures, nor the power of God. For in the resurrection they neither marry, nor are given in marriage, but are as the angels of God in heaven. But as touching the resurrection of the dead, have ye not read that which was spoken unto you by God, saying, I am the God of Abraham, and the God of Isaac, and the God of Jacob? God is not the God of the dead, but of the living. And when the multitude heard this, they were astonished at his doctrine. (Matthew 22:23–33)

First century Judaism was subdivided into several segments, each of whom held to their own ideas about God, His person, and His work. Of all these groups, the Sadducees were likely the least religious in any respectful sense of the word. Likely the most conservative, and probably the most faithful to Old Testament teachings, were the Essenes. We do not read specifically about them in the New Testament. Most New Testament writings deal with the scribes, those Jews who were responsible for copying and preserving the text of the Old Testament, the Pharisees, and the Sadducees.

As a class, first century Sadducees were wealthy and politically influential. It appears that they likely held control of the high priest's office (Acts 5:17) and possibly a majority of seats on the

Sanhedrin Court. As noted in other studies, a simple respect for the accepted definition of the word "resurrection" affirms that the dispute between the Sadducees and other sects of first century Jews had to do with what they believed about the literal resurrection of the body in the last day. The Geneva Bible includes a simple and informative footnote on this passage.

> Christ affirms the resurrection of the flesh, as opposed to the Sadducees.[1]

No Gnostic-like mystical explanation of the resurrection that implies any other meaning can survive this simple definition.

What did the Sadducees believe? Most important to our question is Scripture itself. From information provided by the various mentions of this sect in the New Testament, they denied the resurrection, and they rejected the existence of angels and of life after death.

> The most prominent doctrine of the Sadducees was the denial of the immortality of the soul and of the resurrection of the body. The Pharisees believed that Moses had delivered these doctrines to the elders, and that they had in turn handed them on to their successors. The Sadducees rejected all these traditions. From Acts (23:8) we learn that they believed in neither "angel or spirit." As appearances of angels are mentioned in the Law, it is difficult to harmonize their reverence for the Law with this denial. They may have regarded these angelophanies as theophanies. Josephus distinctly asserts (Ant., XVIII, i, 4) that the Sadducees believe that the soul dies with the body. They deny, he says, divine providence (BJ, II, viii, 14). Their theology might be called "religion within the limits of mere sensation."[2]

Given the manner in which the three synoptic Gospel (Matthew 22:23-33; Mark 12:18-27; Luke 20:27-38) writers introduce this

---

[1] Copied from SwordSearcher Bible software, Matthew 22:23.

[2] *International Bible Encyclopedia*, 1939. Copied from SwordSearcher Bible software, Matthew 22:23.

dialogue, it appears that the Sadducees likely posed this question in their effort to expose Jesus as a messianic pretender. It is also likely that they had used this question in many debates with the Pharisees. "Levirate" marriage was taught in Moses' Law.[3]

The Sadducees framed their argument on the premise that whatever relationships exist in this life must necessarily carry over in the resurrection. Jesus rejected their logic, as well as their denial of the resurrection.

Ye do err, not knowing the scriptures, nor the power of God. For in the resurrection they neither marry, nor are given in marriage, but are as the angels of God in heaven. Any error drawn from a twist on Scripture's teaching can be refuted by Scripture. This is especially true if we accept that Scripture is divinely inspired and preserved. In fact, Jesus charges the Sadducees with two core errors that lead them to their denial of the resurrection. For Jesus to so directly rebuke the leaders of a leading and influential first century Jewish sect would have infuriated these people. They may have entered the discussion as something of an entertaining idea. Jesus had confronted and refuted the Pharisees. If the Sadducees were to debate with Him and succeed in confounding Him with a question regarding their fundamental belief, they would gain substantial political power.

To their surprise, Jesus doesn't react to their question with confusion. He directly exposes the profound depth of their error, even by their own standards of measuring truth. The Sadducees accepted the first five books of the Old Testament, the "Law" of Moses. It is no coincidence that Jesus uses a familiar passage from Exodus, one of those five books, to refute their belief. To say to the Sadducees, "Ye do err, not knowing the scriptures..." and "...have ye not read..." quite emphatically repudiated their errant beliefs.

The Sadducees built their false beliefs on two flawed and errant premises.

---

[3] The word "Levirate" refers to a brother-in-law. The practice involved a woman's brother-in-law, her husband's brothers, marrying her if her husband died, and the couple had no children to carry on their family heritage to future generations. (Deuteronomy 25:5-6; the Book of Ruth deals with this practice in greater detail)

1. They did not know the Scriptures, even the five books of Moses, nearly as well as they prided themselves and thought to know them.
2. Likewise, they grossly underestimated God's power.

The combination of two errant beliefs of this magnitude flawed the Sadducees' thinking and beliefs.

Jesus cited a well-known and simple passage from the third chapter of Exodus, part of God's conversation with Moses at the burning bush. He didn't create a complex or vague argument. He framed the simplest of points on the simplest of passages. At the time God spoke to Moses, Abraham, Isaac, and Jacob had been dead for centuries. That God used the present tense verb "I am" in His response to Moses was sufficient to prove that the Sadducees' twisted view of the small portion of Old Testament Scripture that they did accept was hopelessly flawed.

We read the various accounts of Jesus confronting and rebuking the various leading Jewish sects of the first century, but we may fail to grasp the depth and richness of the value these accounts hold for us. Not only do we see Jesus' teachings clearly, in this case His affirmation of the resurrection, but we also may learn how He approached those people. While we cannot approach believers who happen not to agree with us with the same authority as Jesus, we can well learn as much about *how* to engage believers of a different view as we can learn about the truth that Jesus taught.

How do believers of different and often conflicting ideas engage each other in dialogue regarding their differences? Do we find an acceptable model in Jesus' teachings to understand how we should engage other believers regarding areas of disagreement? I suggest that Jesus gives us a powerful example. Sadly often, sincere and well-meaning believers will follow the Sadducee model of trick questions and debate strategies to win their point, often far more bent on winning the argument than learning the truth of Scripture. They sadly fail to grasp that the word "debate" appears in the New Testament under lists of "...all unrighteousness" (Romans 1:29), *never* under the heading of admirable or desirable traits for believers to cultivate. Without necessarily intending to do so, they display an offensive and unbiblical smug attitude of "I'm right, so if you disagree with me, you are wrong. You simply do not know as much about the Bible as I know." This attitude consistently alienates people and leaves the person who displays it showing more ego than grace; "I intend to win this discussion one way or the other." Try as they might, they simply cannot reconcile this egotistical attitude with the model of Scripture (2 Timothy 2:23-26).

Folks who practice this attitude have failed to learn the most basic principle of Biblical discipleship. They do not understand that the very word "disciple" is defined as a student, a learner, not someone who has learned it all, or who conveys the attitude of knowing more than any other believer about Scriptural teaching. When a believer engages another believer with the attitude that he knows more and better than other believers, he effectively says that he does not need to be taught; he already knows more than anyone within his circle of friends can teach him. He/She fails to grasp that this very attitude excludes them from the description of a disciple of Jesus.

The plight of such believers often slowly slips into ever-increasing loneliness as the people around him/her simply and quietly avoid engaging them in dialogue on the Scriptures—or much of anything else for that matter. Most believers intensely dislike conflict, and they especially dislike exposing themselves to verbal bullying. While most believers respond to the verbal bully who tries to compel agreement with him most of the time quietly withdraw and avoid the errant believer, they should follow Scripture (Matthew 18 and Luke 17:1-6 as clear examples). We should not forget. We may err from Scripture as quickly by our words and attitudes as by our actions.

None of us, even the most studied and rightly informed, can speak with personal authority as Jesus spoke. He alone had such knowledge and authority. Even with that knowledge, He described His disposition toward His followers with "…I am meek and lowly in heart" (Matthew 11:29). The only escape for a "debating" believer is to repent of that fleshly, ego-feeding attitude and to strive to regain Jesus' example of meekness and lowliness of heart. If he/she hopes to follow the Biblical model of discipleship, they will engage other believers as students of Scripture, not as indisputable authorities of its teachings. A student seeks to learn, and, in this case, the errant believer should repent and embrace the attitude of a student desiring to learn from his/her fellow-believer, not of an informed expert who has already learned it all.

The Greek word translated "debate" in Romans 1:29 appears some nine times in the New Testament. In those passages, the same word is translated by English words that leave no question about its meaning.

1. "Debate" in Romans 1:29.
2. "Strife" in Romans 13:13.
3. "Contentions" in 1 Corinthians 1:11.
4. "Strife" in 1 Corinthians 3:3.
5. "Debates" in 2 Corinthians 12:20.
6. "Variance," a work of the flesh, in Galatians 5:20.
7. "Strife" in Philippians 1:15, a context that deals with believers who teach the truth of Jesus with wrong motives.
8. "Strife" in 1 Timothy 6:4.
9. "Contentions," something that believers should avoid, not cultivate or develop to a base art, in Titus 3:9.

Given these passages, no believer can or should defend or cultivate an argumentative or debating attitude toward other believers.

Further, given the severity of this trait, believers who encounter another believer who has fallen into this sinful attitude, or one who is flirting with it, should be approached by his/her brothers and sisters in kind grace—and, most of all—in faith toward God (Luke 17:1-6). To ignore a brother or sister in such error is equivalent to throwing them away by cold isolation. To approach and admonish them in faith, grace, and godly love is to seek their recovery to profitable edification.

Scripture consistently establishes that the teaching authority in a church setting is the pastor, whose primary role is that of teacher (Ephesians 4:11). The debating believer will often either reject or contradict his/her pastor's authority and often attempt to supplant the pastor by becoming a respected teaching authority in the church of his/her membership. Yes, I have observed almost as many women in churches who fell into this errant attitude as men. The point from Scripture is clear. We should avoid, not imitate the argumentative or debating mindset of the Pharisees and Sadducees in favor of the meek and lowly in heart example of Jesus.

We should never expect to truly win an argument with another believer by words alone, unless our attitudes and actions model Jesus. While we cannot speak with personal authority as Jesus spoke, "But I say unto you..." we should appeal to Scripture for our beliefs. And, as we appeal to Scripture, we must avoid our private, often esoteric ideas in favor of the more obvious and accepted interpretations of other believers in the church. Scripture affirms the point. The Lord's church, not a self-proclaimed expert in the church, is the "...pillar and ground of the truth" (2 Timothy 3:15).

Whether in the form of ancient Sadducees or, more contemporary to the apostles, the teachings of ancient Gnostics, a fundamental premise of Biblical truth that forms the essential foundation for other Biblical truth is this doctrine of the resurrection (Acts 17:8). One of its basic principles is one of its practical realities. We shall spend eternity in glory, resurrected body, soul, and spirit, praising God for redemption (Revelation 5:9). How then do we treat each other, and thereby, indirectly Jesus (cf. Matthew 25:40), because we know this glorious truth?

12
Between Now and Then?

And one of the malefactors which were hanged railed on him, saying, If thou be Christ, save thyself and us. But the other answering rebuked him, saying, Dost not thou fear God, seeing thou art in the same condemnation? And we indeed justly; for we receive the due reward of our deeds: but this man hath done nothing amiss. And he said unto Jesus, Lord, remember me when thou comest into thy kingdom. And Jesus said unto him, Verily I say unto thee, To day shalt thou be with me in paradise. (Luke 23:39–43)

God has a marvelous way of teaching some of the Bible's most profound truths in the simplest of ways. Sadly often, preachers and Bible teachers work to complicate their explanations of Bible truths, while Jesus gives us one example after another that urges us to simplify our teachings. Not only did Jesus direct Peter to feed His sheep, but He also commanded him to feed His lambs (John 21:15).

We should know the story well of Jesus' time on the cross. Early in the day, Scripture indicates that both thieves railed against Jesus, but our study passage unfolds the miracle of tender mercy. One of the two thieves quite abruptly changes his words from railing on Jesus to praying to Him. How do we account for this change? How does this thief know that Jesus did "...nothing amiss"? Why did he call Jesus "Lord"? How did he come to think that Jesus was a king, and more than a king? Any explanation that stops short of a miracle of merciful grace fails to make any sense of the sudden reversal in this man's words.

Jesus told the disciples that their belief in Him as "...the Christ, the Son of the living God" (cf. Matthew 16:17) was the result of God's revelation, not of their wisdom or insight. We live in an age when many sincere Christian folk have all but forgotten the Bible accounts and teachings of God's involvement in the lives of His people, particularly His revelations of Himself and His work to them. It is sadly common for people to proclaim quite loudly that God simply cannot reveal Himself to anyone apart from the gospel, the gospel preached by man. In their minds, the only way that God can reach people who have never heard the gospel is for preachers to take the news to them. God intended that His people publish the good news of the gospel far and wide, but He has not reduced Himself to a wooden statue in the preacher's hands. He revealed to Peter and the other disciples that He was "...the Christ, the Son of the living God." He revealed Himself to this thief, even as He hung on the cross in unimaginable pain from the torture of crucifixion. And He taught the disciples, and us, that He regularly reveals Himself to His people (Matthew 11:25-27). As a foundational truth of the new covenant, God in prophecy proclaimed that men would not teach other men to "...know the Lord," because God's provisions in the covenant would result in "...they shall all know me, from the least of them unto the greatest of them" (Jeremiah 31:33-34).

Let's put ourselves as much as possible into this scene. The two prisoners were probably taken out of a jail cell and marched summarily to the hill where their crosses, the Roman instrument of capital punishment, were awaiting them. On their arrival, they realize that a third man was facing the same torturous execution as they. By the time we read the words of our passage, all three men have been suspended on their crosses for some time. From Luke 23:44, we learn that the exchange between Jesus and the thief occurred around mid-day, the sixth hour of the day. When the Romans put someone on a cross, they weren't kept there for a few hours and released. They would only be taken off the cross after their death. Only intense pain and the certain knowledge that more pain remained in their lives until death gave them merciful relief.

Given this setting, our passage becomes all the more enlightening. The man who spoke these words to Jesus was not a Jewish scholar who knew the Old Testament. He was a criminal. Earlier he had been as loud in his railing against Jesus as the other thief.

"And he said unto Jesus, Lord, remember me when thou comest into thy kingdom." Not only does the thief believe that Jesus is a king, but he also believes that Jesus intends to conquer death itself. Look around. There were no trained armies waiting for the word to rescue Jesus from the Jews and the Romans. The thief has some sense of life after death, along with a sense that Jesus shall be in a position to do gracious things after the day's cruel charade has ended.

"And Jesus said unto him, Verily I say unto thee, To day shalt thou be with me in paradise." People who choose their own private ideas over Scripture have worked long and hard to twist Jesus' words in this verse. Those who reject the Biblical truth that we go from death immediately and consciously into the glorious presence of the Lord must twist these words so as to leave the impression that Jesus didn't at all say what He so clearly and simply said. Consider one bizarre explanation from a major group that teaches the unbiblical idea of "soul sleep." According to their explanation, Jesus didn't tell the thief anything about what they would experience after death that day.

The explanation of this aberrant movement interprets Jesus as saying, "Verily I say unto thee today, thou shalt be with me in paradise." Notice the relocated comma. When Jesus spoke the words, "Verily I say unto thee," there was no need to add "today." He wouldn't say, "I say unto thee tomorrow," or "I say unto thee yesterday." The present tense verb suffices. Jesus told the thief about something that they both would experience together on that same day. Both of them would "…be in paradise." Jesus never used confusing or superfluous words.

Scripture consistently describes our experience between death and the Second Coming in terms of consciousness, either in glory with the Lord or in hell and righteous punishment. Sincere studious believers differ in their interpretation of the lesson of Lazarus and the rich man (Luke 16:19-31). Some view it as a parable, while others view it as a literal narrative about two men who lived and died. While I definitely hold the literal view of the lesson, for purposes of this study, the question is immaterial. Why? Jesus never built His parables on myths. He always built them on literal, everyday reality, a farmer with his crops, a shepherd with his sheep, etc. Thus, even if we view this lesson as a parable, we must acknowledge the underlying literal reality of the lesson, and that reality strongly affirms continued consciousness after death for both the saved and the unsaved. And this truth Jesus affirmed to the thief in our study passage.

When Paul, at the time under house arrest, wrote the Philippians, he described a personal dilemma (Philippians 1:23-24). The Romans might decide to execute him; he would then depart and "...be with Christ." Or they might tire of guarding him and choose to release him. Then he could "...abide in the flesh," an option that Paul described as more needful for the Philippians. In his assessment, Paul effectively weighs two choices, 1) depart and be with Christ, 2) remain in this world and be with the Philippians. There is no implication that Paul intended to equate unconscious nothingness with active spiritual interaction with the Philippians.

In 2 Corinthians 5:1-10, Paul deals with our "intermediate state," what we experience between death and the Second Coming. He does not teach us that God shall give us a temporary physical body to inhabit until the resurrection. However, he does clearly describe consciousness from now till then. How are we then "clothed" during this intervening time? Paul answers the question beautifully and comfortingly, "...that mortality might be swallowed up of life" (2 Corinthians 5:4b).

If the idea of soul-sleep were true, we must deal with a major problem. To hold the view consistently, we must not only prove by Scripture that every person who dies—or has died—slips into this unconscious nothingness, but we must also come to grips with the obvious dilemma. During the three days from death to resurrection, did Jesus' soul sleep? Or was He actively engaged with the Father in dealing with the glorious results of His sufferings and death for our sins, typified in vivid details in the Old Testament Levitical priesthood, and confirmed in the New Testament Book of Hebrews? Nothing in the Levitical order and priestly processes allowed for the priest to "sleep on the job." During every moment of his annual work on the Day of Atonement, each act of a busy schedule was scripted and commanded by God.

We cannot imagine the experience of the thief who prayed to Jesus on the cross. Shortly after Jesus' death, the Roman soldiers broke his leg bones, accelerating his death. Thus, he arrives in Paradise very shortly after Jesus, an early witness who experienced the benefits in Paradise that Jesus accomplished in His sinless, atoning death. In a moment, this thief went from jail cell to glory as an eyewitness of Jesus in His crowning glory with the Father. No, we cannot even approach getting our minds around this glorious reality.

Serious Bible students will hopefully not take offense that I raise the senseless and unbiblical idea that, upon death, children of God become angels in heaven. I shall never forget my surprise years ago when I heard a preacher's widow (he already knew the truth, for he had gone to glory) say, "Oh, everyone knows that, when we die, we become an angel." Based on Scripture, God created angels. They are different created beings from us. And we should not forget that we who have been blessed with the gospel and therein "…rejoice with joy unspeakable and full of glory" experience something that "…angels desire to look into" (1 Peter 1:8, 12). If we become angels when we die, why would we forget the most fundamental truth of Scripture's good news about our salvation?

What does this lesson give to us? It reminds us in simple and understandable words what we also should anticipate and rejoice to experience. As the thief did not suffer a detour to an in-between abyss or simply slip into unconsciousness at his death, even so we have the same conscious, joyful experience to anticipate when we leave this world. If the gospel now, fully embraced in faith, gives us "…joy unspeakable and full of glory," what shall we experience when we arrive in glory, in "Paradise," and see our risen and now glorified Lord?

13
Jesus' Resurrection: Literal and Physical

And as they thus spake, Jesus himself stood in the midst of them, and saith unto them, Peace be unto you. But they were terrified and affrighted, and supposed that they had seen a spirit. And he said unto them, Why are ye troubled? and why do thoughts arise in your hearts? Behold my hands and my feet, that it is I myself: handle me, and see; for a spirit hath not flesh and bones, as ye see me have. And when he had thus spoken, he shewed them his hands and his feet. And while they yet believed not for joy, and wondered, he said unto them, Have ye here any meat? And they gave him a piece of a broiled fish, and of an honeycomb. And he took it, and did eat before them. (Luke 24:36–43)

W e could appeal to any number of New Testament passages that affirm the specific character of Jesus' resurrection, but they all speak to the same truth. His resurrection was literal and physical. It involved His physical body, that same body that was born of a virgin, lived as a man for around thirty-three years, suffered at the hands of the Romans and the religious leaders in Jerusalem, was crucified by the Romans, buried, and—yes indeed—arose three days later.

Our study passage goes to great length to affirm the literal reality of Jesus' resurrection. No Gnostic or mystical explanation of a "spirit body" can withstand the vivid witness of Jesus' literal body that stood before the disciples. Based on John's writings, especially 1 John, one of the earliest heresies to invade first century Christianity was a Gnostic fantasy that denied that Jesus had a human body at all or that, if He had a human body, that it arose from the dead, much less entered heaven at the ascension. According to John, this belief assaults one of the most fundamental and essential truths of Biblical truth. How strongly does John reject the Gnostic heresy?

*And every spirit that confesseth not that Jesus Christ is **come in the flesh** is not of God: and this is that spirit of antichrist, whereof ye have heard that it should come; and even now already is it in the world.* (1 John 4:3; emphasis added)

This verse assaults the foundation of the Gnostic error. John will not permit any tampering with the literal reality that he had experienced personally. The Jesus whom John knew was a real human, though obviously more than mere human. He lived in a real human body, a body that consisted of molecules just as real as your body or mine. That body grew tired, rested, ate, drank, and lived an active life. That same body suffered indescribable torture in scourging and crucifixion was quickly prepared for burial by two disciples, buried, and just as literally arose three days later. John begins his first letter with this truth.

That which was from the beginning, which we have heard, which we have seen with our eyes, which we have looked upon, and our hands have handled, of the Word of life. (1 John 1:1)

I suggest that most of John's New Testament writings address the gnostic error, not just First John. Think of this verse, and compare it to the opening verses of John's gospel.

*And the Word was **made flesh**, and dwelt among us, (and we beheld his glory, the glory as of the only begotten of the Father,) full of grace and truth.* (John 1:14; emphasis added)

Early Gnostic beliefs varied widely. We should expect nothing different, given that these ideas were based on mystical ideas that stood on the imagination of the movement's leaders, not on any physical evidence or verifiable facts.

Let's consider two scenarios.

1. Gnostic ideas of a spirit who appeared to be human lived among men for a time. Although people saw an image and thought it to be a real human, he never possessed a literal human body.
2. God literally entered into the world that He created as the real man, Jesus Christ. He lived, suffered, died, was buried, arose, witnessed his resurrection to many for forty days, and ascended in that body into Paradise.

Let's examine our study passage to see which view best matches the facts stated.

1. *Jesus himself stood in the midst of them.* Does a spirit "stand" in the midst of real people with the appearance of a literal body?
2. *But they were terrified and affrighted, and supposed that they had seen a spirit.* This is the very point made by the various Gnostic ideas. If the Gnostic idea were true, these men had very good reason to be "...terrified and affrighted." However, if they were mistaken, if Jesus stood in their midst in His real, resurrected human body, they had no reason to be so frightened.
3. *Behold my hands and my feet, that it is I myself.* Any idea of a non-material "spirit" fails this point miserably. Jesus lived in a body that had hands and feet, hands that healed, and feet that walked among His followers with living grace. "...it is I myself." The same body that lived with these men, the same one who ate that last celebratory meal with them and then surprised them by washing their feet, now reminds them that He, the same He whom they had come to know, love, and follow, now stood before them, living proof that He had risen from the dead, conquering death by His personal and quite literal resurrection. The same body that was buried arose, victor over death's sting.
4. *...handle me, and see.* We can't "handle" a spirit. Other than angels when their divine assignment requires that they

physically appear to us, we can't see a "spirit." On this point, revisit 1 John 1:1. If Jesus intended to show the disciples that He was a spirit and that He had ***not*** arisen with the same literal body in which He lived among them, He chose a strange and deceitful way to do so. However, if He intended to show them that He had literally arisen and that the body that they saw before them was indeed the same body in which He had dwelt among them, He quite wisely demonstrates the same grace and wisdom that characterized His whole time in the flesh.

5. *...for a spirit hath not flesh and bones, as ye see me have.* He could not have more clearly or forcefully made the point. What the disciples saw before them was not a spirit, but was rather the same flesh and bones in which He had lived among them. If Jesus actually appeared before the disciples in a spirit form, these words become the greatest lie ever told, not to mention a cruel and intentional deception.

6. *And when he had thus spoken, he shewed them his hands and his feet.* If Jesus appeared only in spirit, He had no hands and feet to show the disciples. Again, if the Gnostic idea of a spirit, void of a literal human body, had been the facts, Jesus spoke deceitful and misleading words that are inexcusable in leading the disciples to believe a hoax, not the facts.

7. *Have ye here any meat? And they gave him a piece of a broiled fish, and of an honeycomb. And he took it, and did eat before them.* A bodiless spirit cannot pick up a piece of fish and eat it. Jesus goes to the simplest and most convincing length possible to show the disciples that the image they saw was real, that they were looking upon the same body in which He lived while He taught them and prepared them for His final glory.

In every detail of this lesson, the facts stated in the passage speak to the obvious truth. Jesus arose from the dead in the same literal, physical body in which He lived, suffered, and died. Now in resurrection, His literal resurrected body, He proves to the disciples that He is God Incarnate, God temporarily living in human flesh among them.

Forty days later Jesus will take these disciples just outside the city limits of Jerusalem, where He will literally, physically disappear in a cloud of glory before their eyes. He—the real He—in that same body in which He lived, and in which He convinced the disciples that He had arisen, would then ascend into Paradise, but with this promise.

> *And while they looked stedfastly toward heaven as he went up, behold, two men stood by them in white apparel; Which also said, Ye men of Galilee, why stand ye gazing up into heaven? this same Jesus, which is taken up from you into heaven, shall so come in like manner as ye have seen him go into heaven.* (Acts 1:10-11)

The abiding hope of believers from that day till the Second Coming is clear. No less on that future day than during His past time in the flesh, He shall return, but not in humiliation or with the need to atone for sins by suffering and dying. He shall return in crowing, victorious glory to resurrect and to claim His "...purchased possession," including specifically the bodies of His beloved and chosen people from death's grip.

Our study passage documents at least seven vital points that affirm the fact of Jesus' literal, physical body, even after His death, burial, and resurrection. If He did not possess a literal physical body at the time of these events, His conduct was inexcusably deceitful. When Paul began his "Magnum Opus" on the resurrection (1 Corinthians 15), he started with a detailed proof of Jesus' literal bodily resurrection. He rightly reminded the Corinthians that, if Jesus did not arise in that literal physical body, their hope, their faith, the gospel, their baptism; everything that they associated with their faith in God was vain and empty of value or meaning.

Our choice is simple. 1) Choose a myth that is void of Biblical support, one that actually contradicts the consistent New Testament record. Or 2) believe the simple and obvious Bible record of Jesus' life, death, sufferings, resurrection, and ascension in a literal physical body, a body that shall return when He comes to resurrect and to claim His own at the Second Coming. I choose the Bible account. Will you join me?

14
Jesus' Resurrection: Literal and Physical
Continued

Marvel not at this: for the hour is coming, in the which all that are in the graves shall hear his voice, And shall come forth; they that have done good, unto the resurrection of life; and they that have done evil, unto the resurrection of damnation. (John 5:28–29)

As a passage that simply and clearly establishes cardinal truths, John 5 excels. Jesus affirms an oft-rejected truth in John 5:24-25, that the new birth is not a cooperative effort between Him and the believer, but rather a work wholly and exclusively accomplished by God alone. He further emphasizes this truth in John 5:39; Scripture testifies of Him; it does not impart eternal life to those who study it. Verses 28-29, our study passage, also utterly rejects the idea of annihilation of the wicked. Both righteous and wicked are raised at the same time. In the greater context of the chapter, we see a powerful affirmation of His deity, His godhood. In seven specific ways, Jesus affirms that He possesses the same prerogatives of godhood as the Father, verse 19.

1. He does the same work as the Father (verses 17-18; the Jews understood His calling God His "Father" as claiming equality with the Father, and Jesus did not correct their understanding. Nor does John; see John 1:1).
2. The Father has committed all judgment to the Son, temporal and eternal (verses 22-23, 27).
3. He has the power to give life to whom He chooses (verses 21-29; these verses cover both new birth life and final resurrection life).
4. To dishonor the Son is to dishonor the Father also (verse 23).
5. He gives eternal life sovereignly (verses 24-25).

6. His voice shall raise the dead (verses 28-29).
7. He shares the exclusive right of self-existence with the Father (verse 26).

Verses 28-29 simply set forth the Biblical doctrine of the resurrection at the Second Coming. Contradicting the contemporary split rapture madness, Jesus leaves no doubt that both righteous and wicked shall arise in one hour, not two hours, separated by some debated lapse of time. Do not miss the article, "...*the* hour." Jesus in no way indicates two distinct and separate hours

The Bible doctrine of the Second Coming and resurrection is so simple that a dying child can grasp its comforts. The contemporary confusion of secret rapture and split "comings" is so complex that a rocket scientist would struggle to make sense of it—and would likely fail; it is nonsensical when analyzed against the teachings of Scripture. A doctrine that never saw the light of day prior to 1825-27 is about 1,800 years too young to be a sound Biblical truth. The dominant concepts of modern dispensationalism didn't exist prior to this time.

Paul also affirms a single resurrection.

*And have hope toward God, which they themselves also allow, that there shall be **a** resurrection of the dead, both of the just and unjust.* (Acts 24:15; emphasis added)

How many resurrections did Paul acknowledge in this verse? Only one; "...there shall be **a** resurrection...." Further, in that one resurrection, both just and unjust shall rise at the same time. One shall arise to life; the other to judgment, damnation, a legal verdict of "guilty as charged," followed by the righteous sentence against them. To make the point simply, Scripture leaves the "Left Behind" doctrine behind!

In the context of our study passage, Jesus goes to great length to document His claims by witnesses. Deuteronomy 19:15 requires two or more witnesses to a matter. Take note. This passage does not require added witnesses only when an existing witness is not credible. Even with the most honest and credible of witnesses, the passage requires more than one witness. While Jesus spoke truth and only truth, and while He needed no witness to verify that truth, He accommodates His own Law by documenting that the truth that He teaches is verified by more than two witnesses, even if we exclude His own testimony. Why would He make this point? Simple; He intended to leave no doubt whatever about His teachings. Every word that He spoke was true and verified by multiple witnesses.

1. Though He did not need a human witness, He reminds us that John bore a true witness of Him (verses 32-35).
2. The Father bears witness of every word that He spoke and every deed that He did (verses 36-37).
3. Scripture bears a faithful witness of Him (verse 39).

Let's reconstruct and try to follow Jesus' simple explanation of His resurrection truth.

1. "…the hour is coming." First, Jesus contrasts this miraculous event, all future, with another event that He described as both present and future (John 5:24-25). That event refers to the new birth. Jesus described it as the result of one hearing His voice, not His voice plus a mortal man's voice. His voice alone works in new birth. Further, Jesus described the new birth as preceding belief, not occurring simultaneously with belief or subsequent to belief. The hearing believer is, presently already born again (John 5:24). How then can our belief contribute, either causatively or instrumentally, to our new birth if the new birth precedes it? It cannot. As Jesus' voice speaks with sovereign and efficacious power in the new birth, so also He shall speak at the Second Coming. Lazarus heard His voice and left the tomb; all that are in the graves at that day shall hear His voice and come forth. No one shall be "Left Behind" then, shall they?
2. "…all that are in the graves…." Jesus knows nothing of some hearing and coming froth, while others remain. At that

epochal moment, all graves shall be emptied. All shall come
forth, both righteous and wicked, both those who shall hear
the joyful "Come ye blessed of my Father, inherit..." and
those who hear "Depart from me...." Friends, you don't need
to have an advanced degree in theology to understand Jesus'
teachings about His return. It is not so complicated as to stir
endless debate. Example: dispensationalists are hopelessly
divided over when the Second Coming shall occur relative to
their view of the "Great Tribulation." Does He come before
it, in the midst of it, or after it? His teaching is simple. He
comes, He raises the dead, He judges, and He takes His
beloved children to glory to be forever with Him in glory.
   3. There is no annihilation of the wicked in Jesus' words. Both
      righteous and wicked are raised.

  Does Jesus teach that we in some way contribute to our eternal
salvation by our faith or by our good works in His description,
"...they that have done good...and they that have done evil"? I
suggest that the answer is no. Otherwise, we must deal with a
contradiction between Jesus and numerous other New Testament
writings that repeatedly and clearly affirm that our eternal salvation
is all of God and "not of works, lest any man should boast"
(Ephesians 2:9).
  Rather than teaching that our works contribute to our eternal life
with Him, Jesus is teaching that His grace has made a difference in
the moral and spiritual character of those whom He by grace has
saved from their sins. Scripture does not give us the liberty to set
imaginary hurdles of certain moral or spiritual height or difficulty
over which we must pass to gain or to know that we have eternal
life. Every effort to impose such hurdles eventually leads to
insidious legalism and excessive judging by people regarding who,
in their opinion, is and who is not born again. Scripture rather
forbids such self-righteous judgments and warns us to leave all such
judgment in the hands of Him to Whom the Father committed this
judgment (John 5:22-23, 26-27, 30). Leave the identification of

wheat and tares to Him who knows how to distinguish between the two.

If we try to assess Jesus' words as His judge, a foolish posture for frail mortals, we might quibble about whether or not His judgment is just. If we examine His words and judgment in the passage from a more objective legal perspective, something that most of us are somewhat limited to do, we will conclude that Jesus engages in a straightforward, concise, and righteous judgment of those who appear before Him. And that is a good conclusion. I suggest that, in our present sinful mortality, none of us is remotely capable of assessing the justice of the sentence pronounced upon either class. Given Scripture's consistent description of our God as being wholly righteous and merciful beyond our comprehension, we best serve our faith by praising Him for these two traits, even if we cannot fully grasp them in this setting.

In our finite perspective, we often view righteousness and mercy as being more opposed to each other than as complimentary. However, this tension should lead us to the heart of the gospel. In Jesus, these two tension-set principles come together in perfect harmony.

Mercy and truth are met together; righteousness and peace have kissed each other. Truth shall spring out of the earth; and righteousness shall look down from heaven. (Psalms 85:10-11)

Only in the Person and work of the Lord Jesus Christ can we see God's mercy and the truth of our sinful condition come together in a joyful resolution for us. Hallelujah! What a Savior!

15
A General Resurrection, Not a Multi-Staged Event

But this I confess unto thee, that after the way which they call heresy, so worship I the God of my fathers, believing all things which are written in the law and in the prophets: And have hope toward God, which they themselves also allow, that there shall be a resurrection of the dead, both of the just and unjust. (Acts 24:14–15)

What do we mean by a "general" resurrection? The term historically refers to the belief that all humans who have ever lived shall be raised from the dead at one time. In contrast, the idea that one specific group might be raised, while others remain in the grave, would be described as a specific resurrection, specific to the group being raised. We find any number of passages in addition to our study verses that teach the same principle.

When Paul wrote, "Behold, I shew you a mystery; We shall not all sleep, but we shall all be changed, In a moment, in the twinkling of an eye, at the last trump: for the trumpet shall sound, and the dead shall be raised incorruptible, and we shall be changed" (1 Corinthians 15:51-52), the word that he used, translated in our King James Bible as "moment," is the Greek root for our English word "atom." No surprise, it is defined as a moment of time so small that it cannot be further divided into a shorter moment. Our contemporary culture might refer to it as a "nanosecond."

To give practical insight to his point, Paul clarifies, "...in the twinkling of an eye." He didn't refer to our blinking the eyelid, but to the insightful twinkling that you see in a person's eye when they discover something new and exciting to them. The response is instantaneous, and that is Paul's point. The resurrection shall be an instantaneous event for all human beings, just one instant in which all who are in their graves, "...both of the just and unjust," shall arise.

*And many of them that sleep in the dust of the earth shall awake,
some to everlasting life, and some to shame and everlasting
contempt.* (Daniel 12:2)

Do not misread the point. "Many" simply refers to a very large
number. It does not in any way exclude the universal principle that
includes all.

The dominant point of the lesson affirms our primary focus in our
present study. The final resurrection at the Lord's return shall
include both righteous and wicked. Daniel describes the two classes
based on the outcome of their judgment, "some to everlasting life,
and some to shame and everlasting contempt." As we saw in our last
study, this passage also refutes the idea of annihilation of the
wicked. Their shame and contempt are everlasting, something that
could not be if they were raised and shortly thereafter annihilated.
Like his New Testament inspired counterparts, Daniel sees only two
classes of people in his revelation of that Day.

*Behold, he cometh with clouds; and every eye shall see him, and
they also which pierced him: and all kindreds of the earth shall
wail because of him. Even so, Amen.* (Revelation 1:7)

If we examine the literary structure of this context, this verse is the
very first thought that John writes after his formal introduction of
himself and the letter of Revelation. This truth should form the "go-
to" anchor with every step that we take through the Book of
Revelation.

As we confront one frightening and ominous appearing adversary
after another, as we anticipate final deliverance only repeatedly to be
shown that deliverance is repeatedly delayed for a time, we need to
go back to this foundational thought. He is coming, and His coming
shall be in glory and victory. Those who pierced Him shall see Him,
but they shall no longer be able to inflict pain or ridicule upon Him.
All kindreds of the earth shall see Him and wail because of Him.
While those who lived and died "...of the earth" wail because of

Him, those whom He redeemed shall immediately praise Him for redemption. They shall realize that they stand securely and joyfully in His presence and by His side!

And again, I will put my trust in him. And again, Behold I and the children which God hath given me. (Hebrews 2:13)

The idea that the final judgment shall go on interminably while every person who ever lived gives a boring and detailed account of every thought, word, or deed committed cannot be supported by Scripture. What man perceives as taking a symbolic "eternity" shall be completed hastily, but thoroughly. True eternity for the family of God shall not suffer delay from a torturously long judgment.

Our inquisitive mindset may wonder why God did not provide redemption from sin for all humanity. I offer a few thoughts as suggestions, I hope with Biblical reasons.

1. From Genesis the first chapter, Scripture reveals God as a moral being, not, like so many of the pagan imaginary deities, a self-indulgent amoral hedonist. While we might draw practical insights from the Hebrew word translated "good" in the first chapter of Genesis, the word also carries a distinctly moral quality of goodness. A morally good God would be expected to create a morally good universe, and so He did. This fact sheds insight into God's wrath at Adam's sin and the judgment that followed. It therefore stands to reason that a supremely righteous and moral God would choose to demonstrate both His mercy and His moral character.

2. All of these passages consistently reveal the same separation of humanity into two distinct groups, one that shall experience the merciful joys of God's person and presence and the other than shall face His righteous judgment, resulting in "…shame and everlasting contempt." This point rejects both errant doctrines: 1) the total annihilation of the wicked shortly after judgment, and 2) universalism, the soft-

hearted, and unbiblical idea that God shall, in the end, bring all humanity into His favor and eternal life.

3. The sentence pronounced in both cases is a righteous, just sentence. The sentence of eternal joy is righteous based on the person and work of the Lord Jesus Christ on their behalf, not based on their personal works. Jesus fully earned our eternal blessing based on God's righteous judgment. The sentence against the wicked shall likewise be altogether righteous and just. We occasionally look at the severity of the penalty described in Scripture, and we tend to minimize the "Crime" committed. However, we must not forget that our judgment is wholly biased. We cannot possibly assess God's judgment from a purely neutral or righteous perspective. How close do we lie in conduct and in sentiment to those who shall hear the grave sentence pronounced against them? How much impact touches us from the realization, "There, but for the grace of God, am I"? We cannot possibly grasp the righteous character and perspective of God who created man and gave man His moral law. We are obviously therefore incapable of passing judgment against the nature or severity of the sentence that Scripture describes against the wicked. Our inclination is likely to think of an imperceptible eternity of "payment" compared with such a minor, brief time of sin. Do you not see the bias in such a judgment? Can you, even remotely, grasp the depth of offense that man's sinful disposition and actions charge against God? I say no. We cannot.

4. I offer the most obvious and glaring of testimonies to be considered in favor of God on this question of justice. The elect who shall praise God in glory for eternity were born into the world as sinners. We do not anticipate that glorious day based on our lack of sin, do we? Think long and carefully. On what basis did God remit the infectious moral weight of our sins? He would accept nothing less than the sinless offering of His own darling Son. In no way did God compromise or "look the other way" and pretend that we

didn't commit any of the sins that stain each and every one of us. God remained faithful to His moral character, even in atoning for our sins. We could have no greater testimony to God's moral character and to the propriety of His judgment than to think of His own Son, scourged and assaulted by sinful men, hanging on a tree, the most torturous death contrived by wicked men. And yet, to accomplish our redemption, God required far more than mortal man could do to His righteous Son. No wicked man, with all of his depraved torture against our Lord, contributed anything whatever to our redemption. Immediately upon His death on the cross, Jesus took His life, His sinless, righteous life to Paradise where He presented Himself to the Father as the one and only acceptable payment that would settle our moral debt of sin. I cannot imagine any deed that more commands and deserves the adoring worship and faithful-unto-death devotion and service, can you?

At the Second Coming, when the Lord returns, Scripture affirms that both His righteous judgment against sin—and sinners—as well as His unfathomable mercy shall be fully displayed in His final act of judgment.

Given the depth of mercy, we should not be surprised when we read the reaction that Jesus says the elect shall give to the knowledge that they were included. "When saw we thee...?" They are the most surprised of all people at the knowledge of their inclusion! Not a one of them smugly responded, "Well, of course; after all, look at all the good works that I did." To a person, they react with amazement that they, of all people, are included. Hallelujah! What a Savior!

16
An Instructive Analogy: A Shepherd at Work

When the Son of man shall come in his glory, and all the holy angels with him, then shall he sit upon the throne of his glory: And before him shall be gathered all nations: and he shall separate them one from another, as a shepherd divideth his sheep from the goats: And he shall set the sheep on his right hand, but the goats on the left. Then shall the King say unto them on his right hand, Come, ye blessed of my Father, inherit the kingdom prepared for you from the foundation of the world: For I was an hungred, and ye gave me meat: I was thirsty, and ye gave me drink: I was a stranger, and ye took me in: Naked, and ye clothed me: I was sick, and ye visited me: I was in prison, and ye came unto me. Then shall the righteous answer him, saying, Lord, when saw we thee an hungred, and fed thee? or thirsty, and gave thee drink? When saw we thee a stranger, and took thee in? or naked, and clothed thee? Or when saw we thee sick, or in prison, and came unto thee? And the King shall answer and say unto them, Verily I say unto you, Inasmuch as ye have done it unto one of the least of these my brethren, ye have done it unto me. Then shall he say also unto them on the left hand, Depart from me, ye cursed, into everlasting fire, prepared for the devil and his angels: For I was an hungred, and ye gave me no meat: I was thirsty, and ye gave me no drink: I was a stranger, and ye took me not in: naked, and ye clothed me not: sick, and in prison, and ye visited me not. Then shall they also answer him, saying, Lord, when saw we thee an hungred, or athirst, or a stranger, or naked, or sick, or in prison, and did not minister unto thee? Then shall he answer them, saying, Verily I say unto you, Inasmuch as ye did it not to one of the least of these, ye did it not to me. And these shall go away into everlasting punishment: but the righteous into life eternal.
(Matthew 25:31–46)

Not only in His parables, but in His other teachings, Jesus used the simplest and most understandable analogies available. His

objective was obviously to communicate His truth clearly and
simply to His hearers. In the lesson we now study, Jesus used the
analogy of a shepherd at work, something that His first century
audience knew well.

Matthew 25 continues the lesson that Jesus began in Matthew 24.
At the beginning of chapter twenty-four, the disciples and Jesus had
a brief conversation in which Jesus made a point that the disciples
questioned. They asked Jesus three questions; some commentaries
make the number two, but we should not doubt that the questions
were distinct, not merely a redundant duplication. By so directly
telling the disciples that the magnificent temple they were viewing
would become a ruin, Jesus alarmed the disciples. They had no
thought of such a thing. If we attempt to find Jesus' answer to all
three (or two) questions in the twenty-fourth chapter, we will never
arrive at a simple, clear answer. However, by acknowledging the
obvious, that His answer continued to the end of the twenty-fifth
chapter, His answers to the questions more simply and logically
appear.

*Tell us, when shall these things be? and what shall be the sign of
thy coming, and of the end of the world?* (Matthew 24:3b)

Let's sort out the three questions and at least suggest the nature of
Jesus' answer.

...when shall these things be? This question refers to Jesus'
alarming news that not one stone would soon be standing on another
in the temple before them. How could such a catastrophe occur?
Why? When, especially when? Jesus answered the first two
questions in the twenty-fourth chapter.

...what shall be the sign of thy coming? In this context, and set
forth in Jesus' answer, the first thought of the disciples, if their
beautiful temple were to be destroyed, the event must be part of a
signal event of divine judgment. If so, Jesus would come in
judgment, something that He warned the unbelieving Jews of His
day was imminent in the Olivet Discourse, "Behold, your house is
left unto you desolate" (Matthew 23:38). Not only would their house

be left desolate, but it would be wholly destroyed in the judgment that their sin and unbelief brought upon them. In the twenty-fourth chapter, Jesus answered these first two questions. Daniel and other Old Testament prophets had prophesied of this catastrophic event. Rather than give a specific date, though He did give them a clear limit, Jesus answered the question with details of the event that linked it to those prophecies. And He also warned them of the time envelop that would see this event unfold. "Verily I say unto you, This generation shall not pass, till all these things be fulfilled" (Matthew 24:34). Prior to this verse, Jesus repeatedly warned the disciples to flee into the mountains when they saw the signs of this coming judgment, a nonsensical action to take at the time of the Second Coming, but the right action when they saw the events that He described unfolding. In both points, Jesus affirmed that they would live to see the sad fall of the temple, and of God's solemn judgment that accompanied that fall. The event occurred in March-August, 70 A. D., some forty years later.

...and of the end of the world? The third question takes us beyond the fall of the temple and God's judgment against first century Jews. Some commentaries define the "...end of the world" in this verse as the end of the Jewish world, the Old Testament era. Perhaps this is possible, but it is difficult. Jesus marked the end of the Jewish era and the beginning of the gospel era with John's preaching, not some later date (Luke 16:16).

If the Jewish era had already ended, and if the temple in Jerusalem was soon to be utterly destroyed so that one stone would not be left on another, what was to follow? What should they and future believers expect from that date till the Second Coming?

Jesus answers these questions in the twenty-fifth chapter. The kingdom of God was not linked to the temple or any other material building structure, or to one race or culture of people, not any longer. At the time of this event, God's kingdom would be comparable to a wedding celebration in which some of the invited guests took the invitation seriously and prepared for the wedding, while others, the unbelieving Jews of the first century who brought that severe judgment against them, were wholly unprepared. Once the kingdom transitioned primarily from a Jewish national kingdom to a spiritual kingdom made up of all kinds of people, the kingdom of God would be comparable to a master who entrusted his servants with a treasure. Some of the servants respected their master and invested the treasure under their care wisely. Others, in contempt for their master, refused to invest the funds committed to them at all. Rather than effectively judging a whole nation, as with the destruction of the temple, in this new era of the kingdom of God, the wise and faithful servants would be rewarded, and the unfaithful would be punished and dishonored. This scenario would repeat itself and would characterize the Lord's kingdom until the Second Coming, an event that Jesus characterizes in the closing lesson of Matthew 25 with the analogy of a shepherd separating sheep from goats.

We shall linger with this lesson. It is necessary to frame the actual lesson in its extended context to grasp the clarity and the full scope of Jesus' teaching in this extended message. Today we live in the era of the Master's treasure, committed to us in stewardship, a stewardship that requires full and personal accounting directly to Him for our wise or foolish use of His treasure. We look forward joyfully to the day when He returns and separates humanity in preparation for the righteous punishment of the wicked and the eternal inheritance of the elect.

A word of caution: Analogical language is not to be interpreted as allegory, forcing every finite detail to take on symbolic meaning. Parables and general analogies in Scripture should be interpreted with a more "broad brush" interpretation. Look at the "big picture" of the lesson. Let's consider just a few of the major factors that Jesus introduces in this lesson.

1. He compares His separation of humanity to a shepherd separating sheep from goats. What distinguishes a sheep from a goat? If behavior, mental or physical, is the final basis on which the elect enter glory, Jesus chose a poor analogy. The distinction between a sheep and a goat is not behavior. The two animals are distinct species. No goat has ever

"behaved" his way into becoming a sheep; nor has any sheep ever acted his way into becoming a goat.

2. The basis on which Jesus specifically assigns for the elect entering eternal glory is inheritance, not reward for behavior. "Then shall the King say unto them on his right hand, Come, ye blessed of my Father, inherit the kingdom prepared for you from the foundation of the world" (Matthew 25:34). In fact, Jesus actually assigns two bases for the announced and blessed verdict: 1) they are "...blessed of my Father," and 2) they are told to enter based on His inheritance. Yes, He also describes their conduct, as He describes the conduct of the wicked, but He assigns the basis for their eternal blessing as an inheritance, not as a reward or wage earned.

3. The basis on which Jesus assigns the wicked to eternal separation is indeed their behavior. He does not interject any other grounds for their final judgment other than the wicked things that they did.

4. In the new birth, the Holy Spirit alters our moral and spiritual compass. He changes our perception of values. We should avoid the attitude of setting moral or spiritual litmus tests to determine who really is or is not born again, an attitude that typically leads people to become arrogant and judgmental toward others. In principle, Jesus forbids this often self-serving arrogance in the Parable of the Wheat and the Tares. It is not easy to distinguish a wheat plant from a tare plant, so the servants in the parable are liable to mistake one from the other and thereby inadvertently damage wheat plants. Leave such judgments to God who is quite capable of making the right judgment. However, we should not at all hesitate to make the point that the new birth alters a person's values, as well as their spiritual nature. According to Scripture, a born-again person becomes so by a supernatural birth, not by behavior. Based on the Scriptures, it is as nonsensical to think that our behavior or actions cause our new birth as to think that a natural goat may simply change its behavior and become a sheep. Jesus states the basis for

the elect entering eternal glory as an inheritance, followed by His description of their conduct, actions compatible with the work of grace that He accomplishes in the new birth.

5. Interestingly, and typically wholly overlooked by commentaries and Bible teachers, both the elect and the wicked react with surprise at hearing their sentence. Even the elect are surprised to hear the words, "Come, ye blessed of my Father...." Notice the note of surprise, "Then shall the righteous answer him, saying, Lord, when saw we thee an hungred, and fed thee? or thirsty, and gave thee drink? When saw we thee a stranger, and took thee in? or naked, and clothed thee? Or when saw we thee sick, or in prison, and came unto thee?" (Matthew 25:37-39) And we should also take note of Jesus' answer to them. "And the King shall answer and say unto them, Verily I say unto you, Inasmuch as ye have done it unto one of the least of these my brethren, ye have done it unto me" (Matthew 25:40). Forget playing up to your favorite believers or to those whom you hope might give you a favor. Forget courting the politically connected folks who might be able to show you a special kindness. Jesus measures and values our kindness based on how we treat those who have no ability to reciprocate or to return the favors that we show to them, "...*the least of these* my brethren." Sadly often, I have been disappointed and at times amused at the conduct of people who go out of their way to patronize someone whom they think might show them some special favor. To the extent that we go out of our way to patronize other people, whatever their ability to favor us, we demonstrate a similar lack of regard for the Lord's favor.

This lesson overflows with rich and comforting truth. We shall study it further.

17
How Long?

And these shall go away into everlasting punishment: but the righteous into life eternal. (Matthew 25:46)

O ccasionally sincere and well-meaning Bible students engage in something of a hairsplitting idea that attempts to distinguish the difference between "eternal" and "everlasting." Is there a difference in meaning between the two words? Let's start with the English words. Listed below you will see the definitions of the two words from the *Shorter Oxford English Dictionary*.

Eternal. That will always exist; that has always existed; without a) beginning or an end in time; everlasting. b) Pertaining to eternal things; having eternal consequences; not conditioned by time; not subject to time relations.

Everlasting. Lasting for ever; infinite in future, or past and future, duration; Isa. 9:6 (*The mighty God, the everlasting Father*); J. Updike (*His soul has gone to everlasting fire!*); everlasting death; everlasting life; lasting so long as to seem or be treated as eternal.

Do not miss the obvious. The dictionary uses "everlasting" in its definition of "eternal," and it uses "eternal" in its definition of "everlasting."

What about the original first century language in which the New Testament was written? If you check that language, the two words in our study verse were translated from the same exact Greek word. What is the meaning of this word?

*ai**ōn**ios* (The English rendition of the Greek word).   ...pertaining to an unlimited duration of time—'eternal.[1]

When I have engaged those who attempt to distinguish the two words to learn what they think defines the difference in meaning, the most common answer is this. Supposedly, "eternal" means without beginning and without end, while "everlasting" means with a beginning, but without an end. Perhaps somewhere an English dictionary conveys this idea, but, as documented above, the idea is not apparent in the *Shorter Oxford*. Nor is it at all present in the first century Greek word, for both English words are used interchangeably in the King James New Testament for the one Greek word.

The idea of different meanings becomes highly problematic when we realize that the King James Bible uses "everlasting" to refer to God, as in Isaiah 9:6, the reference mentioned in the *Shorter Oxford Dictionary* under its definition of "everlasting." If, as alleged, "everlasting" refers to something—or someone—that has a beginning, but no end, how can we reconcile this idea to the existence and immutability of God? Does God have a beginning, but no ending? Isaiah 9:6 is by no means an isolated case or exception.

Consider a few other passages that refer to God as everlasting; Genesis 21:33; Deuteronomy 33:27;[2] Psalm 41:13; 90:2; 106:48; Isaiah 40:28; Romans 16:26. The fact that all of these verses refer to God as "everlasting," coupled with the passages that also affirm His eternal immutability, His unchangeableness, should dispel the idea that the two words were intended to convey some different meaning.

---

[1] Johannes P. Louw and Eugene Albert Nida, *Greek-English Lexicon of the New Testament: Based on Semantic Domains* (New York: United Bible Societies, 1996), 641.

[2] This verse is highly problematic for the idea of this supposed distinction. Read the verse. Are we to conclude that God is eternal, but that His arms are only everlasting? What do we make of God during the supposed time before His arms came to exist? How do we reconcile this idea with Scripture's emphatic assertion that God is immutable, unchangeable? Obviously, in this verse, Moses is emphasizing that God, including all of His power and essential attributes, is eternal. He, in all of His deity, is eternal and immutable, unchangeable.

I struggle sufficiently with the English language; I cannot claim that my name is Webster or that I am an Oxford official. I choose to respectfully believe the definitions that I read in these authoritative sources instead of attempting to write my own dictionary. Further, the repeated practice of the King James translators to use "eternal" and "everlasting" to translate the one Greek word *aionios* in its various word forms should in and of itself settle the question. Given the King James translators' passion to give the English reading world a literal translation of the Bible, their repeated interchangeable use of the two English words to translate the one Greek word speaks loudly that they viewed the two English words as equal in meaning in their representation of the one Greek word.

The greater task of the serious Bible student is not to split imaginary hairs, but to regard the whole passage in its contextual setting, thereby seeking to understand the Holy Spirit's intended meaning in the passage. The distinguishing words in our study verse are not "everlasting" and "eternal," but "punishment" and "life." Let's pursue these words and seek to learn what the lesson teaches.

That the wicked shall be consigned to endless separation from God and all of His deliverances is a strongly and clearly affirmed truth of Scripture. Advocates of double predestination appear to compromise this point by implying that God as positively predestinated the punishment of the wicked as the joyful deliverance of the elect. Scripture does not agree. Whenever Scripture deals with the final state and punishment of the wicked, it always associates their state with their sinful conduct, never with a divine act apart from their sins. Paul leaves no doubt on this question.

For the wages of sin is death; but the gift of God is eternal life through Jesus Christ our Lord. (Romans 6:23)

What is the difference between wages and a gift? Wages are earned based on what the wage-earner works for and deserves to collect for his actions. A gift is freely given apart from what the recipient earned or didn't earn. The two principles stand in vivid contrast.

If, as some believers assert, we either earn or in some degree contribute to our eternal life, Paul's fundamental point in this verse is wrong. If we contribute to our eternal life, both the wicked and the elect spend eternity based on wages earned. However, if we cannot possibly do anything to merit our eternal life, as Scripture asserts, our receiving it in the end is the result of God's loving and merciful gift, not wages earned. Paul leaves no doubt. The sentence against the wicked shall be based on wages, on actions that earned the sentence and that deserve it.

In our study passage, Jesus has already established the true basis for entrance of the blessed into eternal glory with Him. He refers to them as "...blessed of my Father," and He tells them to "...inherit the kingdom prepared for you from the foundation of the world" (Matthew 25:34). Our entrance into eternal bliss shall occur as the result of these two divine actions: 1) the Father blessed us with something that we didn't earn and that we didn't deserve; and 2) we shall enter into that glorious place and state based on the Father's will, an inheritance based on a family relationship that God established, not we.

Jesus' juxtaposing "punishment" with "life" commands our interest. Both states are identified as equal in duration (remember: the Greek word from which both "everlasting" and "eternal" is the same word). While the primary meaning of the Greek word behind both of the English words refers to duration, it also inherently conveys a sense of quality, as well as duration. Anything that lasts for eternity must possess a quality beyond our imagination. Duration alone does not complete the "...hope of eternal life...which God, that cannot lie, promised before the world began" (Titus 1:2). To support such hope, the word must also convey a sense of quality, of intimate fellowship, of true "life" with God for the duration. The Geneva Bible adds two footnotes to Titus 1:2.

1. Hope is the end of faith.
2. Freely and only from his generosity.

God's promise of eternal life did not originate as He anticipated or saw in advance whether we would believe or perform good works. It comes to us "freely and *only* from his generosity." In harmony with Jesus' words, those who shall finally enjoy this eternal life are "...blessed of my Father," and they inherit that life based on a family relationship with God that God alone established in and for them.

Of the wicked in Matthew 25:46, Matthew Poole writes, "They shall go into everlasting punishment, not a punishment for a time, as Origen thought." The punishment that the wicked shall experience is of exactly the same duration as the inheritance of the elect, not for a limited time, followed either by annihilation or by transition from punishment to glory. It shall be a permanent experience, "everlasting punishment," just as the elect shall rejoice in "eternal life."

The presence of both "Father" and "inherit" in this context nudges a central point to the lesson, a point confirmed throughout Scripture. God's election and our eternal (review the word in the definition above, something that has eternal consequences, not conditioned by time) life with God is presented in Scripture as a family matter. "Behold I and the children which God hath given me" (Hebrews 2:13b). And the development of God's family is a matter that God brings about exclusively Himself, sovereignly, and lovingly. "The LORD hath appeared of old unto me, saying, Yea, I have loved thee with an everlasting love: therefore with lovingkindness have I drawn thee" (Jeremiah 31:3). We do not cause our new birth or our family identity with God. Nor do we contribute to that relationship causatively or instrumentally, any more than we caused our birth into our earthly family. In both cases, it occurred prior to our being able to cause anything. But our future is lovingly secured with our heavenly family. What a day that will be!

18
God's Effectual Drawing

*All that the Father giveth me shall come to me; and him that cometh to
me I will in no wise cast out. For I came down from heaven, not to do
mine own will, but the will of him that sent me. And this is the Father's
will which hath sent me, that of all which he hath given me I should lose
nothing, but should raise it up again at the last day.* (John 6:37–39)

Occasionally Bible students observe that Scripture often uses
"shall" in a strong, decisive way. The word in our present
context leaves no ground for doubt or uncertainty as to the outcome.
When God in His eternal (remember the Shorter Oxford English
Dictionary's definition from our last study, having eternal
consequences) and redemptive purpose declares that He "shall" do
something, we cannot doubt His intention or His ability to
effectually bring that consequence to pass.

Jesus begins our study passage with such a sentence structure.
"All that the Father giveth me *shall* come to me...." Jesus takes the
question of whether they come to Him or not off the table. *They
shall come!* They shall not be cast out.

In this context, Jesus specifically identifies the "eternal
consequences" of His work; "...raise it up again at the last day."
Yes, in the chapter, Jesus deals with His being the bread of life, but,
even in that analogy, His application of bread to His own body and
blood nudges us to think of the chapter in terms of eternal
consequences.

The Roman Catholic view that this chapter interprets Jesus' body
and blood as Communion, that the bread and wine of Communion
mystically become the body and blood of Jesus, leaves advocates of
this view open to the charge of cannibalism, and its defenders work
to defend their view against this charge. However, once you hold
that the bread and wine become the body and blood of Jesus, and

you eat the bread and drink the wine, you have no real defense against the charge.

Scripture never teaches that the bread and wine are changed in chemical or effective substance during Communion. You eat unleavened bread and drink wine, that is, if you follow Scripture's teaching on the correct symbols for Communion, the same items that Jesus used when He instituted it. Jesus uses an analogy in this chapter, but His analogy refers to His intimate, personal relationship with each of His beloved children, particularly His nurturing and protecting them securely in His care. There is no basis in the context of John 6 to think that Jesus was teaching on Communion by His reference to eating His flesh and drinking His blood. Thus, no defense against cannibalism is necessary in this chapter, nor, for that matter, in Communion if we hold the right view of Communion. The bread represents Jesus body, broken and died for us; the wine represents His blood, His life, freely and sacrificially given for us. Communion is a representation of His body and blood; the elements do not change, literally or mystically.

Any analogy that depicts the child of grace as an entity outside the Lord Jesus Christ makes that child a parasite, invading and consuming the Lord's body. But a healthy body, nourishing itself and maintaining its immune system to ward off invading disease, is a powerful lesson to remind us of the Lord's abundant care and provision for His beloved children, His "body." Only when we discover the proper perspective of the lesson do these silly problems go away. If the child of grace belongs to the body of Christ, is actually a part of His body, then the child eating His flesh and drinking His blood becomes a simple and rational process of the body nurturing, feeding, and keeping all of its body parts healthy and vital.

And hath put all things under his feet, and gave him to be the head over all things to the church, which is his body, the fulness of him that filleth all in all. (Ephesians 1:22-23)

For we are members of his body, of his flesh, and of his bones.
(Ephesians 5:30)

*And not holding the Head, from which all the body by joints and
bands having nourishment ministered, and knit together,
increaseth with the increase of God.* (Colossians 2:19)

In Ephesians 1:22, the church to which Paul refers is far broader
than any given local church, or all local churches for that matter. As
members of His body, feeding on Him is a routine part of our
permanent and loving family relationship with Him. As we live in a
dirty, sin-diseased world, He constantly feeds and protects us from
the invasion of the sin disease that could drag us down into eternal
woe.

Thus, even in the bread of life sections of this chapter, Jesus is
teaching the truth of His loving, effectual drawing and sustaining
power over His elect. It is He who keeps you alive spiritually and in
a fixed loving union with Him. What is the final note of this lesson?
"…that of all which he hath given me I should lose nothing, but
should raise it up again at the last day."

If we ponder the analogy of the body that Jesus uses in this
chapter, we must deal with two facets of "food" and the body. 1)
The person chooses and eats food to satisfy his body's needs. 2)
This person's body breaks down the food that he has eaten and
digests its nutrients into the blood system, from which the blood
system delivers oxygen, nutrition, and antibodies to every part of the
body. In John 6, Jesus is not dealing with the first of these food
dynamics, but the second. Jesus teaches us that He lovingly and
sufficiently nourishes and protects His whole body from danger or
loss. He shall "…raise it up again at the last day."

Further, in John 6:44, Jesus clarifies His role in this "coming" to
Him. This *coming* is not an act of believer's willing and voluntary
obedience, but rather the result of God's divine drawing. The Greek
word translated "draw" in this verse is a powerful word. It is used
elsewhere in the New Testament of a net full of fish being drawn
into a boat. The question begs to be answered. Did those fish in

some way volunteer to be taken into the ship? Were they required to exercise their "free will" before the fishermen could draw them? Were they required to look up to the fisherman and respect him as their lord and master before he agreed to "really" draw them into the boat? Does their being drawn into the boat by a power outside themselves and their control mean that the same power also controlled or "orchestrated" their every action before the net, while they lived in the water? Of course not.

When Jesus teaches extended lessons such as we see in John 6, He sets the context. He frames the lesson as He intended. The greater lessons of John 6 clearly include two distinct truths or principles. The first principle is relational and eternal in its consequences. He gives life to the world. Do not twist the language. No amount of wresting can morph the meaning of Jesus' words from giving life to the world into the common construction of offering life on a "take it or leave it" proposition. Nothing in the verse (John 6:33) so much as implies that Jesus came down from heaven and offered life to anyone. *He gives it*. People who formerly had no life (spiritual, eternal life) now have it, and their having it resulted from His gift, not from their accepting His offer (Ephesians 2:1-9). He didn't offer it; He gives it.

The question of interpretation in this verse deals with the meaning of the "world" named, not with whether Jesus offers or gives life to that world. The simple fact that the verse states that Jesus gives life to this world should shock folks who hold the populist view into serious reconsideration.

Both in first century Jewish culture and our own culture today, "world" often is used to refer to a specific subculture, such as the political world, the religious world, etc. First century Jews referred to anyone outside their culture as part of the world. John obviously uses this idea in another passage, "And we know that we are of God, and the whole world lieth in wickedness" (1 John 5:19). John distinguishes two classes of people in this verse: 1) one class belongs to God; 2) the other class, identified by John as "the whole world," resides in wickedness. Clearly those who are "of God" do not belong to the "whole world" of wickedness.

Sometimes we can learn much about a passage by simply acknowledging that it says either too much or too little for any given interpretation. In this case, John 6:33 says too much, far too much to support the populist view of the day that Jesus died for every human being who ever lived, and that He offers eternal life to anyone who will make a decision for Him, believe in Him, or whatever the various facts of this belief system impose as their requirements on the individual to obtain this salvation himself. The verse doesn't indicate a conditional offer, but an unconditional gift, fully bestowed and conveyed. He "...*giveth life* unto the world."

Jesus did not teach universal salvation in this verse. He identified that He gives, ***never offers***, eternal life to a specific group of people, a gift based on His own love and purpose, and a gift that required His personal work to remove their debt and transform them into members of His own body. As part of His body, He gives them life. Their whole life in His body depends on Him. As part of His body, He also feeds them, nourishes them to keep them healthy and free of damning disease. Nothing can so infect them or damage them as to endanger their position and security in His body. That is the basic point of Jesus' words and lesson in this chapter.

From this point of coming down from heaven and giving life to the world, Jesus next speaks the words of our study passage. What Jesus said in our text relates specifically to His giving life to the world. The "world" to whom He gives life is the world that the Father gave to Him for safe keeping and redemption. All individuals in that world, according to Jesus (could we find a better spokesman?) shall come to Him, not be cast out, but be raised again at the last day. He gives this world life. He preserves and sustains this world. And, at the last day, He shall raise this world and glorify it (them) to be like Him and to be with Him in joyful and endless glory.

We shall praise our God and Savior throughout eternity in ways that we cannot fathom. Are we praising Him as we should now?

19
Resurrection: God's Example for His Glory

When Jesus heard that, he said, This sickness is not unto death, but for the glory of God, that the Son of God might be glorified thereby. (John 11:4)

If we stop to think of what life might have been like had we lived in Jesus' time and had been a close friend, our imagination could easily run out of control. Rather than chase imaginations, Scripture gives us occasional glimpses of that life. John devotes a lengthy chapter to one incident in the life of a family that enjoyed a close friendship with Jesus. We shall linger with this lesson.

When we face grave danger or loss, we long for our close friends to be with us to help us work our way through the trial. Thus, when we read that Lazarus became ill, likely a grave illness of some kind, his sisters, Mary and Martha, send word to Jesus. They likely had more in mind than merely His comforting company, for later we read that they believed, had He been present, Lazarus would not have died. They believed that He who had healed so many other people and even raised some from the dead could heal their brother.

Although Jesus healed many people during His brief public life, we read the inspired notation that an incident occurred for the glory of God on two special occasions. The other occasion appears in John 9 with the man born blind. Jesus gives him sight. But, when the disciples asked Jesus the nonsensical question about the man's blindness being caused either by sin committed by the man's parents or by the man himself, Jesus corrected their error. The man was born blind for a good reason, "...that the works of God should be made manifest in him" (John 9:3b).

Occasionally, sincere believers will run their minds off the track of God's truth in Scripture and adopt a pagan-originated fatalistic attitude. In such cases as these two in Scripture, they will leap from

two men who experienced major illness or untimely death, stated in
the Scripture as occurring for God's purpose and glory, to the
fatalistic and illogical idea that all illness, all birth defects, and all
death occurs by God's causing intervention for His glory. This
wrong-headed conclusion egregiously commits the parts-to-the-
whole logical fallacy.

The parts-to-the-whole fallacy examines only one part of a larger
and more complex system and errantly concludes that, since this one
part manifests certain characteristics, the whole system must also
possess the same characteristics. In this case, these folks conclude
that since the man born blind in John 9 was so born so that God's
works should be manifest in him, all birth defects are caused by God
for the same reason. And, since Lazarus became deathly ill for the
glory of God, all illnesses are divinely caused for the same reason.

Let me give you a simple illustration that clearly shows the
illogical thinking of this fallacy. If I walk into my garage and
examine my automobile, I notice that it has four round wheels
covered with rubber tires. If I follow the parts-to-the-whole logical
fallacy, I then conclude that my whole automobile consists only of
round wheels covered with rubber tires. I errantly think that this one
part of the car makes up the whole car.

As I ponder the various errant ideas that I have encountered over
the years, I have never seen any single error that must rely on so
many logical fallacies to support its bizarre house of cards errors as
various threads of fatalistic belief. At the heart, all forms of fatalism
eventually make God the active cause of all events that occur. No
surprise, when put to the test, advocates of this fatalistic view of
predestination must spend large amounts of time trying—
unsuccessfully—to explain how God can cause illness, death, and all
acts of cruel and diabolical human depravity without being, in the
end, the actual cause of those things. He causes them, but He isn't
the cause of them? The idea is utterly nonsensical and as utterly
unsupported by Scripture.

Jesus tells us that these two occasions are special situations that
God intended to use for His glory, a revelation that would be wholly
unnecessary if He taught that all birth defects, illnesses, and deaths,

untimely or otherwise, were divinely caused. In the case of Lazarus, Jesus didn't cause the illness, but He was obviously aware of it and knew that He would intervene and raise Lazarus from the dead.

John 11:5 tells us that Jesus loved these three people. Thus, His reaction, described in verse six, catches us by surprise. Rather than immediately leaving to go to his beloved friends, Jesus remained in His present location for two whole days. Only after two days does He tell the disciples that it is time to go to Lazarus and his two sisters. Given that Martha tells Jesus that Lazarus has been dead for four days when He arrives, we may conclude that Jesus and the disciples are at least a two day journey from their home. When someone is gravely ill, much can change in four days, and so it does with Lazarus.

"Our friend Lazarus sleepeth; but I go, that I may awake him out of sleep" (John 11:11b). Folks who believe in the errant idea of "soul-sleep" often quote this sentence as supposed proof of their idea. Wrong citation; in this comment, Jesus refers to Lazarus' body, not to his soul. The reference to Lazarus sleeping when, in fact, Jesus knows that he has died, conveys a comforting and simple truth to our minds, a truth that Jesus specifically states in the comment. Jesus is now going to Bethany to awaken Lazarus out of his sleep. Even though Lazarus is dead, like natural sleep, Jesus will awaken him and restore him to his former life.

Then said Jesus unto them plainly, Lazarus is dead. And I am glad for your sakes that I was not there, to the intent ye may believe; nevertheless let us go unto him. (John 11:14–15)

When Jesus referred to Lazarus as sleeping, the disciples likely thought that Lazarus' illness had broken, and he was now sleeping restfully in recovery. How often during those three and a half years the disciples failed to understand what Jesus said to them, though He spoke quite simply and clearly. However, we should remember that He often spoke words to them of things so heavenly and so far beyond the norm of this world that they found it difficult to grasp, just as we would have struggled similarly with His words, had we been with them.

Jesus brings the disciples back to the reality of the situation, a reality that they were not at all prepared to witness. Their friend Lazarus had died. By the time they arrived back in Bethany, he would have been dead four days. Nevertheless, Jesus would raise Lazarus from the dead and restore him to his life with his two sisters.

Be honest. Had you been with Jesus and the disciples at the time, would you have understood the imminent miracle that was soon to unfold? Perhaps if someone died, and Jesus almost immediately arrived and spoke to him, revival might occur, but four days. This lapse of time stretches our material perceptions beyond comprehension. If the human brain is robbed of oxygen for a bare few minutes, permanent damage occurs. But, in four days, all of the body's intricate systems would have fallen into significant decay. Any thought of revival would be the last thing we—or they—could imagine. But the fact of this record in Scripture, in Jesus' own words no less, teaches us undeniably of His power to raise the dead, however long they may have been dead.

In this comment, still in their distant location, Jesus doesn't specifically tell the disciples that He intends to raise Lazarus from the dead, but He distinctly tells them that He intends to do something that will convince them to believe things about Him that they do not presently believe, even after spending those three years with Him.

Contemporary Christianity sadly holds a myopic view of belief in Jesus. Based on much of this accepted teaching, if you have, even for a moment, a shred of unbelief in Jesus, you are probably not even born again. This thinking grows out of a belief that people control their new birth instead of God controlling it. So if they think they are born again, and the contemporary preacher thinks they may not be born again, they can just, for the benefit of the doubt, run themselves back through the same routine that they followed to cause their new birth initially.

Resurrection: God's Example for His Glory   113

This idea, first of all, contradicts Jesus' categorical teaching regarding the new birth. We do not control it, and we do not do things to produce it.

The wind bloweth where it listeth, and thou hearest the sound thereof, but canst not tell whence it cometh, and whither it goeth: so is every one that is born of the Spirit. (John 3:8)

Jesus didn't say—or even remotely hint at the idea—that we "blow" where we please and produce our new birth. Exactly the opposite; He said that the wind, translated from the same Greek word as "Spirit," blows, breathes, where He pleases, not where people "invite" Him to blow.

Further, Jesus also eradicates the notion that people may gain the new birth by one of any number of vehicles. "...so is every one that is born of the Spirit." The new birth occurs exactly the same way in every single case with every child of grace. And that way is the work, the personal, intimate breathing of the Holy Spirit, not by something that we think or do.

When God formed Adam of dust, He "...breathed into his nostrils the breath of life; and man became a living soul" (Genesis 2:7). Likewise, when the miraculous moment arrives, the Holy Spirit breathes the breath of eternal life into the soul of a child of grace, and that breath produces immediate eternal life in that individual. We add no more to our new birth by what we think or do than Adam added to his becoming a "...living soul" by thinking or doing something. How could he do anything before that moment? He was a glorious composition of dust! Nothing more. He could think and act only after God gave him life. Likewise, our spiritual thinking, acting, and believing occur after our new birth, not before.

Based on the teachings of Scripture, this lesson included, the disciples struggled with unbelief toward Jesus even after His resurrection. Jesus prepares them for an event related to Lazarus' death that will enable them to believe, an obvious commentary to the fact that they did not then believe as they should.

Just a few days later, as Jesus was preparing the disciples for His departure from them, He reinforced this same reality with them.

> *Let not your heart be troubled: ye believe in God, believe also in me.* (John 14:1)

In both first century Greek and contemporary English, "believe also in me" is a directive, a commandment to the disciples to do something that they were not, at the moment, adequately or rightly doing. Respected New Testament Greek authority, A. T. Robertson, affirms what a simple and believing read of the King James language already tells us.

> **Ye believe ... believe also...**So translated as present active indicative plural second person and present active imperative of πιστευω [*pisteuō*]. The form is the same. Both may be indicative (ye believe ... and ye believe), both may be imperative (believe ... and believe or believe also), the first may be indicative (ye believe) and the second imperative (believe also), the first may be imperative (keep on believing) and the second indicative (and ye do believe, this less likely). ***Probably both are imperatives*** (Mark 11:22), "keep on believing in God and in me."[1] (emphasis added, "Probably....")

At the moment, the disciples believed in God, but apparently, based on Jesus' words, even more simply stated in our King James text than Robertson's technical explanation, they did not yet believe in Jesus, in the same way that they believed in God. And Jesus teaches them that they need to believe in Him as God, just as they believe in God. Ah, if the modern salvation-by-human-cooperation theologian had been present, he would have immediately warned the disciples, "If you don't believe in Jesus, you may not be born again. Get to work." Not Jesus, His words instruct and nurture the disciples to grow in their belief. They are born again. They are His children and

---

[1] A.T. Robertson, *Word Pictures in the New Testament* (Nashville, TN: Broadman Press, 1933), Jn 14:1.

His disciples, but they, as you and I, needed to grow in their belief in Jesus.

God help us to study the lesson of Lazarus and thereby come to believe in Jesus more fully and deeply than we have ever yet believed in Him.

20
Resurrection and the Lord's Return

Then Martha, as soon as she heard that Jesus was coming, went and met him: but Mary sat still in the house. Then said Martha unto Jesus, Lord, if thou hadst been here, my brother had not died. But I know, that even now, whatsoever thou wilt ask of God, God will give it thee. Jesus saith unto her, Thy brother shall rise again. Martha saith unto him, I know that he shall rise again in the resurrection at the last day. Jesus said unto her, I am the resurrection, and the life: he that believeth in me, though he were dead, yet shall he live: And whosoever liveth and believeth in me shall never die. Believest thou this? She saith unto him, Yea, Lord: I believe that thou art the Christ, the Son of God, which should come into the world. (John 11:20–27)

We so quickly judge or criticize Biblical characters, thinking to ourselves that, had we lived in their world, we would have been more faithful than they. I think not. Martha held onto a false belief that Jesus had to be physically present to perform a miracle. "If thou hadst been here…."

Think about some of your recent spiritual struggles. Perhaps the burden became so heavy that you bowed and took the matter to the Lord. However, during your prayer, you had no special sense of His presence or of a "silver bullet" answer to your problem. And, even as the trial lingered on, depleting your spiritual energy, you tried to pray over and over. Each time the follow-up was the same. You never received a sense of peace or awareness of His presence. In the end, did you not build your expectation of the outcome more on what you felt or, in this case, didn't feel than on His Biblical promise? If you had truly sensed His presence and blessing, you'd have immediately concluded that He had answered your prayer and now came to deliver you.

But absent that personal sense of His presence, you resign yourself to the trial and give up hope for deliverance.

How are you different from Martha? She thought that Jesus had to be present so she could see Him, touch Him, and hear His voice, or He could do nothing for Lazarus. In our trials, we react similarly. Unless we consciously realize that deep peaceful sense of His presence, we conclude that He hasn't answered our prayer. Nowhere in Scripture does the Lord promise to make Himself known emotionally every time He is present. Considering the Biblical teaching that God wholly transcends the material universe that He created and that He is always ever present, that is, "omnipresent," must we "feel" His presence for Him to be present? No. "Feel" Him or not, Scripture teaches that He is present, always and intimately so.

Mormon teaching exemplifies the imbalanced reliance on what we feel or do not feel by their "burning in the bosom" idea. We have a far better guide to gauge the Lord's presence. According to Scripture, He is always present no matter our personal location at the moment and no matter our feeling or not feeling His presence (Hebrews 13:5-6). So you see, we walk almost exactly in Martha's footsteps. We certainly fail to walk a higher spiritual road than she walked.

We read in this chapter that Jesus knew of Lazarus' illness, although He was a two-day distance from Bethany. He told the disciples that Lazarus was dead, but that they were now going to Bethany to raise Him. In these points, we have specific evidence in the passage that Jesus did not need to be physically present to know or to help His child in need.

But I know, that even now, whatsoever thou wilt ask of God, God will give it thee. Before we come down too harshly on Martha, we should ponder these words. Her brother has been dead for four days and is in the tomb. Nothing short of a miracle from God can resurrect him, and Martha voices just such confidence in Jesus. We read other accounts of Jesus resurrecting people who had just died, but we find no other record of His raising someone who has been dead for such an extended time. We should not criticize Martha's faith in Jesus.

Martha saith unto him, I know that he shall rise again in the resurrection at the last day. Resurrection, last day; Martha has a clear and concrete understanding of final things. Occasionally, deceived but well-meaning Christians will deny the Bible doctrine of the resurrection. However, the essential meaning of the English word cannot be twisted to agree. Note below the definition of the word from the *Shorter Oxford English Dictionary.*

> **resurrection.** ...from Late Latin *resurrectio*(n-)... from Latin *resurrect-* (stem of *resurgere*) Noun.
> 1 Christian Church. The rising of Christ from the dead; also (chiefly historical), a church-festival commemorating this – dramatic, pictorial, or other representation of the resurrection of Christ. e. g. *The men that condemned Christ were the first to be made aware of His resurrection.*
> 2 Christian Church. The rising of the dead at the Last Judgment. e. g. *Mrs. Cousins believed in the resurrection of the dead.*

From Job ("...yet **in my flesh** shall I see God"–Job 19:26b; emphasis added) to John ("...but we know that, when he shall appear, **we shall be like him**; for we shall see him as he is"—1 John 3:2b; emphasis added), Scripture consistently affirms a literal, physical, bodily resurrection, not a bodiless mystical resurrection, as taught by ancient Gnostics and subsequent ideas that build on a Gnostic foundation instead of Scripture. Any notion of "resurrection" that in any way falls short of accepting that the same body that died shall be resurrected and restored to life, indeed a glorified life far different from the life we now live, falls short of Biblical revelation and typically mimics the Gnostic error that ignores the meaning of the word and rejects the basic teaching of Scripture.

Jesus did not in any way correct Martha's point. He did not tell her that she had erred, as He told the Sadducees who denied the resurrection, "Ye do err, not knowing the scriptures, nor the power of God" (Matthew 22:29b). Take note: Jesus never allowed error to go unchecked in His presence, so His acceptance of Martha's stated belief strongly affirms that she believed rightly.

I am the resurrection, and the life: he that believeth in me, though he were dead, yet shall he live. As comforting as Martha's belief in the resurrection at the last day may have been to her, Jesus enlarges and enriches her faith to see His power in the here and now. Jesus adopts the timeless present tense verb, just as God did with Moses in Exodus 3, "I AM...." Take note of the number of times in John's gospel that Jesus used this "I am" term to refer to Himself. The resurrection at the last day is not a Bible doctrine to be iced away and held in store for the future. It is a Bible truth that enriches and empowers our present faith and conduct. Jesus didn't tell Martha, "I shall be the resurrection and the life," but "I am...." Every sermon on the resurrection should include a strong and clear point regarding the present impact of the resurrection on life as we live it in the here and now. John makes the point in terms of personal conduct.

And every man that hath this hope in him purifieth himself, even as he is pure. (1 John 3:3)

In addition to its impact on our personal conduct, the doctrine of the resurrection can eliminate or soften grief and hopelessness as we face the many trials and disappointments of life.

Comforting as the truth of resurrection at the Second Coming is, Jesus takes Martha beyond this truth. She shall shortly witness perhaps the greatest miracle that Jesus performed during His Incarnation, His time dwelling in human flesh. He shall raise her brother and restore him to her and Mary, even though he has been dead for four whole days.

Why is such a lesson necessary in the gospel? It is necessary to show us in concrete terms that Jesus has power over death and the grave. If He can raise someone who has been dead for four days, He can also raise someone who has been dead for four years, or four hundred years, or four thousand years, for that matter.

What does this "I am the resurrection and the life" point mean? It means that every facet of our hope of personal resurrection relies on Jesus. In 1 Corinthians 15:20, Paul refers to Jesus' resurrection as the "...firstfruits of them that slept." "Firstfruits" refers to the Old Testament practice of Jewish farmers. Early in the growing season, as the very first clusters of grain or other crops would appear, the farmer would gather that cluster and offer it to God as his "firstfruits" offering. Making this offering gave assurance that God would grant a bountiful harvest of the whole crop at harvest time.

When Jesus came out of the grave, He declared for all His family to know that the kingdom of death had been conquered, not only for Himself, but for all whom He represented in His death. Our identity with Adam ensures our death; our identity with Jesus ensures our resurrection. When Jesus arose from the dead, Scripture declares—

Knowing that Christ being raised from the dead dieth no more; death hath no more dominion over him. (Romans 6:9)

When He came in human flesh, virgin born, He fully subjected Himself to our humanity, including death. But when He arose from the grave, He conquered death. It was not possible for death to maintain its grip on Him (Acts 2:24). He broke the grip of the despot death, not only for Himself, but also for you, me, and all of those for whom He died and arose.

Jesus' point to Martha is not that He shall accomplish the resurrection, but that *He is*, personally, Himself, the resurrection and the life. Martha and Mary would have their beloved brother restored to them temporarily, though all three would eventually face the temporary obstacle of death, but Jesus' words to Martha marked deliverance for Lazarus and for all of the Lord's beloved children of grace. We have reason to worship Him today!

21
Lazarus Alive!

Jesus said, Take ye away the stone. Martha, the sister of him that was dead, saith unto him, Lord, by this time he stinketh: for he hath been dead four days. Jesus saith unto her, Said I not unto thee, that, if thou wouldest believe, thou shouldest see the glory of God? Then they took away the stone from the place where the dead was laid. And Jesus lifted up his eyes, and said, Father, I thank thee that thou hast heard me. And I knew that thou hearest me always: but because of the people which stand by I said it, that they may believe that thou hast sent me. And when he thus had spoken, he cried with a loud voice, Lazarus, come forth. And he that was dead came forth, bound hand and foot with graveclothes: and his face was bound about with a napkin. Jesus saith unto them, Loose him, and let him go. (John 11:39–44)

As we observe the reality of death taking those whom we love, we can more appreciate Martha's struggle. When the proverbial "rubber hits the pavement," can Jesus actually restore life to a man whose body has been dead for four whole days? Medical science measures the maximum time of oxygen starvation to the human body in minutes, not hours, much less days. Permanent damage occurs in the brain in less than ten minutes without oxygen. Martha does us a favor by reminding us of the degree of the miracle that Jesus shall perform in raising her brother from the dead. Jesus literally reversed the cellular degeneration that had occurred, but He did far more. He restored that wonderful mysterious link of life to Lazarus.

Said I not unto thee, that, if thou wouldest believe, thou shouldest see the glory of God? Jesus does not impose a condition on Lazarus being raised, but on Martha seeing God's glory. Take careful note. God likely works miracles far more frequently in our lives than we realize. Whether we recognize the miracle and see God's glory or not depends on our faith. Are we looking for His miracle or not? One person may experience a miracle and celebrate "good fortune," or thank an excellent surgeon for his skill. Another person may experience exactly the same event and thank the Lord for the miracle. How often do we blind ourselves to the Lord's gracious miracles by our unbelief? Our own unbelief robs us of the joy and comfort of seeing God's glory.

When our oldest daughter was barely two years old, one Saturday morning I put her in my car (of course, no seat belts then—Mom or Dad's arms were baby's "seat belt") to drive to the local home improvement store to get supplies for my day of chores. I had my route well memorized. I'd drive to the stop sign on Taylor and cross the street for my most direct route to the store. Taylor was a four lane through street with a 35 mph speed limit. I stopped at Taylor, looked both ways, and saw no cars approaching near the intersection. I moved my right foot from the brake to the gas pedal, fully thinking of driving straight across Taylor. Almost immediately, my mind "heard" as clearly as if someone had shouted at me, "Turn right!" Without thinking, I immediately sharply turned the car to my right. At that moment, a car went through the intersection, likely going in excess of 70 mph. Had I driven across the street as planned, that car would have "T-boned" my car and killed both of us. I haven't had many such experiences, but I had one that day. To my last breath, no one could convince me that the Lord didn't speak to me to spare Kelli and me. And I thank Him often for that moment of merciful and loving deliverance.

Sadly, some folks seem to have the idea that they can ask the Lord for just about anything they wish, and, if they ask "in Jesus' name" or otherwise go through the right motions, God is obligated to grant their petition. Not so. Let's suppose that you go through all the supposedly right motions and words with Petition A, and I go through all the same right motions, but I pray Petition B, the mirror opposite to your request. Obviously, the Lord will not grant both requests. Godly prayer may well address our deepest needs and problems—and it should—but, in the end, every prayer should be framed with the desire and request that the Lord do what is most fitting to His glory. Jesus framed His prayer to the Father in this way when he responded to Martha.

Father, I thank thee that thou hast heard me. And I knew that thou hearest me always: but because of the people which stand by I said it, that they may believe that thou hast sent me. We are prone to think in terms of answered prayers and unanswered prayers. We chalk up our answered prayers to God hearing us and our unanswered prayers to His not hearing us. Make no mistake. The Lord hears every prayer. He may answer some of our prayers by denying our request rather than granting it. James explains, "Ye ask, and receive not, because ye ask amiss, that ye may consume it upon your lusts" (James 4:3). God not only weighs our request; He also considers our motive. Do we pray for a certain thing with the motive of greater glory to God or greater comfort and convenience for ourselves?

Don't overlook that Jesus knew that the Father always heard His prayers, along with the implication that the Father always granted them. Jesus never prayed with a bad motive or for a foolish petition to be granted. Jesus didn't pray on this occasion for His sake, but to aid His children who stood by and observed the events of the moment. When Lazarus revived and came out of the tomb, Jesus intended that they know why. Bless Martha; she needed this prayer from Jesus fully as much as others who stood by.

Both Jesus and the Holy Spirit intervene in our godly, faith-filled prayers (Romans 8:26-27). When we so pray, our words do not go before the Father as orphans. They go with the united petition of the Lord Jesus and the Holy Spirit. And the Father grants. Remember; the Father never fails to respond to Jesus' prayers. Every prayer you ever prayed that was granted went through this loving, gracious intervention and endorsement.

...that they may believe.... Jesus adds another filter to the prayer question. His intervention, His joining our prayers and sending them on to the Father aims at increasing our belief in Him, "*...that thou hast sent me."* Think about one of your recent prayers. How much thought did you give to these two filters, God's glory and your believing in Jesus? Did you think in these terms at all? Or were you

absorbed in your personal pain or sense of need so deeply that you neglected these filters?

Any belief that we experience is as good or as bad as the facts or non-facts that we embrace as true. If we believe that something is true when it is in fact false, our belief is nothing more than self-deception. It sets us up for cruel disappointment. It was not Mary's or Martha's belief that prompted Jesus to raise Lazarus, though He obviously felt deeply for their grief. He raised Lazarus to thereby give glory to God and to deepen the disciples' faith in Him. Believing something doesn't make that thing true or false. Our belief puts our minds in harmony with the facts of the situation. Our belief in Jesus' power to raise the dead doesn't cause the resurrection, but it richly frames our minds to praise God and to believe all the more in Him than ever in the past.

Lazarus, come forth. Three words…just three words. You and I could utter a thousand words, and Lazarus would remain lifeless in the tomb. However, when Jesus spoke those words, Lazarus got up and stumbled out. Notice the description of Lazarus' burial state. His body was bound, similar to the Egyptian method of preparing the body for burial. That same body that had reached a pervasive state of degeneration came back to life. That brain that was dead for four days processed the sound of Jesus' voice, understood its meaning, and obeyed. He got up and, despite the grave wrappings, walked out of the tomb.

And he that was dead came forth. Occasionally people who claim to believe the Bible to be God's inspired word try to deny that it teaches anything at all regarding a literal, physical bodily resurrection. They have a major problem with this passage! Lazarus didn't revive in another body, but in the same body that he occupied up to that point in his life. When Jesus confronted and refuted the Sadducees who denied the truth of the resurrection, He charged them with two foundational problems that fed their unbelief. They didn't know the Scriptures, and they didn't understand the power of God. He cited one simple passage from the third chapter of Exodus to prove that they didn't know the Scriptures. In addition to denying the resurrection, the Sadducees also denied any life after death.

When God appeared to Moses in the burning bush, He told Moses "I AM" was His name. He enlarged the point.

Moreover he said, I am the God of thy father, the God of Abraham, the God of Isaac, and the God of Jacob. And Moses hid his face; for he was afraid to look upon God. (Exodus 3:6)

Abraham, Isaac, and Jacob had been dead literally for centuries when God spoke these words to Moses. Yet God didn't say, "I was the God of...." He said, "*I am* the God of...." Abraham, Isaac, and Jacob, though their bodies were dead, were very much alive in glory with the Lord. By making this point, Jesus refutes the Sadducees' denial of life after death, and, by implication—Jesus' implication, mind you—He also affirmed the resurrection. Any belief system that acknowledges continuing life after death, but rejects a literal, physical, bodily resurrection is no better than first century Sadducee error. Scripture affirms that the resurrected body shall undergo an amazing change, but it affirms that it is the same body in which we lived—and died—that shall be so changed.

*Behold, I shew you a mystery; We shall not all sleep, but **we shall all be changed**.* (1 Corinthians 15:51; emphasis added)

You can't "change" something unless you are dealing with that same "something" in the first place. If God didn't raise the body in which we lived, He couldn't "change" it, could He? If God gives His children a new heavenly or "spiritual" body at death or at the resurrection, there is no resurrection, and there is no "change."

Job states this fact. The same eyes that saw the world around him while he lived shall see his Redeemer in glory (Job 19:25-27). Job also reminds us that this glorious view of his Redeemer shall occur after his body has decayed. In likely the first book written that makes up our Bible, and in John's gospel, one of the latest books of the Bible to be written, God affirms the same truth; the resurrection is real, and it involves His reviving and glorifying our literal, physical, human body, that same body in which we lived our lives.

22
He is Alive. What Now?

And he that was dead came forth, bound hand and foot with graveclothes:
and his face was bound about with a napkin. Jesus saith unto them, Loose
him, and let him go. Then many of the Jews which came to Mary, and had
seen the things which Jesus did, believed on him. But some of them went
their ways to the Pharisees, and told them what things Jesus had done.
Then gathered the chief priests and the Pharisees a council, and said,
What do we? for this man doeth many miracles. If we let him thus alone,
all men will believe on him: and the Romans shall come and take away
both our place and nation. (John 11:44–48)

Loose him, and let him go. Martha, Mary, or any of their friends could not raise Lazarus from the dead. They could only grieve his death and bury him. Nor could they in any way contribute to Jesus raising Lazarus from the dead. They neither caused his resurrection, nor were they instrumental in his resurrection. Jesus alone was capable of raising a man from the dead. It is sadly common in some Christian circles in our day for sincere believers to believe that they cannot cause the new birth—and they are correct in that point—but they think that they must be "instrumental" in Jesus bringing about the new birth. If they fail to provide the "instrument," they believe that Jesus will not—or cannot—produce the new birth in anyone.

Jesus Himself used the analogy of death and life when teaching on the new birth.

Verily, verily, I say unto you, He that heareth my word, and
believeth on him that sent me, hath everlasting life, and shall not
come into condemnation; but is passed from death unto life.
Verily, verily, I say unto you, The hour is coming, and now is,

*when the dead shall hear the voice of the Son of God: and they
that hear shall live.* (John 5:24–25)

Based on the stated beliefs of these dear folk, they must be
instrumental in bringing an unregenerate person to the point of
belief. If they are instrumental in bringing someone from unbelief to
belief in Jesus, they believe that Jesus will produce the new birth.

Jesus quite clearly contradicts and refutes their idea in this
passage. While our friends believe that they are instrumental in
producing the new birth, in a manner conditioning the person for
Jesus to then bring about the new birth, Jesus says that the believer
"...*is passed* from death unto life." In English, "is passed" identifies
a past action now complete, not an action in prospect of occurring or
even an action in the process of occurring. When you see a person
legitimately believe in Jesus, you are looking at someone who was
born again at some time prior to that belief, for at the moment of
belief, he is already born again. He has already passed from death to
life.

How then did this new birth occur, according to Jesus Himself?

*The hour is coming, and now is, when the dead shall hear the
voice of the Son of God: and they that hear shall live.*

Although human science has not reached the point of sophistication
to accept a "voice print" as binding legal evidence, the unique
speech patterns that identify one and only one person as the speaker,
it increasingly asserts that our speech patterns are as unique to us as
our finger prints. No two people speak with precisely the same voice
patterns.

Do not miss the point that Jesus did not say, "The hour is coming
and now is, when the dead shall hear the words that the Son of God
spoke...." **He specifically refers to His own personal voice.** He
speaks the words, not a faithful missionary or gospel preacher or
praying family member. He alone possesses a voice that has the
power to give life to a dead Lazarus or to a dead sinner who has not
yet experienced the new birth. It is "...*the voice* of the Son of God"

that imparts life to the dead sinner, not the voice of the witnessing believer speaking Jesus' words. No one possesses "...the voice of the Son of God" other than *the Son of God*."

Several years ago, I was listening to John MacArthur on the radio as he explained his personal belief in the exact dynamics of gospel instrumentality in bringing about the new birth. He described a situation in which you enter a room for the first time. You are tired and want to sit down to rest. You see an unoccupied chair. It appears inviting. You look at the supporting framework of the chair, and you reach the conclusion that the chair is quite capable of holding your weight, so you "believe that the chair will hold your weight," and you therefore sit down in it. According to MacArthur's explanation, quite clearly explained in his message, you must see and hear the gospel, and you must so assess its message as to believe that Jesus can save you, so that you in fact make the conscious decision to trust Him—to believe in Him—before He will actually produce the new birth in you.

This analogy flies in the face of Jesus' words in John 5:24-25. MacArthur says that you must hear his sermon and believe it before Jesus will produce the new birth in you. Jesus says that the hearing believer on Him gives evidence that he already possesses "...everlasting life, and shall not come into condemnation, but is passed from death unto life." MacArthur says you must believe on Jesus first. Jesus says that He must produce the new birth first. I choose to believe Jesus. New birth first; belief follows.

Another advocate of this idea of gospel instrumentality was questioned about the truth-content of what is preached to someone who has not heard the gospel before and who therefore does not presently believe it. This man responded with his—no doubt—sincere belief that, if a person hears about Jesus from a Methodist missionary (God bless the good Methodist folks; we could learn much from them about compassion for hurting people, but their belief is firmly based on the salvation by works teachings of James Arminius, and I believe Scripture teaches that salvation is by God's grace—all of God's grace), the person who hears this representation of the gospel "...will at least go away believing in Jesus." Hmmm...

Let's once again consult Scripture and compare Scripture with a man's stated beliefs.

*I marvel that ye are so soon **removed from him** that called you into the grace of Christ unto another gospel: Which is not another; but there be some that trouble you, and would pervert the gospel of Christ. But though we, or an angel from heaven, **preach any other gospel unto you than that which we have preached unto you**, let him be accursed. As we said before, so say I now again, If any man preach any other gospel unto you than that ye have received, let him be accursed. For do I now persuade men, or God? or do I seek to please men? for if I yet pleased men, I should not be the servant of Christ. (Galatians 1:6-10; emphasis added.)*[1]

Paul says that believing another gospel in effect means that you are "...removed from **him** that called you...." Think of the utter inconsistent absurdity; a false gospel about another Jesus is supposedly capable of producing the new birth, enabling the hearer to go away "...at least believing in Jesus," but Paul devotes an entire New Testament letter to refuting the idea. Do we believe the modern witness, or do we believe the inspired words of Scripture? I choose Scripture.

Almost every time you read in Scripture about the gospel being preached, you will see the hearers sharply divide into two opposite camps. One group will be convinced by what they hear and believe it. The other group will be more incensed by what they hear and will fiercely oppose it. No one could deny that Lazarus died. Multiple witnesses could give their personal testimony of his death and burial, a burial that lasted for four days. All of these men knew that Lazarus was now alive. He was dead, dead for four days, and now he lives. This fact was not in dispute. It could not be. The question before these men was *how*. How could this be? How could a man

---

[1] A careful study of Galatians indicates that the false gospel that the Galatians believed—and the false Jesus to whom they removed themselves—was in large part a gospel of salvation by works.

die, much less remain dead for four whole days, and then be brought back to life? One group accepted the evidence and rightly concluded that only God could raise the dead, so Jesus must be God Incarnate, God presently living in human flesh. The other group analyzed the same information wholly in terms of its potentially bad effect on them in the eyes of the Romans.

If we let him thus alone, all men will believe on him. So what is the problem? Is this a bad thing? Many very sincere believers get tripped up when they read words in Scripture that, on the surface, sound universal, terms such as we see in this sentence, "all men will believe on him." But notice the very next sentence from the mouth of these unbelievers, "...*the Romans shall come and take away both our place and nation.*" Are the Romans "men"? If "all men" was as universal a term in the Jews' thoughts as some folks try to make it, would not "all men" include Romans as well as Jews? And, if the Romans believe on Him, again, what is the problem?

First century Jews imbedded their religious thinking into a myopic perspective that included Jews and only Jews. If they thought or spoke in terms that included more than just Jews, they might logically use such terms as "all men," intending Jews and Gentiles, people of all race, culture, and background, not just Jews.

Let's see if Scripture supports this idea.

And we know that we are of God, and the whole world lieth in wickedness. (1 John 5:19)

John identifies two groups or classes of people in this verse, "we," and "the whole world." Are believers real human beings? Do they literally live in this world? Or are they mere phantoms who appear to live in this world, but they really don't? Obviously, in this case, the universal sounding term "whole world" refers to a specific class of wicked unbelievers, not to every person in the "whole world" of our created universe, or, for that matter, to the whole of the created material universe.

John draws a clear contrast. In his mind, "we" and "the whole world" are mutually exclusive. No one can be part of both the "we" and part of the "whole world." Ah, then "whole world" refers to some group of people, by definition, less inclusive than all humanity. It cannot include the "we" whom John defines as being of God.

A careful study of these broad sounding terms in Scripture will consistently show in the context that the term refers to a defined class of people, not to all humanity. This fact becomes central to our belief when we study passages dealing with the big question, "For whom did Jesus die"? And Scripture consistently teaches that Jesus did not die to give all humanity the opportunity to consider whether they desire to be born again or not. It teaches that all for whom Jesus died shall surely and effectually be born again by the work of God alone, not by any human instrumentality. "...so is every one that is **born of the Spirit**" (John 3:8b).

I suspect that almost every person who takes the time and interest to read this writing fits distinctly in the category of those men who considered the evidence and believed in Jesus, not in the group of unbelievers who sought to kill Jesus because He performed so many undeniable miracles. And I encourage you, therefore, to examine such Bible passages as John 5:24-25 and 1 John 5:1, concluding with Scripture that your belief is evidence of, not instrumental or causative in your new birth.

Jesus alone raised Lazarus from the dead. He personally used the analogy of death and life when He taught on the new birth, something that He taught that He alone brings about. He is our complete Savior, not our salvation facilitator.

23
A Strange Prophet – A True Prophecy

Then gathered the chief priests and the Pharisees a council, and said, What do we? for this man doeth many miracles. If we let him thus alone, all men will believe on him: and the Romans shall come and take away both our place and nation. And one of them, named Caiaphas, being the high priest that same year, said unto them, Ye know nothing at all, Nor consider that it is expedient for us, that one man should die for the people, and that the whole nation perish not. And this spake he not of himself: but being high priest that year, he prophesied that Jesus should die for that nation; And not for that nation only, but that also he should gather together in one the children of God that were scattered abroad. Then from that day forth they took counsel together for to put him to death. Jesus therefore walked no more openly among the Jews; but went thence unto a country near to the wilderness, into a city called Ephraim, and there continued with his disciples. (John 11:47–54)

In this brief reading, we learn much about the dark hearted state of the Jewish people, at the least their leaders, in the first century. The ordinary priests and Pharisees feared what the Romans would do against them because of Jesus, should He continue in His ministry, especially in His references to His kingdom and kingship. Obviously, they were interested in a way to eliminate this man who increasingly was becoming a problem for them and for their carnal view of their faith.

Jesus is always a problem for carnal religion. Caiaphas, if we draw a likely motive from his words, has a solution, cold hearted and wicked, but a solution in his mind. Why should the Jews intervene on Jesus' behalf when the Romans finally give way to their concerns about Jesus and His "Kingdom"? If Jesus offends the Romans, let the Romans have Him.

And this spake he not of himself: but being high priest that year, he prophesied.... If God can speak His words by the mouth of a donkey, as He did in the Old Testament, we should not be surprised that He would also speak by the mouth of a wicked man (Numbers 22; 2 Peter 2:15-16). On occasion throughout Scripture, God prophesies by surprising and unexpected means and men. Yes, this method represents an exception. Ordinarily, God spoke through His called and faithful prophet. It behooves us to take note of these exceptions—and to follow Scripture in regarding them as an exception, not as the primary and normal means of divine prophecy.

God used the man in the office of high priest to utter this prophecy, even though the man grossly dishonored that office. If we hang up our thinking on this point, we shall surely miss the beautiful truth that God revealed in this unusual prophecy. And that truth is the most important point of this prophecy. Its message means that God is speaking something of tremendous value to His people. What is His message, regardless of the man He used to declare it?

...he prophesied that Jesus should die for that nation; And not for that nation only, but that also he should gather together in one the children of God that were scattered abroad. For whom did Jesus die? The prophecy answers the question.

"...that also he should gather together in one the children of God that were scattered abroad." John's interpretation of Caiaphas' prophecy reveals two central truths regarding Jesus' purpose and work in His coming into the world: 1) He shall die for others, not for Himself; 2) He shall gather together in one, not in isolated cultural, racial, or theological groups, all the children of God, children who have been scattered by persecutors by their own failures and unbelief, and by false teachers. Further, His death shall not be exclusively for the benefit of Jews only, *"...not for that nation only."*

Take careful note. John carefully defines those for whom Jesus died as *"...the children of God that were scattered abroad."* When the angel assured Joseph of Jesus' supernatural conception, he used a similar manner of speech, "He shall save his people from their sins" (Matthew 1:21b). The people whom Jesus shall save by His coming into the world are "...his people." Caiaphas' prophecy as John translated it meant "...*he should gather together in one the children of God that were scattered abroad.*" The prophecy does not at all indicate that He would gather those who would, at some future time, make a decision to be a child of God. At the time of the prophecy, in some sense, though obviously not the sense of new birth, these people were already His people, "the children of God." At the time of the prophecy, they were children of God, but they were at that time yet scattered abroad. In fact, John's interpretation states that these children *were* scattered abroad, past tense. Their scattering had occurred at some past time. He would gather them together "...in one," in Himself.

Contemporary Christianity builds its views of Jesus' death on a strange contradiction. Folks with this view are adamant that Jesus must have died potentially for the benefit of every human being who ever lived. However, based on its various conditions and prerequisites of human response and behavior, they also openly acknowledge their belief that only a small fraction of humanity shall spend eternity with God in glory because only a few faithfully respond to his "offer."

What is the point? If Jesus died to give everyone an opportunity, knowing that most would refuse or ignore that opportunity, what is the purpose? As God, Jesus was/is all-knowing, so He fully knew from the beginning who would believe in Him and become His faithful disciples and who would not. Why choose a method of salvation whose inefficiency results in actually saving so few people? An engineer would evaluate that system from an efficiency perspective and conclude that it is abominably inefficient. Shouldn't God, all-wise, and all-powerful, devise a more efficient system of saving people from their sins?

This question grows more intense as we ponder the many Scriptures that describe what Jesus came to do—and did—and what He actually accomplished in that work. Consider.

He shall see of the travail of his soul, and shall be satisfied: by his knowledge shall my righteous servant justify many; for he shall bear their iniquities. (Isaiah 53:11)

If Jesus and the Father were fully satisfied with the work that Jesus accomplished, it becomes increasingly difficult to rationalize the idea that Scripture actually describes the number of God's elect people as a small number, especially as a small number who themselves performed the actual conditions that resulted in their new birth and eternal salvation. In fact, this verse contains a distinct commentary on that point.

I would ask these dear folks "the elephant in the room" question. Is God truly satisfied with the small number of people whom you believe shall actually be saved based on your system of salvation? You quote Scriptures and make impassioned pleas to people that God is not presently satisfied and that he wants everyone to be saved. How can we then rationalize that He saw what Jesus did and was satisfied with its outcome? In fact, the next thought in this same verse makes the very point of the number whom He shall save.

...by his knowledge shall my righteous servant justify many; for he shall bear their iniquities.

How many people does God's "righteous servant" justify by "his knowledge"? The verse qualifies the number as "many;" yet you say the number is few, in fact, minuscule. "Many" is not all; Scripture does not teach universal salvation of all humanity. Hell shall be occupied. However, "many" is also not a minuscule few either.

How do you explain this contradiction between the number whom you claim shall be saved and Scripture's emphatic assertion of "many"? In harmony with Isaiah's prophecy, John writes a relevant commentary to the number and even the constitution of those who actually enjoy heaven.

And they sung a new song, saying, Thou art worthy to take the book, and to open the seals thereof: for thou wast slain, and hast redeemed us to God by thy blood out of every kindred, and tongue, and people, and nation. (Revelation 5:9)

After this I beheld, and, lo, a great multitude, which no man could number, of all nations, and kindreds, and people, and tongues, stood before the throne, and before the Lamb, clothed with white robes, and palms in their hands; And cried with a loud voice, saying, Salvation to our God which sitteth upon the throne, and unto the Lamb. (Revelation 7:9-10)

After going into some detail regarding the hundred forty-four thousand who were sealed, John introduces this infinite number, a number "…which no man could number" who came from "…all nations, and kindreds, and people, and tongues" who stood precisely where we would expect to see God's redeemed, "saved" people, singing the glorious song of "Salvation to our God…."

False teachers often obsesses about the finite number, 144,000, who were sealed, but John will not stop with them. He goes on to emphasize the infinite number that cannot be numbered by any human effort or scheme, and they all praised God for salvation. Honestly now, does this sound as if God shall have only a small fragment of humanity in heaven praising Him throughout eternity?

Where in Isaiah 53:11 do we find the idea of an offer of salvation, or the idea of merely giving everyone a "chance"? God's righteous servant, Jesus, God Incarnate, ***actually, factually justifies many by actually, factually bearing their iniquities***. His death, the theme of this whole prophetic chapter, does not merely give people a good opportunity, a "chance," or a generous and sincere "offer" to be saved. It factually, literally "justifies many" by His "bearing their iniquities." Praise God for salvation accomplished!

Occasionally, folks who hold these views will try to split hairs and say that Jesus actually removed all the sins of all humanity with one exception. He didn't die for the sin of unbelief, and, unless you believe, you shall die alienated from God because of your sin of unbelief. Where in these verses do we see any indication, however remote, of an exception? It simply isn't there, "…he shall bear their iniquities." Is unbelief an iniquity? Indeed it is. Then He bore that sin as well as all their other sins.

Consider Matthew 1:21. Is unbelief a sin? Of course it is a sin. Where in "...he shall save his people from their sins" do we find any basis whatever for an exception? There is none. In our study passage, the true meaning of the prophecy is not that Jesus would give all of "...the children of God that were scattered abroad" an opportunity to accept Him and thereby gain salvation, but that "...he should gather together in one" all of His children.

Based on the consistent teaching of Scripture, unbelief consistently disqualifies a person from God-glorifying discipleship. It dishonors God, and it brings the Lord's severe chastening on His children who refuse to believe Him and His glorious work. The Lord's chastening, consequently, brings pain and a painful reminder of our disobedience, urging us to repent. But it does not bring death to the child! What kind of parent, under the guise of chastening, murders his child? A despicable parent, not the loving and merciful Father and Savior of His people that we see in Scripture.

The prophecy shall not be complete, fulfilled, until Jesus actually, factually gathers "...*together in one the children of God that were scattered abroad.*" After something more than two thousand years, visible Christendom is more scattered, more divided by variations in belief and in practice, the form and manner of public worship, than ever. Despite Scripture's description of the gospel as bringing God's children together, public Christianity becomes increasingly splintered and divided.

Let me make a simple observation: some of the messages that are declared as being the gospel are obviously not the gospel, in that they do not bring God's people together; they separate them. Sadly, a significant number of messages openly declare that, if we do not believe exactly as they believe, and perform our Christianity as they teach us to live it, we are not children of God at all. How obviously this kind of narrow belief contradicts John's description of those who sang salvation's glorious hymn in heaven!

I preach most Sunday's to a small congregation, but I preach a gospel that declares for any and all to consider. Belief of my sermon does not define who is going to heaven and who is not. My God's family is broad and wide. Its tenets fully and gloriously—mercifully and lovingly—embrace God's people across this globe in every culture, language, and family. And there is coming a day when we shall all join together in one voice and one heart, praising our God alike for His loving, merciful, and gracious deliverance. Friends, we shall all join together in singing that glorious hymn. By God's grace, I shall continue to preach that theme till I preach my last sermon.

When shall this prophecy realize its fulfillment? There is coming a day, a day like no other day that ever dawned. In that day, God's creation shall be shocked by a shout that it never heard before. No ear shall fail to hear that shout. Even those who died across the centuries shall hear that shout, and its power shall bring them back to life and out of their graves. And, finally, at long, but glorious last, the prophecy, Jesus' death and His full and complete bearing of "His people's" sins shall be realized. All the children of God who were scattered abroad by Adam's sin, by never-ending human folly, by false teachers, by their own failure to grasp, believe, and rejoice in Jesus and what He did for them, shall then "…be gathered together in one," in their glorious, reigning, and victorious Savior. And Scripture punctuates this comforting truth.

…and so shall we ever be with the Lord. Wherefore comfort one another with these words. (1 Thessalonians 4:17b-18)

24
God's Answer for a Troubled Heart

Let not your heart be troubled: ye believe in God, believe also in me. In my Father's house are many mansions: if it were not so, I would have told you. I go to prepare a place for you. And if I go and prepare a place for you, I will come again, and receive you unto myself; that where I am, there ye may be also. And whither I go ye know, and the way ye know. (John 14:1–4)

If we examine the four accounts of Jesus' incarnation (His time on planet Earth as a man), based on each writer's focus as revealed by the amount of "ink" he devotes to each season of Jesus' life, we quickly and clearly discover a strong emphasis in all four on the last week of Jesus' life, including His arrest, trial, crucifixion, and resurrection. That emphasis should nudge us to keep our focus on Him and the things that He accomplished during that time.

Paul's preaching emphasized, "...Jesus, and the resurrection" (Acts 17:18b). We live in a time when focus on any specific Bible doctrine is strongly discouraged. We read much about "seeker-sensitive" preachers, preaching, and churches. Should we not rather focus, as Paul did, on Jesus and the resurrection?

I've encountered several people who say, "Love unites; doctrine divides. Let's stop preaching doctrine and work on loving each other." The idea sounds appealing to our superficial senses. However, without exception, every time I ever mentioned a Bible doctrine that one of these folks disagreed with, the reaction I witnessed was anything but love. It smacked far more of the opposite.

Only one such doctrine will make the point. Polarized dispensationalism is so emotional that many very sincere preachers who do not believe it have given up altogether on preaching anything about the Second Coming because of the emotional reaction they must endure for their rejection of this idea. While I do not accept historical pre-millennialism, it should be noted that modern dispensationalism and historical pre-millennialism are not at all the same.

As it is typically taught, dispensationalism had its beginning in the late 1820s with John Nelson Darby. It simply didn't exist prior to that time, leaving this doctrine some 1800 years too young to be a Biblical doctrine. It was generally rejected by historical Christians of most stripe until the early twentieth century with the publication of the Scofield Bible, a Bible that was published with beliefs and study notes by C. I. Scofield printed on each page, along with the Bible text.

Scofield succeeded in popularizing Darby's ideas. Among many other errant ideas, this doctrine emphasizes its belief that the Jewish return to their Middle Eastern land in 1947 was fulfillment of Biblical prophecy, wholly ignoring and contradicting Jesus' own words (Matthew 23:39; does modern Israel acknowledge Jesus, the One who came in the "…name of the Lord"?).

As Jesus slowly moved the disciples from the mount of Transfiguration in the northern edge of the nation to Jerusalem for that last visit, we see Him increasingly teaching the disciples that He would be rejected and taken from them. At times, it appears that they may have caught a glimpse of His point, but mostly they seemed oblivious to it. On that last evening when He would be arrested later that night in Gethsemane, Jesus made the point so directly that the disciples could no longer mistake or misunderstand his point.

Location when Jesus taught the lessons contained in John 14-16 is not relevant to the truths that He taught. They could no longer doubt what He told them. Even then, they still didn't fully grasp His meaning, as evidenced in their overwhelming sadness at His words.

I have yet many things to say unto you, but ye cannot bear them now. (John 16:12; add to this a study of the disciples' reaction to Jesus' words in these three chapters)

They would not begin to fully understand His teachings until the promised Holy Spirit descended on them at Pentecost with special power and revelation.

Let not your heart be troubled. For a moment, try to put yourself in the disciples' place. Increasingly over the last few weeks, Jesus has warned you that His personal presence with you is coming to an end. What then? The question looms greater and greater. The hostility of the leaders in power at Jerusalem is growing white hot by the day. Things are shaping up for what you perceive as a disastrous change, but Jesus seems perfectly calm, even as He talks more about His imminent experience of all these things. How can He be so calm when it seems to you that your whole world, your world that has Him in its center, is ready to implode, at least as you perceive it?

And, of all things that Jesus could say, at this confusing and emotional moment for you, he speaks these words. How can you be anything but troubled in heart?

...ye believe in God, believe also in me. Every time I engage an in depth study of the Bible, I am increasingly thankful that we have a literal, word for word translation of the Bible in our King James translation. The simplest English explanation of this thought is not a mystery. "...ye believe in God" states a fact. Jesus tells the disciples something that they would have considered so basic as to need no reminder. Yes, they believed in God, the specific and only one God of Old Testament Scripture.

...believe also in me. And just as simply, these words issue a directive, a commandment to the disciples to do something that they apparently have not fully done at this moment. Do not understate their belief in Him. Each of them left his career and followed Jesus for the last three plus years. Yet even this degree of belief falls short of what Jesus here commands them. He is telling them to do something in words that build on the idea that they are not presently obeying. You don't command someone to do what they are already doing, do you?

What Jesus is commanding the disciples is possible and logical only if they fully understand that he is God Incarnate, God—fully and wholly God—living in a human body, the very point that John will make in the opening words of his written account of Jesus (John 1:1-18). Jesus is commanding the disciples to believe in Him as God, no less than they believe in God as God.

Jesus makes this point quite clearly in His discussion with Thomas, verses 5-9. Believing that Jesus was a righteous and insightful rabbi was not enough. Believing that He was a sent prophet from God was not enough. What Jesus commands in this verse rises immeasurably above any such belief. No more than we, those disciples could not possibly embrace Jesus' words regarding what He was about to do and where He was soon to go if they believed anything less about Him. They already believed in Him in many commendable ways. Would you abandon your career and livelihood and follow a man for over three years whom you did not believe?

But clearly their belief in Him still fell short of what He here commanded. He commanded them to believe in Him in the same way that they believed in God. In short, they must believe that He is God Incarnate, God living in human flesh and dwelling among them. If He was anything less, they could not believe that He could go anywhere through death to prepare anything for them.

Even in the fresh shadow of Jesus raising Lazarus from the dead, to believe that they had lived with God in human flesh for these last three years was almost more than the disciples could imagine, much less truly believe. Yet this is precisely what Jesus commands them to believe. For them, death remained as the black wall. If they believed their Old Testament writings, death certainly was not the end of existence for them. But the idea of Jesus dying and consciously doing things, even more miraculous things that they had witnessed Him doing while they were with Him, and then rising from the dead, was simply more than they could wrap their minds around.

Study the Scriptures that reveal the disciples' reactions after Jesus' crucifixion. Ponder their surprise when they witness His presence, His physical, literal, bodily presence after His resurrection. One response from two disciples will bear ample testimony to their state of mind.

> *And he said unto them, What things? And they said unto him, Concerning Jesus of Nazareth, which was a prophet mighty in deed and word before God and all the people: And how the chief priests and our rulers delivered him to be condemned to death, and have crucified him. But we trusted that it had been he which should have redeemed Israel: and beside all this, to day is the third day since these things were done. Yea, and certain women also of our company made us astonished, which were early at the sepulchre; And when they found not his body, they came, saying, that they had also seen a vision of angels, which said that he was alive. And certain of them which were with us went to the sepulchre, and found it even so as the women had said: but him they saw not.* (Luke 24:19-24)

When faced with the idea of resurrection, for the moment, the disciples fell prey to the same flaw as the Sadducees who denied the doctrine of the resurrection. They did not at that moment believe the Scriptures or the power of God.

Given the details of doubt and unbelief among the disciples immediately following Jesus' resurrection, we can more fully appreciate why Jesus so directly commanded them "…believe also in me." They could only understand the full reality of the resurrection, His or theirs, on the premise of believing that He was God manifest in the flesh, including God over death, not a man subject to it. No mere man could possibly accomplish what Jesus increasingly tells the disciples that He intends to do. The modern occasional claim that Jesus never so much as suggested to the disciples that He was God, when weighed in the light of Scripture, is pure fantasy. Jesus taught this truth from the beginning. Only after the disciples were empowered by the Holy Spirit on the Day of Pentecost did they begin to truly understand and believe this truth. Someone has said that, if you do not believe in Jesus and the resurrection, you are liable to fear everything; but if you do believe in Jesus and the resurrection, you fear nothing. So true!

25
How Many and How Glorious?

Let not your heart be troubled: ye believe in God, believe also in me. In my Father's house are many mansions: if it were not so, I would have told you. I go to prepare a place for you. And if I go and prepare a place for you, I will come again, and receive you unto myself; that where I am, there ye may be also. And whither I go ye know, and the way ye know. (John 14:1–4)

Building on the commandment to the disciples to believe in Him as they believed in God, Jesus teaches the greatest truth that had the potential to comfort and sooth their troubled hearts. While He would leave them in this world, He was going away to put the final touches on another place where they would join Him and enjoy even greater fellowship and blessing than they had experienced with Him during the last three years. And, during His time away from them, He would send the Holy Spirit, an ever-present Comforter who would be just as present and effective a companion and helper as He had been to them. They would not be left alone.

When people confuse passages dealing with discipleship and passages dealing with eternal life, they inevitably conclude that the relative number of people whom God saves, eternally saves from their sins, is small. This conclusion must ignore any number of passages that state the mirror opposite, that the number of people whom the Lord saves and who shall enjoy Him for eternity is relatively large. Jesus adds yet another such passage here.

In my Father's house are many mansions. Jesus didn't give a precise number, but He did give a relative point, **many** as contrasted with *few*. Jesus reinforces the point; "...*if it were not so, I would have told you.*" If He intended to prepare heaven—and populate it— with only a few people relative to all humanity, He says that He would have told the disciples that fact. This comment in and of itself tells us that we cannot interpret any of Jesus' "few" comments as a reference to eternity and the relative number of the elect. A careful study of those passages in context will show that they focus on discipleship, not eternity. And Scripture abundantly warns us that the difficulties and required self-denial of discipleship will render the number of faithful disciples to be few indeed.

Jesus' use of the term, "many mansions," adds further to Scripture's revelation of our future with the Lord in glory. The dwelling place for the Lord's people in heaven is not a shanty hut that might last for a brief time, but is so flimsy that it shall soon fall to the ground. That place is not a temporary tent. It is a place suitably luxurious—luxury measured by the Lord's standards, not ours—to be an appropriate dwelling for all eternity.

I go to prepare a place for you. Jesus here associates His many dwelling places, or "mansions," with people. There shall be no empty, unoccupied dwelling place in heaven, not even one. Several years ago during the housing crisis in California, Sandra and I occasionally drove through a very nice upscale street near where we live. As we drove along this street, more than half the houses were vacant with foreclosure signs in the front yard. It felt as if we were driving through a ghost town. Just a few months earlier we had driven this same street and seen children playing in the yards, parents working to make their home comfortable and attractive, and cars parked in driveways. What happened? How could so many dreams be shattered? In fact, every vacant home on that street represented a family with a shattered dream.

Will heaven be filled with reminders of shattered dreams and unrealized potential? No, Jesus completed the work—and this passage is all about reminding us of this truth—necessary to ensure that every "mansion," every glorious dwelling place in heaven shall be occupied.

I go to prepare a place for you. ...for you, Jesus identifies that His going to prepare this place is not for some vague someone who will make a decision, believe the gospel, or otherwise supplement His work to gain their access to this place. A modern dodge to the Bible doctrine of election builds on this errant idea. As the idea goes, since Isaiah 42:1 in prophecy identifies Jesus as God's "elect," all Bible election has to do only with Him personally. According to this idea, if you will take the necessary steps to put yourself into Jesus, then you become identified with Him as God's elect. Paul writes—

Therefore if any man be in Christ, he is a new creature: old things are passed away; behold, all things are become new. (2 Corinthians 5:17)

By specifically defining that anyone who is in Christ is a new creature, the product of a new creation, Paul defines "creation" as the process and excludes any other process by which a person may find himself "in Christ." The person who is truly "in Christ" is not a new evolution. He is not a new self-made man. He is in Christ by a creative work that occurred outside himself. The natural world didn't actively contribute to its creation in Genesis 1. God created it exclusively by Himself (Genesis 1:1). The product of creation must attribute his existence to his Creator, not to himself.

Further, when Jesus taught Nicodemus about the new birth, He concluded His lesson with an analogy of blowing wind. You hear its sound blowing through the trees, but you are not in charge of wind. You can't tell where it blew before it blew at your location, and you can't tell where it will blow in the next ten minutes.

Jesus states the fact. He left the disciples to accomplish a work that only He could complete, and the recipients of that work's benefit are as specific as the work itself, "…for you." A story will illustrate the point.

A young man came to believe that God had called him to preach. In his denomination's tradition, a man in his situation must graduate Bible college or seminary. He enrolled in his denomination's seminary and started his training. As he studied his Bible, he increasingly came to see the Bible doctrine of election. When he started talking to people about his beliefs that He had discovered in his Bible, word soon got to the administrators of the college. They called him to a hearing for his beliefs that contradicted the college's and the denomination's stated freewill beliefs. The college had one professor who believed the doctrine of election; he was so respected in the denomination and by his students that they quietly tolerated his belief. This man happened to be on the hearing board that heard this young man's case. After the young man simple stated why he had come to believe in Biblical election, he was dismissed, and the board discussed his case privately. The professor who shared this belief argued for the young man. He had immersed his mind in the Bible. What was wrong with that? He had discovered an unpopular, but clearly taught doctrine in his studies of the Bible. What was wrong with that? The board decided to allow the young man to continue his studies. Subsequently, the young man and the professor who shared his belief in Biblical election became good friends. The professor took the young student under his wings and guided him through his studies. Sometime later in a general assembly of the students, the college president used the gathering to preach a brief sermon on his beliefs in man's free will. Near the end of his sermonette, the president quoted a verse that he believed supported his idea, Revelation 22:17.

The president added volume and intensity to his voice as he stated, "I believe the *Whosoever wills* of the Bible." The professor who believed the Bible doctrine of election was a very short man. When he sat in the seats in the auditorium, his feet didn't touch the floor. In the quiet of the audience, the professor seated by his adopted student friend, jumped from his seat, landed his feet on the floor with a thump, and shouted, "But what are you going to do with all the *Whosoever will nots* in the Bible?" No answer.

No two Bible doctrines, rightly divided and rightly understood, contradict each other. Revelation 22:17, rightly divided, in no way contradicts the equally clear teachings of Scripture regarding God's election of a chosen, specific people to be His family throughout eternity. The only people who are in fact willing to come to Jesus are people who were previously born of His Holy Spirit. They possess eternal life.

Jesus affirmed that the believer in Him already possesses eternal life (John 5:24; a truth that John affirms in 1 John 5:1). If eternal life is already a fact at the time we believe, our belief cannot possibly be either causative or instrumental in our coming to possess eternal life. Those who are willing to respond to the gospel as they come to believe in Jesus have already been born again. They are already children of God. They are both elect and born again.

A person's will is a function of his nature; a dead person has no will. A person's willing faith and obedience to the Lord and to His gospel is manifestation that he presently is a living, born-again child of grace (Ephesians 2:1-10; Paul specifically equates our condition prior to being saved by God's grace as "...dead in trespasses and sins," a state that God in kind grace reverses by giving us eternal life).

I will come again, and receive you unto myself; that where I am, there ye may be also. Jesus arose from the dead after three days in the borrowed tomb. He appeared to the disciples and taught them for forty days. He then ascended out of their sight in glory, returning to the Father (Acts 1:9-11). However, in this ascending, Jesus did not take the disciples with Him. They remained behind. His promise of returning and receiving them to Himself remains unfulfilled, but it is no less certain today than when Jesus spoke the words of promise.

Today we abide in the same hope that stirred the disciples' faith in the first generation of the faith. We do not know the time. It will come unannounced and unexpected, but it shall surely come. And when it comes, our Lord shall appear in glory and receive to Himself His chosen and beloved children, the "Many" children for whom He prepared "many" mansions.

At that day, we shall hear our Lord speak the glorious and joyful words, "Behold I and the children which God hath given me" (Hebrews 2:13b). When we appear before the Father, we shall be nestled in our Lord's loving embrace, for He shall then receive us to Himself. From that moment and throughout timeless eternity, we shall be with Him where He is. We shall never know a moment of lonely gloom, looking for His appearing. We shall never feel a touch of anxiety, wondering "When shall He come?" We shall never visit a cemetery to remember our loved ones who have gone before us. For a joyful eternity, we shall be with Him where He is.

If you have friends in gloryland
who've left because of pain,
There'll be no pain in gloryland;
they'll suffer not again.

So weep not friends, I'm going Home.
Up there we'll die no more.
No coffins will be made up there,
no graves on that bright shore.

- The Primitive Quartet

26
The Foundation of Christian Joy

Then the same day at evening, being the first day of the week, when the
doors were shut where the disciples were assembled for fear of the Jews,
came Jesus and stood in the midst, and saith unto them, Peace be unto you.
And when he had so said, he shewed unto them his hands and his side.
Then were the disciples glad, when they saw the Lord. (John 20:19–20)

Then saith he to Thomas, Reach hither thy finger, and behold my hands;
and reach hither thy hand, and thrust it into my side: and be not faithless,
but believing. (John 20:27)

I can't imagine the state of mind that prevailed in the room where
the disciples gathered on the evening of Jesus' resurrection. A
few of them had seen Him and told the others. Some believed and
some doubted, we know at least one. After almost a week of
stronger emotions than they'd likely ever experienced in their lives,
they must be emotionally drained. They simply had more on their
"plates" than they could process. What do you make of it all? Is He
raised? Did He really defeat death and come back to them? Then He
appeared to them. It really was Him alive and standing there. It was
not a spirit or an illusion. Not only did they see Him, but they heard
His voice. He even showed them His hands and side, the evidence of
His crucifixion.

The gospel that we preach is based on facts, on true information
about events and people, in particular, one person, in real human
history. It is not a fabricated fiction story. Later when Paul strives
with all his reasoning and heart to regain the Galatians who heard
and believed the truth that he preached, but then stumbled at the
false gospel that his detractors preached, he reminded them that his
gospel was literal and factually true.

*O foolish Galatians, who hath bewitched you, that ye should not obey the truth, before whose eyes **Jesus Christ hath been evidently set forth**, crucified among you?* (Galatians 3:1; emphasis added)

Jesus was not crucified in Galatia, but the evidence of His literal crucifixion and His equally literal resurrection were both key elements in the gospel that Paul had preached to those people. In his preaching, Paul taught the literal reality of what Jesus did for our sins, and the Galatians believed it. Whatever else Paul taught them, this truth was central to his message. And so it must always be.

When Paul wrote his first letter to the Corinthians, he wrote, *"For I determined not to know any thing among you, save Jesus Christ, and him crucified"* (1 Corinthians 2:2). Yet as we read First Corinthians beginning to end, we see Paul reasoning with them about a long and varied list of errant ideas and practices that they had carelessly embraced as a church. They were so focused on the personality of individual preachers that they had forgotten this truth. They became confused about such practical issues as diet, meat offered to idols, and how believers should live in pervasive and kind respect for each other, not take each other to a human judge and court to settle their personal differences. They had wholly discarded the matter of church discipline and boasted of their broad-minded tolerance of moral sin, rather than grieving it and separating themselves from their member who had so sinned. They had corrupted the Lord's Supper, turning it more into a collective meal than an act of worship. They were highly confused regarding spiritual gifts; Paul devoted three whole chapters out of sixteen to this topic. Some of them had denied the doctrine of the resurrection.

Paul writes this confused church about each of these issues and many more. Yet the one central truth that pulled all these issues together and made sense of his whole message was the same. Paul's whole letter was not sixteen chapters about Jesus' sufferings and death. Nor should our preaching today be so. However, our preaching should always build on this truth, just as Paul's First Corinthian letter and the varied topics covered therein builds on it.

What was the disciples' reaction to Jesus' appearance and words to them? "Then were the disciples glad, when they saw the Lord." How refreshing! After over a week of more confusion and stress than they could have imagined, gladness returned to their hearts. I love the image of people's faces at the moment of spontaneous joy. Surely this moment with the disciples was wholly unexpected. Long droopy faces immediately turned to overwhelming joy. When they say Him, they were **glad**.

Whatever the issue in our lives, however distressing or depressing, refocusing our minds on our resurrected and victorious Lord restores gladness to our hearts. David recalls such a moment.

He brought me up also out of an horrible pit, out of the miry clay, and set my feet upon a rock, and established my goings. And he hath put a new song in my mouth, even praise unto our God: many shall see it, and fear, and shall trust in the LORD. (Psalms 40:2-3)

Joyful, truly "glad" people tend to live generally in a more peaceful manner, both with themselves and with others. Few deep convictions are as pervasive in providing a foundation for kind and godly grace between believers as the Bible doctrine of the Second Coming and resurrection. Peter makes this point in his teaching on the resurrection (2 Peter 3:11-16).

We only prove that we actually believe in the resurrection and the Lord's return by how we treat other believers. If I constantly criticize you and pick faults, real or imagined, in you, I give you no evidence that I believe in the Second Coming and our bodily resurrection: "...what manner of persons ought ye to be...?" We prove what we believe in fact by how we live and, specifically based on this and many other passages, by how we treat each other in the faith.

As a young man in both my faith and in the ministry, I recall meeting a preacher from a region a couple hundred miles from my home. At our first meeting, I liked him and his family. They were friendly and seemed quite sincere and devoted to the faith. I was shocked when I heard the man preach the first time. He started with his text and was nicely building the framework for a good sermon. When he set up a particular point that he wanted to emphasize, he paused, put a scornful scowl on his face, and shouted, "Now you get this" with more hatred than love in his voice. His manner was wholly out of character with his message. Today, I have no recall whatever of his text or subject that night, but I clearly recall his unkind manner in the pulpit.

Believers in Christ who truly do believe in the Second Coming and resurrection should take great care in their manner of life toward other believers. We could so easily find ourselves in the situation of this preacher. People will forget what we believed, but they will long remember how unloving and harsh we were toward other believers. I ask, my friends, is this really how you wish to be remembered?

We show gladness of heart by how we live, the way we treat the people around us—to use a Bible term—"especially unto them who are of the household of faith" (Galatians 6:10b). We are often too inclined to isolate our beliefs from our conduct, packing each into a well wrapped and insulated package. Scripture rejects this fragmented idea of the faith of the Lord Jesus Christ. It integrates our belief with our conduct. Our minds and hearts hold to certain beliefs, and our eyes, ears, hands, feet, and, ah, yes indeed, our tongues either validate our belief or bring it into question.

When Jesus appeared to the disciples in our study passage, they had gone through more emotional trials and stresses than we can imagine. Within the last few weeks, Jesus increasingly told them what to expect, but they simply couldn't bring themselves to believe His words. And, when they did momentarily accept His imminent exit, they fell into ungodly bickering about which of them would be the leader of the group after He left them (Mark 9:34; Luke 22:24). As they entered the city of Jerusalem, they were overjoyed to see the palm leaves and the crowd shouting praises to God at Jesus' entrance into the city. They were likely bewildered and wholly unprepared so soon afterwards to see their leaders openly opposing

Jesus, and eventually arresting Him and turning Him over to the Romans for trial and crucifixion

Peter's reaction to the young woman's notice that he was a Galilean who followed Jesus may tell us much about the other disciples, as well as about Peter. Their minds likely were overloaded with fear, questions, and doubts. Some of them, even after hearing the early reports of Jesus' resurrection, voiced continuing doubt, "But we trusted that it had been he which should have redeemed Israel." (Luke 24:21)

With so much confusion and turmoil in their minds, how can these men be described as "glad"? And here we discover the power of the lesson and the power of "Jesus and the resurrection." (Acts 17:18) "Then were the disciples glad, when they saw the Lord."

In this textual setting, we also see even greater words of comfort. In the number of the disciples, we see one who, even upon hearing more than one of the disciples report that they had actually seen the resurrected Jesus and talked with Him, refused to believe their words. He has earned the cliché, "Doubting Thomas."

"*...and be not faithless, but believing.*" Though Jesus was not bodily present when Thomas voiced his unbelief, He knew. When we voice our own doubts and disbelief today, never doubt; He knows. Jesus singles Thomas out from the others, shows Thomas his hands and his side, and even invites him to touch if that is what Thomas needs to remove his doubt.

How differently Scripture deals with this question of doubt than the typical contemporary preacher of condemnation! Jesus knows His own, even in their moments of doubt or unbelief. Instead of warning them, "I can't give you any assurance that you are really born again unless you believe," Jesus confronts our unbelief with solid evidences that remove that unbelief.

Based on Scripture, the Holy Spirit, not a self-appointed preacher, is the source of assurance to the child of grace in this world. If such a preacher gave you his iron-clad assurance that you were born again, it would mean absolutely nothing whatever. However, if the Holy Spirit gives you His assurance, you join the disciples who were "glad, when they saw the Lord." You rejoice at

His kind grace and at the weight of His testimony to you. Your doubts melt, replaced by joyful belief. Such, my friends, is the true gospel of the grace of God. Never settle for less.

27
What Lies Ahead?

When they therefore were come together, they asked of him, saying, Lord, wilt thou at this time restore again the kingdom to Israel? And he said unto them, It is not for you to know the times or the seasons, which the Father hath put in his own power. But ye shall receive power, after that the Holy Ghost is come upon you: and ye shall be witnesses unto me both in Jerusalem, and in all Judaea, and in Samaria, and unto the uttermost part of the earth. And when he had spoken these things, while they beheld, he was taken up; and a cloud received him out of their sight. And while they looked stedfastly toward heaven as he went up, behold, two men stood by them in white apparel; Which also said, Ye men of Galilee, why stand ye gazing up into heaven? this same Jesus, which is taken up from you into heaven, shall so come in like manner as ye have seen him go into heaven. (Acts 1:6–11)

Our study passage is the only passage that provides a detailed account of Jesus' ascension. Therefore, we should linger with it and probe its rich treasures thoroughly. In the two prior verses, Jesus instructed the disciples to remain in Jerusalem until they experienced a special outpouring from the Father, something that He had told them, but they could not fully understand it till they experienced its reality. He associated this event with John's prophecy of baptism with the Holy Ghost.

Our safest and best interpretation of Scripture is always to take note when one Scripture interprets another. Follow Scripture's interpretation of itself. Jesus associated this unusual baptism with something that these men should experience "...not many days hence," with the implication that the event should occur in Jerusalem, the reason they were to remain in the city. This baptism was not intended as a potential for all believers, but as a special experience for the disciples on this certain day.

I have occasionally been asked my thoughts regarding Peter's citation of Joel 2:28-32 in Acts 2:16-21. The frequent question ignores the simple language of the passage. Peter stated, "But ***this is that*** which was spoken by the prophet Joel" (Acts 2:16; emphasis added). Notice the clear point that Peter made, "But this is that...." He didn't say, "But this is one phase of that," or "But this is a partial fulfillment of that," or "This partially fulfills that...but more is yet to come." Peter's language leaves no question. What happened on Pentecost in Acts 2 fulfills Joel's prophecy. Period. I believe Peter's inspired explanation with no need to add to it or to expand it. "But this is that...." It was this extraordinary outpouring of the Spirit of God that Jesus told the disciples would occur in them in Jerusalem "...not many days hence."

Lord, wilt thou at this time restore again the kingdom to Israel? We could learn far more than we ordinarily consider by pondering this one question. The disciples understood what Jesus told the leaders of Judaism during His public ministry.

> *Therefore say I unto you, The kingdom of God shall be taken from you, and given to a nation bringing forth the fruits thereof.* (Matthew 21:43)

By their words to Jesus, the disciples fully understood that the Jewish people had lost God's kingdom in whatever way they once possessed it.

"...*wilt thou at this time **restore again**....*" Various commentaries take this question from the disciples and catapult it to suppose that the disciples believed in some form of dispensationalism or millennialism, and that they were asking Jesus if the time had come for it to begin. In fact, the disciples were looking back to a previous era when the Jewish people basked in the Lord's glory and blessings as they followed Him in faithful obedience. They never experienced anything remotely akin to the era described by either of these beliefs regarding the future. The disciples were not expecting a future millennial age of Jesus personally ruling planet Earth in righteous and sovereign dominion. They were interested in a restoration of blessings upon the Jews similar to past ages when they obeyed and the Lord blessed them. Their question in fact does not at all lend support to either dispensational or millennial beliefs.

Is it possible that, at some future time, a large number of Jewish people might embrace Jesus and the faith of New Testament Scripture? I would not deny the possibility. However, I doubt that Jewish people as a culture will ever replace Gentile believers in the New Testament Church. When Jesus came and completed His work, He removed the dividing wall that separated Jews from Gentiles, treating one differently from the other (Ephesians 2:11-17). I find nothing in this context to indicate any intent on His part to restore that dividing wall. It was removed and shall not be rebuilt by Him.

Further, we find ample evidence in New Testament Scripture to describe how any person ever finds the Lord's blessings and enjoys the fruits of His kingdom, "...righteousness, and peace, and joy in the Holy Ghost." (Romans 14:17) The process is never culture-wide, but always individual and personal. When Jesus announced His judgment against Jerusalem and the people who then so grievously mismanaged His temple, He included an explanation of how they could reverse that judgment.

For I say unto you, Ye shall not see me henceforth, till ye shall say, Blessed is he that cometh in the name of the Lord. (Matthew 23:39)

Jesus is the One and only One who came "...in the name of the Lord." His judgment indelibly associated their seeing His face in blessings with their praising and blessing Him.

Despite passionate and sincere efforts by dispensationalists in particular to make the Jews' return to their native land in 1947 a fulfillment of Scripture, the character of the present people in Israel contradicts rather than agrees with Jesus' sentence. Try openly preaching Jesus in Israel today and see how your preaching is received. These people have earned the privilege of having a place to call their own as an earthly nation, but they have not at all fulfilled Biblical prophecy.

Jesus' judgment was against the leaders of the nation and religion of that time in Jerusalem. His promise of blessing, of seeing His face again, is made to individuals who, from the heart, say "Blessed is he that cometh in the name of the Lord." Therefore, my answer to those who hope for a national restoration is this. The Lord's church and kingdom today is quite broad enough for every Jew and for every Gentile believer who blesses His name and embraces Him and His message in faith. Neither Jew nor Gentile who so believes in Him is now—or shall ever be—excluded because of their race or cultural background.

As we sweep away the errant interpretations of the disciples' question and Jesus' answer, we get to the truth of the lesson. The disciples longed for restoration of the former ages when their ancestors followed God in the shadow of their great Rock, and rejoiced in the light of His glory. Was that time upon them? "Wilt thou *at this time*..." If we follow the language, they were not at all asking about an eschatological or end-times situation of any kind. They were interested in something that they would witness in their lifetimes.

Jesus answers their question simply and clearly. "It is not for you to know the times or the seasons, which the Father hath put in his own power." Looking into the future was not part of Jesus' assignment to these men as His disciples. It is also not part of His assignment to us. Jesus does not affirm their hope for restoration, and He does not in any way open the door or prophecy of a future millennial era. He simply rebukes the disciples for trying to anticipate what was not in their view or divine assignment.

Jesus prepared them to be His witnesses, to give personal testimony and Biblical evidence, where ever they went, of His coming, fulfilling Old Testament prophecies, and saving "...his people from their sins" (Matthew 1:21). He never assigned them to become future prognosticators or "star-gazers" who thought themselves able to know the future. Living so as to be a credible and faithful witness to Jesus and His resurrection is a full-time assignment. It leaves no time or energy available for star-gazing or prognosticating. The more we or any people invest our time and energy in predicting what we cannot know fully from Scripture robs us of our credibility as His witnesses.

The primary charge that each believer in Christ has received from the Lord is to be His witnesses. That first generation of disciples, the eleven in particular, had witnessed Jesus' life and miracles firsthand. They had also now witnessed Him in glorious resurrection for approximately forty days. He charges them to avoid speculation about what the Father may or may not have in store for the future and to invest themselves in being His faithful witnesses. John reflects this focused assignment of being His witnesses.

That which was from the beginning, which we have heard, which we have seen with our eyes, which we have looked upon, and our hands have handled, of the Word of life; (For the life was manifested, and we have seen it, and bear witness, and shew unto you that eternal life, which was with the Father, and was manifested unto us;) **That which we have seen and heard declare we unto you,** *that ye also may have fellowship with us: and truly our fellowship is with the Father, and with his Son Jesus Christ. And these things write we unto you, that your joy may be full.* (1 John 1:1-4; emphasis added)

If we follow Jesus' commandments today, we must live so that our words, attitudes, and actions are credible witnesses of His love and grace in us, as living evidence of "...Christ in you the hope of glory." After restoring the wild Gadarene, Jesus gave him similar instruction, "Go home to thy friends, and tell them how great things the Lord hath done for thee, and hath had compassion on thee" (Mark 5:19b).

If your relatives, neighbors, or work associates rely solely on your personal conduct, including words, attitudes, and actions, would they gather from your conduct that you have spent time with Jesus? Would they see His grace in you? (Colossians 4:6) Would your personal life motivate them to desire time with both you and Him, or does your conduct motivate them to exit your presence as quickly as possible? The focus of the gospel is always to be on the "whole counsel of God," (Acts 20:26-27), but Scriptures such as we here examine remind us. If we follow Scripture, we shall not only witness its true teachings, but we shall also manifest His presence, love, and grace in our lives. Otherwise, people will see little reason in us to take note of anything that we may care to say about Scripture.

The Christian culture, in the broad sense of that term, overflows with philosophical types who will tell you more than they know about exactly what the Bible teaches, but their words, attitudes, and actions are void of His sweet fragrance and grace. Therefore, their words lack edification and give their hearers no credible reason to hear or to believe them.

Lord help us this week to spend much time praying for the Lord to convict us and to guide us to so live His grace that our whole life speaks the kind grace of Him and of His gospel. Only as we so live can we fulfill His command to be His witnesses in our lives. (John 13:35)

28
He Shall Return as He Went

*When they therefore were come together, they asked of him, saying, Lord,
wilt thou at this time restore again the kingdom to Israel? And he said unto
them, It is not for you to know the times or the seasons, which the Father
hath put in his own power. But ye shall receive power, after that the Holy
Ghost is come upon you: and ye shall be witnesses unto me both in
Jerusalem, and in all Judaea, and in Samaria, and unto the uttermost part
of the earth. And when he had spoken these things, while they beheld, he
was taken up; and a cloud received him out of their sight. And while they
looked stedfastly toward heaven as he went up, behold, two men stood by
them in white apparel; Which also said, Ye men of Galilee, why stand ye
gazing up into heaven? this same Jesus, which is taken up from you into
heaven, shall so come in like manner as ye have seen him go into heaven.*
(Acts 1:6–11)

When Paul faced the challenge of defending the faith before
Greek philosophers on Mars Hill, he started with their own
past philosophers, quoting from two of them, but interpreting their
words quite differently from their ideas. He quickly launched from
that point into his primary focus, "Jesus, and the resurrection" (Acts
17:18). Throughout New Testament teaching, Jesus' resurrection
serves as the foundation for our belief that we shall also be raised,
not to inhabit an ideal world on this planet, but, like Him, to ascend
"…into heaven."

Jesus' ascension into heaven was not in spirit only. The disciples
saw His body ascend into a cloud, I suggest a cloud of glory, not of
fog. Further, the angels who spoke to them affirmed His bodily
ascension, "…this same Jesus, which is taken up from you into
heaven…." Did the disciples' experience with Jesus for three and
one-half years include His physical body? Yes, and that Jesus, body
included, was taken into heaven. That same Jesus, body included,

shall also return "...in like manner." He ascended in glory; He shall return in glory. He ascended victorious; He shall return victorious.

Although he does not go into details about the image, Paul tells us that he saw the resurrected Jesus, fully qualifying him to be one of Jesus' chosen apostles. The most likely occasion to which he referred was the recorded encounter that he had with Jesus on the road leading into Damascus (Acts 9:1-8; 22:1-11; 26:9-18; 1 Corinthians 15:8). John begins Revelation with an account of Jesus appearing to him on his prison island (Revelation 1:10-16). He describes a physical body, but a body so changed in glory that the glory shines far brighter than the physical image.

The centrality of Jesus' literal, physical, bodily resurrection and ascension is foundational to every major New Testament doctrine, not just its teaching regarding our personal bodily resurrection (Philippians 3:20-21). Consider just one example.

For there is one God, and one mediator between God and men, the man Christ Jesus. (1 Timothy 2:5)

In this key passage on Jesus' mediatorial work, Paul makes specific reference to "the man Christ Jesus." At the least, "the man" includes some reference to Jesus' physical body that He inhabited during His time on earth. Paul didn't say, "...the spirit Christ Jesus," but "...***the man*** Christ Jesus."

If we follow Paul's reasoning in this verse, if Jesus does not inhabit that same body today in heaven where he went at His ascension (Acts 1:11), we have no mediator. When Christians refer to Jesus' time on earth as His incarnation, they are liable to leave the question of His present bodily status unaddressed. He didn't occupy a human body just during those thirty three plus years. He occupies it today in heaven, crucial to His present work as Mediator between God and men.

We find no Scripture to indicate when on our calendar Jesus shall return. Just during my lifetime, I have observed several men, often radio or television preachers, who claimed to have discovered some hidden truth that enabled them to tell people precisely when Jesus would so return. One of them, Harold Camping, got it wrong, but didn't learn. At least twice after missing the specific date of Jesus' return, he tried again, but each time he was wrong. His predicted date for the Second Coming came on the calendar and went, but Jesus didn't sound the trumpet or return.

If we follow Scripture, we learn that date-setting is not to occupy our minds or distract our testimony to Jesus and His resurrection and glory. If you play the prophet only to see the passing of time bear incontrovertible testimony to your error, your whole testimony to Him loses its credibility. In our study passage, Jesus rebukes the disciples for seeking a supposed restoration date and directs them to invest their spiritual energy to their testimony of Him.

Often the simple Scriptures reveal far more to us than we grasp. While we strain at gnats and swallow camels in our pursuit of "big truth," we become inexcusably ignorant of the simple truths of the gospel that we should know and manifest by the testimony of our life's conduct. Our failure to manifest Jesus' life and ethics in our daily conduct, and especially our interactions with other believers, will utterly destroy our credibility as witnesses to Him and to His truth. "If ye love me, keep my commandments" (John 14:15). When we promote ourselves as theological experts, but fail to practice what Jesus taught us to practice in our daily life, again especially toward other believers, we reduce ourselves to theoretical philosophers, and we lose all credibility to bear personal witness to our Lord and to His grace in our lives.

The witness of Jesus is as valid through the testimony of the gospel as it was to the disciples who were eyewitnesses of His life, death, resurrection, and ascension. Jesus never physically visited Galatia during His time on earth. He was not crucified there, we know. But, when Paul visited Galatia and preached the gospel to the people there, they saw the evidence of Jesus. When he wrote the Galatians in rebuke for their departure, Paul reminded them of the gospel that he preached to them and that they received.

O foolish Galatians, who hath bewitched you, that ye should not obey the truth, before whose eyes Jesus Christ hath been evidently set forth, crucified among you? (Galatians 3:1)

"...evidently set forth" means that Paul's preaching to the Galatians revealed Jesus' life, sufferings, death, resurrection, and work as he preached to them. Jesus was crucified in the outskirts of Jerusalem, not in Galatia, but Paul's preaching to the Galatians so presented Jesus and His crucifixion with evidence to support this fact that the Galatians were in the same position as those who did witness His actual crucifixion in Jerusalem. Therefore, as Paul reasons, they were foolish and without excuse when they rejected Paul's preaching and believed the false gospel that Paul's detractors taught them.

When Paul wrote the Thessalonian Church, he taught them comforting truth regarding the Lord's return. His objective in teaching this early church the truth of the Lord's return was not to indoctrinate them in one or another dispensational theory, pre-trib, post-trib, or mid-trib. You don't understand these terms? Great! You are blessed not to know them. Paul had a far more important objective when he preached the gospel of the Lord's return.

Wherefore comfort one another with these words. (1 Thessalonians 4:18)

For persecuted, discouraged, and distressed first century believers, the thought that the Lord and His return was so thoroughly designed and would be so precisely executed, all for the Lord's glory and for the eternal joy of His people, nothing they faced in this life could diminish their joy at the thought of His return. And so Paul intended his gospel to them.

For ye are dead, and your life is hid with Christ in God. When Christ, who is our life, shall appear, then shall ye also appear with him in glory. (Colossians 3:3-4)

He shall return as the disciples saw Him ascend. And when He returns, we shall immediately experience a change that involves our whole selves, body, soul, and spirit, all changed to appear with Him in glory forever.

Inspired by the Holy Spirit to write his words, Paul taught a firm and sound belief in the Lord's return that imposed present, immediate, and life-changing power onto those who believe this truth.

If ye then be risen with Christ, seek those things which are above, where Christ sitteth on the right hand of God. Set your affection on things above, not on things on the earth. (Colossians 3:1-2)

John teaches the same truth.

Beloved, now are we the sons of God, and it doth not yet appear what we shall be: but we know that, when he shall appear, we shall be like him; for we shall see him as he is. And every man that hath this hope in him purifieth himself, even as he is pure. (1 John 3:2-3)

"…we shall be like him." If He ascended into heaven and glory in His physical body, so shall we. We shall fully experience Him as He is today in glory when we are resurrected, and body, soul, and spirit unite in heaven to praise Him forever.

Paul and John speak as one voice. Both inspired writers show us the iron-clad link between belief in the Lord's glorious return to how we live now. Do you believe in the Lord's return? In our physical, bodily resurrection? How convincingly do you prove that belief in your daily conduct? In how you interact with other believers in the "household of faith"?

If you rejoice at the thought of eternity praising God for redemption, one voice in the innumerable multitude of His redeemed children, do you show those same people that you love them and cherish their fellowship and companionship today? Do you long to spend time with them? And do you act so that they long to spend time with you? If so, you are learning the lesson of Scripture. If not, you have the Lord's assignment to grow.

29
Jesus' Resurrection: Foundation of Truth & Conduct

Ye men of Israel, hear these words; Jesus of Nazareth, a man approved of God among you by miracles and wonders and signs, which God did by him in the midst of you, as ye yourselves also know: Him, being delivered by the determinate counsel and foreknowledge of God, ye have taken, and by wicked hands have crucified and slain: Whom God hath raised up, having loosed the pains of death: because it was not possible that he should be holden of it. (Acts 2:22–24)

Just a few days earlier Jesus instructed the disciples to wait in Jerusalem, not to leave the city, until they received His power in the form of a miraculous outpouring of the Holy Spirit (Acts 1:4, 8). This was His last recorded word to them before He ascended back into heaven. They didn't know when this miracle would occur; only that they were to wait in Jerusalem until it appeared. Acts 2:2 uses the word "suddenly" to introduce the fulfillment of Jesus' word to them. Something that occurs "suddenly" occurs without warning. The disciples didn't wake up on Pentecost morning and say, "Today is the day." They knew something powerful was coming, but they didn't know when.

What was the form of the Spirit's manifestation? Luke, the inspired author of Acts, indicates that the disciples heard a sound "…as of a rushing mighty wind;" they saw "…cloven tongues like as of fire" that settled on each of them, and they "…began to speak with other tongues, as the Spirit gave them utterance."

The "tongues" languages with which they spoke were not mystical utterances that required translation. Quite in contrast to the modern claims of mystical utterances that no one can accurately understand or interpret, these men spoke, apparently in their native Galilean dialect; those who heard them knew that they were Galileans (Acts 2:7). The miracle appears in the hearers. Jewish people had gathered in Jerusalem from many nations and languages for the Day of Pentecost. Acts 2:8-11 documents at least sixteen different regions representing sixteen different languages. While recognizing that the men were Galileans, they marveled that each man heard the words spoken by the disciples "...in our own tongue wherein we were born" (Acts 2:8, 11). There is nothing mystical about their speech. The miracle occurred in the ears and minds of the hearers. Those who heard the disciples speaking heard in their native-born language, not in mystical utterances that they could not understand.

I do not doubt or question the sincerity of most people who believe that they speak in miraculous tongues today, but none of them ever speaks in the manner that Scripture clearly describes these men as speaking. Rather than requiring translation, the Holy Spirit's miracle was an immediate translation of the disciples' words from their native language simultaneously into the various sixteen different languages represented by the hearers of their words. No mystical utterances occurred. The Holy Spirit used known human languages to produce a miracle that none who heard the disciples' words could doubt or deny with any credibility. Believe the content of what the disciples said or not, they could not deny the miracle of human language that the Holy Spirit produced that day.

When the gospel is preached with the direction and power of the Holy Spirit, it always divides hearers. Some will hear with deep conviction and be stirred to ask questions, to seek more information. They sense something very important for them to know and do that the gospel teaches. Others will hear with rejection, often even with either anger or with a discrediting charge against the messenger. You see an example of this "great divide" in this chapter. Those who rejected the disciples' preaching accused them of being drunk at 9:00 A.M. Those who believed the preaching were stirred, "...pricked in their heart," (Acts 2:37) and asked for more instructions, specifically what they should do because of what they believed in the disciples' preaching.

There is always a link between what people believe and what they do. If they believe error, their attitude and conduct will manifest that error. If they believe the truth, their attitude and conduct will likewise manifest the truth that they believe. Not at all dissimilar to folks who reject the gospel today, the unbelievers on this day sought to discredit the messenger when they heard a message that they didn't like. They refused to consider that the message came from God, so they didn't consider that their attack against the messengers would not in any way neutralize the message.

When someone hurls false and unsavory words against you, your first human inclination is to strike back. While Peter briefly rejected the false charge, he had a far more important message that day than anything to do with himself. He devoted one simple sentence to the personal attack, "For these are not drunken, as ye suppose, seeing it is but the third hour of the day" (Acts 2:15). He then devoted the remainder of his message to the gospel, affirming what his false accusers most feared and hated, that the same Jesus whom they had crucified had arisen from the dead and ascended into heaven from which He sent the Holy Spirit in power, as manifested that day. One of their number later acknowledged the futility of resistance if God indeed had sent these men (Acts 5:34-39).

While we read about many unusual events in Acts that did not continue as permanent manifestations of the gospel after that time, we also see many things that have encouraged and instructed struggling, persecuted saints across the centuries. Whether preaching to a Jewish audience in Jerusalem or to Greek philosophers in Greece (Acts 2, 17), they never strayed far from the central truth of the gospel, Jesus, and the resurrection. When Paul taught the Ephesian elders, possibly his last personal time with them, he reminded them that he had preached all the gospel to them, not just parts of it.

Wherefore I take you to record this day, that I am pure from the blood of all men. For I have not shunned to declare unto you all the counsel of God. (Acts 20:26-27)

Paul preached many things beyond the resurrection, but he kept that truth prominent in his hearers' minds as he preached "...all the counsel of God."

When Paul wrote a deeply troubled and compromised Corinthian Church, he "...determined" not to know anything among them save Jesus Christ and Him crucified. However, as we read the whole first Corinthian letter, we do not read sixteen chapters of nothing but the sufferings and death of Jesus. Paul confronted this compromised church on multiple errors in both their belief and their conduct that deviated from the truth of the gospel. He rejected their preacher loyalty above loyalty to Jesus. He rebuked them for their moral laxity in the church. He shamed them for appealing to human courts to settle personal differences instead of appealing to the Lord's judgment in His church. He dealt in extensive details with the then-sticky question of meat offered to idols. He warned them to study the Old Testament and learn thereby to avoid the sinful bad examples recorded there. He rebuked their errant attitudes and practices regarding the Lord's Supper. He spent three whole chapters on the right understanding and purpose of spiritual gifts. He even taught them regarding the right way to go about giving. And, yes indeed, he wrote a long chapter that specifically taught them regarding their departure from the truth of Jesus, and the resurrection. He challenged and taught them on every point of their errors; he expanded and enriched their minds regarding a far better way (1 Corinthians 12:31). He gave us a powerful example in his two Corinthian letters of what it means to preach all the counsel of God, not just one dimension of it.

However, if Paul had not included his resurrection teaching, his message about Jesus Christ and Him crucified would have been incomplete. And, if he had not challenged the errant beliefs in this cosmopolitan and compromised church, he would have failed to apply the ethics of the gospel to the Corinthians. Based on New Testament teaching, believing all the right things serves as a foundation for living; it is not an end in itself. If you believe in Jesus and the resurrection, God commands you to also "...depart from iniquity" (2 Timothy 2:19).

In the lesson immediately following this verse, Paul draws a rich and instructive analogy about vessels in a "great house." Our faithful obedience, not just what we believe, important as that belief is in Scripture, classifies us as a vessel of honor, "...sanctified, and meet for the master's use, and prepared unto every good work" (2 Timothy 2:21). However, failure to depart from iniquity dooms us to be a vessel of dishonor, not ready for the Master's use and sadly unprepared "...unto every good work."

When Mordecai encouraged Esther to face her honored position boldly for God, he reminded her that perhaps God had raised her up for just that purpose (Esther 4:14). God is quite competent to fill His house with the right vessels that are ready for His use. However, if you or I choose the path of profane and vain babblings that steadily decline to more ungodliness (1 Timothy 2:16), or if we constantly invest ourselves in foolish and unlearned questions that promote strife rather than the "unity of the Spirit in the bond of peace," we reduce ourselves to a dishonorable vessel whom that Master of the "great house" will reject for His use, choosing a clean and prepared vessel instead (2 Timothy 2:23; Ephesians 4:3). Jesus warned the Jewish leaders in His day of just such a judgment that they had brought upon themselves.

Jesus saith unto them, Did ye never read in the scriptures, The stone which the builders rejected, the same is become the head of the corner: this is the Lord's doing, and it is marvellous in our eyes? Therefore say I unto you, The kingdom of God shall be taken from you, and given to a nation bringing forth the fruits thereof. And whosoever shall fall on this stone shall be broken: but on whomsoever it shall fall, it will grind him to powder. (Matthew 21:42-44)

Whether we acknowledge and honor Him as God's sure foundation corner stone or not, Jesus is the Rock on which God builds His church and all of His gracious works. If we choose to oppose Him instead of honor Him, He shall take the kingdom from us. Whether you fall on Him as if He were a small stone that you might stumble over on your path, or whether you turn from Him and His righteous judgments fall on you, refusal to honor Him brings destruction upon you.

Jesus warned the seven churches in Asia (Revelation 2-3) that their refusal to obey Him put them in danger of His falling on them in judgment and removing the candlestick, a symbol in this context of His blessing in honoring them as one of His churches. There is no faithful church in any of those seven cities today. Eventually each of these churches turned from Him and lost their candlestick, a solemn warning to us.

As we gather in our various locations for worship this Lord's Day, let us pray for grace to humble us before Him, for clear conviction to avoid the foolish questions of spiritual immaturity and strife-evoking contention, grave indications and warning that we are not fit for our Master's use or prepared for every good work. Let us pray for the Lord's conviction to direct us to repentance where we need it, to show us what He requires of us to be one of His clean vessels, prepared for whatever good work that He may direct us to do and ready for whatever use He may choose to make of us. If we are not so prepared, we may face the same judgment that fell upon those first century people who lost His kingdom blessings because of their refusal.

Belief in the resurrection of Jesus and of our own resurrection because of His conquering death imposes a powerful ethical obligation onto each of us. If we call His name, have we departed from iniquity? Have we departed from the iniquity of those "Ten Commandment" kind of sins that He forbids? Have we also departed from those sins of foolish and contentious strife that renders us a dishonorable vessel, not prepared for His use and not ready for every good work? We prove our belief in Him and in His resurrection by our faithful and consistent "endeavouring to keep the unity of the Spirit in the bond of peace" (Ephesians 4:3).

And every man that hath this hope in him purifieth himself, even as he is pure. (1 John 3:3)

Hereby perceive we the love of God, because he laid down his life for us: and we ought to lay down our lives for the brethren. (1 John 3:16)

And this is his commandment, that we should believe on the name of his Son Jesus Christ, and love one another, as he gave us commandment (1 John 3:23).

30
Jesus' Resurrection: Fulfillment of Prophecy

Men and brethren, let me freely speak unto you of the patriarch David, that he is both dead and buried, and his sepulchre is with us unto this day. Therefore being a prophet, and knowing that God had sworn with an oath to him, that of the fruit of his loins, according to the flesh, he would raise up Christ to sit on his throne; He seeing this before spake of the resurrection of Christ, that his soul was not left in hell, neither his flesh did see corruption. This Jesus hath God raised up, whereof we all are witnesses. (Acts 2:29–32)

In Acts 2:25-28, Paul quoted from Psalm 16. When David wrote, "Because thou wilt not leave my soul in hell, neither wilt thou suffer thine Holy One to see corruption," though using personal pronouns as if writing of himself, he wrote of Jesus in prophecy of the resurrection. In our study passage, we have the invaluable benefit of inspired Scripture interpreting another inspired Scripture. We need not speculate or appeal to our unsanctified and highly unreliable private imagination. God tells us what He intended when He directed David to write those words.

Based on Peter's words, first century Jews knew where David's grave was, and it remained present and occupied by David's bodily remains at the time. After death, David's body "saw corruption." Folks who deny the resurrection outright or try to impose various mystical private interpretations onto this passage (indirectly trying to deny the resurrection) face an insurmountable problem. Based on the Holy Spirit's personal interpretation of His own prophetic words to David (2 Peter 1:20-21), the prophecy refers to Jesus' "flesh" not seeing corruption by prolonged time in death.

Various Scriptures refer to the composition of an individual as consisting of body, spirit, and soul. Some commentaries and believers view spirit and soul as being the same, making the individual's composition body and soul or spirit. Does either a soul or a spirit have "flesh"? The answer shouts from the pages of Scripture, "No." Our only reasonable conclusion from this passage must be that the prophecy referred to Jesus' physical body and His brief time in death, a time ended in victorious literal, physical, "flesh," bodily resurrection. The tomb in which His body was buried lost its tenant after a brief three days. His body did not remain there.

This Jesus hath God raised up, whereof we all are witnesses. Peter's vivid contrast between David's death and Jesus' resurrection leaves no reasonable view of the lesson other than a reference to Jesus' literal, physical, bodily resurrection. Peter reminds us that his claim that Jesus literally and bodily arose from the grave is not based on his imagination or speculation. Along with several hundred other people who lived at that time, Peter was an eyewitness of Jesus' resurrected body. He could not deny what he had personally witnessed multiple times over several weeks between resurrection and ascension.

More than one skeptic has started his research intent on disproving the Bible's teaching regarding Jesus' resurrection only to discover that the evidence in Scripture is so compelling that the skeptic became a believer. Simon Greenleaf, a highly respected attorney in his day (1783-1853), represents only one such convert.

> Greenleaf, one of the principle founders of the Harvard Law School, originally set out to disprove the biblical testimony concerning the resurrection of Jesus Christ. He was certain that a careful examination of the internal witness of the Gospels would dispel all the myths at the heart of Christianity. But this legal scholar came to the conclusion that the witnesses were reliable, and that the resurrection did in fact happen.[1]

Critics of Christianity devalue the testimony of the first generation apostles by comparing them to the long list of people who believed in a lie, but nevertheless gave their lives in martyrdom for their false beliefs. The skeptics fail. Believers in false teachers and false ideas

---

[1] http://law2.umkc.edu/faculty/projects/ftrials/jesus/greenleaf.html.

who are willing to be martyred obviously believed the lies that they were told. However, first generation Christians died in martyrdom because they could not deny what they had personally witnessed to be true. Eyewitness testimony versus second-hand reports powerfully underscores the validity of the New Testament record of Jesus' life, death, and resurrection. Would anyone falsely claim to be an eyewitness, knowing that he was lying, and still surrender to martyrdom for a known lie? These men died for a factual truth that they personally witnessed to be true (2 Peter 1:16-21). For them, the question was not "Will you die for something someone whom you respect told you?" but "Would you die in denial of what you personally witnessed to be true?"

Based, I believe, on a skewed interpretation of this passage, specifically the reference to Jesus' soul being left in hell, and 1 Peter 3:19, some commentaries teach that, during the three days and nights of His physical death, Jesus in His spirit went to literal hell, or, as they interpret the word, a dark, intermediate "abode for the dead," where He "preached" to those souls who had formerly lived and died. This interpretation wholly ignores and contradicts the teaching of the whole Book of Hebrews.

Based on Hebrews' inspired interpretation of the detailed manner in which Jesus' sufferings and death fulfilled the typology of the Levitical priesthood, when Jesus died, He did not go in spirit to an imagined intermediate place that housed the spirits of people who died in former ages. He went directly to heaven to the Father. In fact, at the moment of His death, Jesus specifically indicated that He was going to the Father, not to a dark intermediate prison for the spirits of dead people.

And Jesus said unto him, Verily I say unto thee, To day shalt thou be with me in paradise (Luke 23:43). In 2 Corinthians 12, Paul refers to being caught up into the third heaven (v. 2). In verse 4, he again mentions being caught up, this time referring to the place as "paradise." Notice the direction. When Paul had this experience, He did not go down into a dark place. He went up. He identifies the place to which he went by two terms, 1) "the third heaven," and 2) "paradise." When Jesus answered the thief on the cross, he told the thief, "To day shalt thou be with me in paradise" (Luke 23:43). Based on these passages, Scripture affirms that true Biblical "paradise" is not a dark nether region below. It is in fact a place that Scripture also identifies as "the third heaven."

"And when Jesus had cried with a loud voice, he said, Father, into thy hands I commend my spirit: and having said thus, he gave up the ghost" (Luke 23:46; Notice Jesus' words: He does not expect to go to a place apart from the Father, but rather into the Father's hands, a place of intimacy with the Father).

He seeing this before spake of the resurrection of Christ, that his soul was not left in hell, neither his flesh did see corruption. If we follow Peter's detailed explanation of Psalm 16 in the context of our study passage, Acts 2, we learn that David's prophecy referred to Jesus' body. Literally, His life, His body, would not be left in the grave. Hell in this prophecy refers to the grave, not to a mythical place for the spirits of the dead. Take note of Peter's direct reference to David's grave where his body remained roughly a thousand years after his death. But his prophecy referred to Jesus whose body would not be left in the grave long enough to see corruption.

...when he had by himself purged our sins, sat down on the right hand of the Majesty on high (Hebrews 1:3). Jesus sat down on the Father's right hand immediately upon purging our sins. Nothing in Scripture in any way implies that Jesus did not purge our sins until His ascension approximately forty days after His death and resurrection. Quite the opposite, Romans 4:25 states that Jesus was "...raised again for our justification."

"For" in this verse carries the idea "because of." Because we had offended God by our sins, Jesus was delivered to death, and, because He accomplished our legal justification during those three days and nights, He arose out of the grave in His literal, physical body. Our justification actually occurred before the Father during those three days and nights.

And for this cause he is the mediator of the new testament, that by means of death, for the redemption of the transgressions that were under the first testament, they which are called might receive the promise of eternal inheritance (Hebrews 9:15; emphasis added). In the moment of His death, Jesus accomplished our redemption. In fulfillment of the Levitical types and His greater and "for ever" Melchisedec priesthood, Jesus offered Himself to the Father in death. Nothing in any of these passages allows time or a logical reason for Jesus to spend three days and nights in a mythological place.

Thus, based on these and many other Scriptures, at His death, Jesus in spirit and/or soul immediately went to the Father in heaven where He offered Himself to the Father as the full atonement for the sins of all His beloved children. If we examine all the rich types of priesthood in the Old Testament, and explained in the New Testament Book of Hebrews, Jesus was busy during those three days and nights with the Father accomplishing our redemption, fully satisfying the Father for our sins. He even sat down beside the Father during this brief time, indicating that He had finished the work prior to His resurrection. Then, atoning, redeeming work fully completed, He returned to occupy His body and thereby arise from death and the grave.

This process precisely describes the meaning of the word "resurrection." If He did not return to reclaim and revive that body in which He lived and in which He was crucified, there was no real resurrection at all. And, based on Paul's reasoning in 1 Corinthians 15, if Jesus didn't bodily arise from the dead, we have no hope whatever of resurrection. But since He did arise, legitimizing the word "resurrection" in the New Testament, we have a lively hope of arising, too.

31
Jesus' Resurrection: Begotten from Death

*And when they had fulfilled all that was written of him, they took him down
from the tree, and laid him in a sepulchre. But God raised him from the
dead: And he was seen many days of them which came up with him from
Galilee to Jerusalem, who are his witnesses unto the people. And we
declare unto you glad tidings, how that the promise which was made unto
the fathers, God hath fulfilled the same unto us their children, in that he
hath raised up Jesus again; as it is also written in the second psalm, Thou
art my Son, this day have I begotten thee.* (Acts 13:29–33)

Over time after the Lord separated and called Paul, the Lord
blessed his labors in Antioch to begin a church and to conduct
much of his ministry and evangelism from that church. Biblical
evangelism should never seek a separate life of its own apart from
the Lord's church. In fact, nothing beneficial in spiritual matters
should ever be approached other than through the function and
authority of a New Testament church. The Lord intends His church
to serve His people as the "pillar and ground of the truth" (1
Timothy 3:15).

No sub-culture or class of people inside the Lord's church are
commanded or permitted in Scripture ever to lord themselves over
the Lord's church, but rather submit to and serve the church. We
never read in Scripture that either preachers or deacons—or any
other group for that matter—are to lord themselves or their ideas
over the Lord's church.

When Paul wrote the majority of his New Testament letters, he
wrote to one or more church, not to a governing board of deacons,
elders, or any other hierarchical body. Hierarchical ruling
subcultures within a church contradict the New Testament model of
the Lord's church. Paul wrote his letters and his teachings to these
churches. When Paul directed them to take action, whether dealing

with the sinning member in 1 Corinthians 5 or collecting for the needy saints at Jerusalem in 1 Corinthians 16, he directed the churches to take this action (1 Corinthians 5:13; 16:1, "...as I have given order to the churches of Galatia, even so do ye"). Paul gave his "order" to the churches), not a hierarchical governing or ruling board of any class or type. Such a hierarchy is conspicuously absent from the New Testament; it should be equally absent from the Lord's churches.

Once people are taught the truth of the gospel they need a place for worship and a fellowship of people with whom to worship. Biblical Christianity is not modeled by multitudes of individual believers all running in their own direction and doing their own thing, nor by forming their "private interpretation" of Scripture and ignoring the teaching structure that the Lord created within His churches. The Lord did not allow the men who wrote the Scriptures to write their private interpretations (2 Peter 1:20), so He certainly does not approve of individual believers forming their private interpretations and ignoring the unique "pillar and ground of the truth" that He established and has preserved across the centuries, His church.

The church, the "pillar and ground of the truth" (1 Timothy 3:15), is the Lord's spiritual vehicle by which He preserves His truth and through which He grows His believing children into spiritually mature members of His body. To the extent that any believer either magnifies himself above or distances himself from this spiritual, New Testament body, he endangers himself to the assaults of the adversary and fails to advance the Lord's truth among His people in this world.

While the "Rambo" mindset may plays well on the screen in entertainment, in the real world where we live, it always fails. The wannabe "Rambo" in the real world, especially in a church, will become self-focused, self-centered, and presume to ignore and to contradict fellow-believers, rather than learning in grace the New Testament bedrock principle of looking up to them, respecting them above self, and actually submitting to them.

In New Testament Christianity, we serve the Lord by serving His people, not by chasing our own windmills and ways (John 13). Jesus literally washed the disciples' feet, a sorely needed reminder to them so soon after they had disputed about which of them would be the chief. What lesson did He teach that we should learn from this action? Do we prove by our attitude and conduct that we have learned it? Or do we contradict that example by our actions? Philippians 2:1-8; failure to honor this consistent New Testament pattern of attitude and conduct always fails to honor the Lord or to bless a church that ignores or contradicts it.

As they ministered to the Lord, and fasted, the Holy Ghost said.... The Lord speaks to His people when and as they minister to Him and serve Him and each other. When we choose our own ways, He remains silent and allows us to grow cold beside the sparks of our own private fire (Isaiah 50:11).

The Holy Spirit directed the church to assist Paul and Barnabas, to "separate me" them to the work that He directed. Paul and Barnabas left Antioch, located in the area of modern Syria, and traveled to the western region of modern Turkey, Antioch of Pisidia. There they entered a Jewish synagogue on the Sabbath. First century Jewish synagogues apparently observed a custom that, after the reading of the Scriptures by the leader of the synagogue, men in the audience were given the opportunity to speak to the gathering. The leader of the synagogue on this day asked Paul and Barnabas if they had any "word of exhortation for the people." As always, Paul readily accepted the opportunity. We are blessed to have a rich portion of that sermon recorded in the context of our study passage.

Paul started his sermon with a brief summary of God's dealings with His people in the Old Testament. You couldn't find a more concise and enlightening outline of early Old Testament history than in these words.

Paul used this summary of Old Testament history as the vehicle by which to preach Jesus and the resurrection to them. Our study passage narrates the beginning of those truths in Paul's sermon. In this study, we examine the first of three Old Testament prophecies that Paul sets forth as being fulfilled in Jesus.

And when they had fulfilled all that was written of him.... You will find more references to Old Testament prophecy in the week leading up to Jesus' crucifixion, ending with His resurrection, than in any New Testament account of any similar time lapse. Obviously, God flooded Old Testament pages with prophecies of the events leading up to Jesus' death. Many Bible students have observed that reading Isaiah 53 and thinking of its words in terms of Jesus' sufferings and death is like reading a headline news account the day after it happened, but Isaiah wrote these words around seven hundred fifty years before Jesus came. When God prophesies, He doesn't guess or consult astrology charts. He knows whereof He speaks, past, present, or future.

But God raised him from the dead. In various passages, Jesus' resurrection is attributed to the Father, to the Holy Spirit, or to Jesus Himself. There is no contradiction. Here Paul makes the one point that needs to be known. God raised Him. The resurrection of Jesus is preeminently a supernatural event. He didn't slip into a deep coma as His time on the cross ended and revive three days later. The disciples didn't fabricate the resurrection story. He really died, and, just as really, He arose from death.

Not only did He arise from the dead, but many people saw Him and talked with Him after His resurrection. It was not a secret event or an exaggerated rumor. His revelations of Himself to His disciples were at times very personal, e. g. His conversations with Thomas and Peter, and at other times quite public, as His appearance to five hundred at one time.

And we declare unto you glad tidings, how that the promise which was made unto the fathers, God hath fulfilled the same unto us their children, in that he hath raised up Jesus again. We rightly rejoice at the rich truths revealed by God in all the Old Testament prophecies and valid types by which God taught His people during that era about His coming Son. But our greatest reason for rejoicing must ever rest on the rock of Jesus' personal life, death, resurrection, and, yes, ascension.

No prophecy is valid unless it is accurate, unless the person or events prophesied come to pass according to the precise information contained in the prophecy. An inaccurate prophecy or a prophecy that is so vague as to find fantasy fulfillment in any number of vaguely similar events is no real prophecy. The more detailed the prophecy and the more detailed and exact the fulfillment the more credibility the prophecy contains. In the case of Old Testament prophecies, Jesus fulfilled every finite detail precisely as described in the prophecy, as in Isaiah 53. The time of His coming is prophesied precisely in Daniel's seventy-week prophecy. His virgin birth is prophesied. His living in Nazareth is prophesied. Judas betraying Him for thirty pieces of silver is prophesied. His dying by crucifixion is prophesied. But, above all other details, His resurrection from the dead is prophesied, even the time He spent in the tomb.

And he was seen many days of them which came up with him from Galilee to Jerusalem, who are his witnesses unto the people. Not only did Jesus fulfill Old Testament prophecy, but he appeared to a multitude of people who became eyewitnesses of His resurrection. If we accept the consistent testimony of eyewitnesses, we must accept the truth of His literal bodily resurrection.

And we declare unto you glad tidings, how that the promise which was made unto the fathers, God hath fulfilled the same unto us their children, in that he hath raised up Jesus again; as it is also written in the second psalm, Thou art my Son, this day have I begotten thee. As in many similar cases, in this lesson, we have an inspired New Testament writer giving us the Holy Spirit's intended meaning of an Old Testament prophecy. Psalm 2 does not teach about a hypothetical origin of Jesus in eternity past. Rather Scripture teaches us that He is co-equal and co-eternal with the Father (John 1:1-3). God intended Jesus to revive and arise from death in precisely the three days recorded in Scripture, just as a pregnant woman gives birth to a child in approximately nine months. Just as the conceived child cannot remain permanently in its mother's womb, even so Jesus could not possibly remain in the grave. God raising Jesus from the dead fulfilled David's Psalm 2 prophecy.

And as concerning that he raised him up from the dead, now
no more to return to corruption, he said on this wise, I will
give you the sure mercies of David. Wherefore he saith also in
another psalm, Thou shalt not suffer thine Holy One to see
corruption. For David, after he had served his own generation
by the will of God, fell on sleep, and was laid unto his fathers,
and saw corruption: But he, whom God raised again, saw no
corruption. Be it known unto you therefore, men and brethren,
that through this man is preached unto you the forgiveness of
sins: And by him all that believe are justified from all things,
from which ye could not be justified by the law of Moses. (Acts
13:34–39)

Paul quoted three Old Testament passages in this sermon in the
synagogue. Although he was preaching to Jewish people who
believed in God and in the Old Testament, the idea of Jesus and the
resurrection was not the message that they heard in their ordinary
Sabbath gatherings. The first passage that he cited was from Psalm
2, "Thou art my Son, this day have I begotten thee." Paul's
interpretation of this verse was that God raised Jesus from the dead.
He continues this focused interpretation of the two passages cited in
the verses that we study here.

I will give you the sure mercies of David. Paul's interpretation of
this passage from Isaiah 55:3 continues his theme, *"And as*
concerning that he raised him up from the dead, now no more to
return to corruption, he said on this wise...." The sure mercies of
David as Paul interpreted the verse, and as the Holy Spirit included
his sermon in the inspired text of the New Testament, relates to
Jesus' resurrection, not to a future restoration of Jewish people to
the blessings of the gospel, or to an end times millennial Jewish
kingdom. Our view of the text should agree with Paul's. The "sure
mercies" that God promised David, though he did not deserve them,
was fulfilled in Jesus, God's prophetic and greater David, not in any
form of national restoration.

Wherefore he saith also in another psalm, Thou shalt not suffer
thine Holy One to see corruption. Paul cited these words from Psalm

16. We saw in Peter's Day of Pentecost sermon (Acts 2) that Peter also used this Psalm in precisely the same way that Paul here interprets it. When the Holy Spirit enlightens a man's mind to see the truth that He reveals in Scripture, you will not hear one private interpretation after another. You will see harmony in his teaching with the teaching of other men who also follow the Holy Spirit's teaching and not their private interpretations.

And the Holy Spirit's teaching always agrees with the words that He directed chosen men to write in our Bible. Claims of a "private revelation" that espouse ideas that contradict Scripture never come from the God. Any of us who regularly study the Bible occasionally may ponder an interpretation of a passage that is a bit different from other interpretations that we've heard or read from other believers. Such a difference should sound a caution to our minds.

The Holy Spirit has been revealing true interpretations of Scriptures to His people throughout the New Testament era. He doesn't change His mind about what a given passage teaches. Nor does He reveal one idea to one Bible student and another wholly different idea to another believer. While Scripture teaches that the Holy Spirit reveals truth to the Lord's people, it never teaches that He reveals contradictory ideas to different believers. He rather reveals consistent truth, *and only truth*, to all believers who seek and listen to His counsel.

Further, His revelation is never mystical or private. It always comes in association with Scripture. "Consider what I say; and the Lord give thee understanding in all things" (2 Timothy 2:7). What Paul "said" to Timothy in this letter is part of the New Testament's inspired text. We may repeat Paul's words only so far as we faithfully preserve his words and teaching.

The Holy Spirit gives eternal life wholly of His own power and apart from agencies or tools of any kind (John 3:8). Scripture describes this life-giving work as being wrought on someone who is dead (John 5:25; Ephesians 2:1-7). However, after the new birth is completed, He leads and teaches the child of grace according to Scripture. Notice; the same truth and lifestyle that we read in

Scripture is the truth and lifestyle that the grace of God teaches "us" in Titus 2:12-14.

Further, the Holy Spirit never singles out one man to understand truth, while leaving other believers in the dark. The fundamental vehicle that God uses to preserve His truth is not individual people, but His church, "...the pillar and ground of the truth" (1 Timothy 3:15).

In sixty years of studying the Bible and observing human behavior, I have seen multiple occasions when one person rejected the mind of the church of his membership and defended his personal interpretation. While I sadly have witnessed churches making mistakes, experience has strongly confirmed the truth of this passage. The peaceful mindset of a church is far more reliable as a mark of Biblical truth than one person's divergent opinion.

We are all vulnerable, and quite sincerely so, to bad interpretations of Scripture, leading us to bad beliefs of error. The Lord's stated vehicle to maintain stable truth that He preserves is "...in the church by Christ Jesus throughout all ages..." (Ephesians 3:21). The Lord preserves His truth by this "pillar and ground of the truth," not by individual believers who claim superior enlightenment or knowledge of Scripture.

More than once I have engaged men in conversation who held to Belief A and later embraced a near opposite and contradictory Belief B. When I questioned their illogical change in belief, they most often claim, "The Lord revealed to me...." In that state of mind, they forget that even our most sincere private interpretations are to be submitted to and tested by Scripture, not by our measure of personal sincerity or by our claims of a private revelation. The community of the Lord's church, His "pillar and ground of the truth," puts our private interpretations and sincere ideas to a test that we should profoundly respect, not despise if it disagrees with our ideas.

The nineteenth century saw multiple major departures from historical Christian faith in our country, and, without exception, every leader of every major departure claimed a divine revelation. When the Lord truly does reveal truth to His people, He always guides them to Scripture as confirmation, not to their esoteric experience. And, with equal consistency, these men degraded the Lord's church, claiming that it had either wholly or substantially died, and that God had singled them out to restore pure Christianity to the world, a patent contradiction of the Lord's promise to preserve His church in Ephesians 3:21.

The Lord's revelation of truth to His people today is by Scripture and by Scriptural-based preaching. It follows the pattern that we see in our study passage and throughout the New Testament. Paul cited three Old Testament Scriptures to the people who heard him preach on this occasion, and he used these Scriptures to affirm the truth of Jesus and the resurrection.

For David, after he had served his own generation by the will of God, fell on sleep, and was laid unto his fathers, and saw corruption: But he, whom God raised again, saw no corruption. Peter enlarges this truth in his Pentecost sermon, teaching the same truth and interpretation from the psalm. When David wrote the words, "Thou wilt not suffer thine Holy One to see corruption," he wrote of Jesus and His resurrection, not of himself or his body. He died and somewhere even today his body lies in a tomb. He saw "corruption." His body decayed and followed the course of death's work on it. But Jesus of whom the Holy Spirit directed David to write spent a bare three days in a borrowed tomb, arising to life and shortly on to glory. He saw no corruption. His body did not decay and decompose in His grave.

Forgiveness and justification, as Paul preached these principles, comes through and by the Lord Jesus Christ. While many Bible students interpret belief in this passage as a further condition for forgiveness and justification, I suggest that belief more properly describes those whom the Lord forgives and justifies than adding an added requirement. Paul didn't say that forgiveness and justification are available, but "you must believe" if you want to obtain them. This interpretation harmonizes with Jesus' words in John 5:24, "...is passed from death unto life," and with John's words in 1 John 5:1, "...is born of God...." In both of these lessons, hearing and/or believing describe a person who has already been born again, has already passed from death to life.

Despite believing in gospel instrumentality for the new birth, A. T. Robertson, **Word Pictures in the New Testament**, in his grammatical explanation of 1 John 5:1, quotes another writer who specifically states, *"The Divine Begetting is the antecedent, not the consequent of the believing."* Robertson could not have stated the point more clearly. The new birth occurs prior to our believing, not because of it or subsequent to it. Thus, whether we are reading in John 5, 1 John 5, or Acts 13, our belief does not precede or serve as a cause or an instrument in our new birth. God produces the new birth sovereignly and irresistibly; then we are empowered to believe.

"...all that believe...." Paul makes no distinction whatever between the Jewish people in the synagogue and Gentiles on the street. God's grace in the heart, not a person's superficial association with a given race, makes the difference. We could frame the point simply, "Salvation is by grace, not race." Paul neither imposes a penalty on the people in the synagogue or gives them an advantage. The ground at the foot of the cross is level ground. No believer in Christ stands on higher ground than another.

Once the Holy Spirit has produced the new birth in a chosen child of grace, eternal (the consequences of what God does are eternal) forgiveness and justification that Jesus secured for His people is a fact, a permanent fact in that person. The gospel preached according to the truth revealed in Scripture brings the knowledge of God's gracious forgiveness and justification to light in the heart and mind of the child of grace.

In this lesson, Paul seems to emphasize that point with his focus on "...all that believe...." Through the knowledge of what God did for us and in us through the Lord Jesus, we discover the joy and the deliverance of knowing about His loving grace. The synagogue congregation to whom Paul preached were looking for that deliverance through Moses' law, and they never found it, never. Paul shows them the path to what they could never find in Moses' law. How sadly often we substitute a legalistic equivalent to Moses' law in our own lives and seek our joy in those things instead of in the loving grace and person of God's Son! We need Paul's sermon.

32
Our Resurrection: For Just & Unjust

But this I confess unto thee, that after the way which they call heresy, so worship I the God of my fathers, believing all things which are written in the law and in the prophets: And have hope toward God, which they themselves also allow, that there shall be a resurrection of the dead, both of the just and unjust. (Acts 24:14–15)

These verses are from Paul's defense before Felix. An "orator" named Tertullus represented the high priest and the Jewish case against Paul. Paul spoke for himself. Rather than dealing with their actual differences of belief, Tertullus followed the sinful path of attacking the messenger when he couldn't deal with the message. He hurled various false accusations against Paul. Paul didn't view his faith as a personal philosophy that required his reputation or his ego to defend. "For we preach not ourselves…" (2 Corinthians 4:5). He ignored the accusations and went directly to the heart of the gospel. The Jews rejected Jesus and the gospel that Paul preached, but he firmly associated Jesus and the gospel with the Old Testament law and the prophets. Only after he had affirmed the doctrine of Jesus and the resurrection did Paul respond to the personal accusations against him. His first concern was not what those people said against Him, but what they said against his Lord and His truth.

Implied in this scenario is the tactic that first century Jews practiced against the church, accuse them of starting a new religion. When the Romans conquered a people, they fully tolerated the religion of that people. However, they were fiercely set against any new religion, so, if someone started a new religion, the Romans would stamp it out. If the Jews could convince the Romans that Christianity was a new religion, Rome would take care of the Christians. Paul understood this tactic and rejected it. He rejected it on solid ground. It was first century Jews, not the Christians, who had forsaken Moses and the prophets of the Old Testament.

In the second century, the Jews continued this tactic, trying to convince the Romans that Christians were a new religion that Rome should fear and eliminate by brute force. Justin Martyr's *First Apology* (*circa* ~150 A.D.) addresses this same accusation. Justin devotes the greater portion of his apology to proving that Christianity is actually a very old religion, not a new one. "Apology" as used by Justin refers to the historical use of the word, such as appears in the field of Christian study that focuses on defending the faith. Justin, as Paul in his speech to Felix, defended the faith against false charges from its enemies.

Paul affirms that he worships the God of his fathers, the Jewish people, and that he believes and teaches the same things that Moses and the prophets taught, what first century Jews claimed to believe, but didn't. Long before Paul, Jesus confronted the Jews for rejecting Moses and the prophets, so Paul simply followed Jesus in his defense before Felix.

...there shall be a resurrection of the dead, both of the just and unjust. In fact, the Pharisees of the first century believed in life after death and in a literal, bodily resurrection. The Sadducees, who often occupied the highest positions of authority in Jewish government, at times including the office of high priest, strongly rejected life after death and a literal, bodily resurrection. Though the Sadducees were likely in the minority in terms of numbers, they held significant influence in political power. There can be little doubt that Paul well knew that he introduced a divisive topic when he focused on the resurrection in this gathering. However, the passage gives no indication that he played the political game for his personal interest. He spoke the truth to honor his Lord, not play political games.

Fellow pastor Elder Ben Winslett recently published a brief article in which he observed the fatal impact on a church of its leaders trying to "manage" the church based on commonly accepted business practices. The Lord's church is not a business that operates for profit or for the ego boost of its leaders. Such a carnal philosophy will kill a church in short order. I would add that trying to "manage" a church based on commonly accepted political practices and attitudes is equally deadly to a church.

When the disciples slipped into a carnal moment by disputing which of them would be the leader, Jesus confronted them with the one right principle of church leadership. If you want to lead in church, work at serving, not at bullying or domineering your ideas over others in the church (Luke 22:24-27). Peter affirms the same principle, not "...as being lords over God's heritage, but being ensamples to the flock" (1 Peter 5:3). Any strategy or attitude that attempts to control people in a church that exceeds this principle, a Christ-like, gracious example—show the way by your feet, not by your words alone—contradicts this Biblical model.

Many years ago I was meeting with the two men who were our church's deacons at the time. Wholly apart from the reason for our meeting, one of them spoke up, "Joe, how may we help you in your work?" I was deeply touched by this true servant's heart and spirit. "How may I help you?" is a far more Biblical mindset than a privately thought "How may I manipulate them to my way of thinking?"

A frustrated pastor may grow weary of seeing people leave his church and return to the world. What pastor would not? However, for a pastor facing this dilemma to alter his doctrinal preaching, shifting from solid grace to threats or questions about the person's eternal standing is inexcusable. "If you depart, I can't give you any assurance that you are born again." This sentiment in a pastor falsely usurps the position of assurer that the Holy Spirit claims in Scripture. The strategy is as much a manipulative control tactic as a doctrinal issue, though it is an unsound doctrinal issue. At its heart, this and any similar manipulative or control strategy that people in leadership positions in a church practice beyond their gracious godly example contradicts Jesus' words to the disciples and Peter's word to his readers.

Paul introduced the core facts of the gospel to Felix with no regard for his personal gain or loss. He preached Jesus whose coming and work fulfilled literally hundreds of Old Testament prophecies and all the legitimate types that God inserted into the Old

Testament Scriptures to foreshadow His coming and work. The crowning glorious principle of both Old Testament teaching and of Paul's preaching was one, Jesus and the resurrection.

Most modern teaching regarding the end times is so complicated and confusing that you must often struggle to find just a few men who actually agree on all the details. In admirable contrast, Scripture's teaching on end times is gloriously simple and comforting for tired, struggling pilgrims looking forward to home. There shall be one resurrection that includes both just and unjust. Paul mirrors Jesus' teaching (John 5:28-29). There shall be one hour when all the dead, just and unjust, shall arise.

Neither Jesus nor Paul taught multiple resurrections or comings, some secret and some public. When Paul outlined these principles to the Thessalonian Church, he concluded his teaching with "Wherefore comfort one another with these words" (1Thessalonians 4:18). The doctrine of the Lord's final and glorious return appears in Scripture to comfort children of grace, not for intellectual challenges beyond the ordinary believer's ability to unravel or to understand.

Our study passage also distinguishes Paul's teaching on the resurrection contrasted with the Pharisees or other Jews who believed in the resurrection: "...which they themselves also allow." They "allowed" the idea of resurrection, but apparently it didn't form the bedrock of their belief. While they "allowed" the idea of a resurrection, Paul believed that "...*there shall be* a resurrection." For Paul, the resurrection was not an optional belief that one could rightly take or leave, or simply "allow."

To deny the resurrection puts one outside the pale of orthodox and accepted faith. The word "resurrection" literally defined requires the return to life of a literal, physical body that died. It cannot be fulfilled by a mere mystical or immaterial energizing. Thus, folks who claim to believe the Bible, but also deny the Bible's teaching of a literal, physical, bodily resurrection, must make a credible case that every appearance of the word "resurrection" in its various forms in Scripture are symbolic, something that cannot be done.

In our present culture, people may claim to believe just about anything they imagine about Jesus and carry on their life without interference or persecution, so long as they don't make too much noise about it. We are increasingly facing greater threats against outspoken Christians who hold to historical, Biblical definitions of Christian faith. For Paul, speaking out boldly about Jesus and the resurrection before a Roman governor could possibly have cost him his life. Yet he spoke with boldness. This truth was just that important, that central to right faith for Paul. He could not compromise or downplay this truth.

A few years ago, I had a sadly enlightening discussion with a pastor from a different denomination. He spoke of his belief in the historical, Biblical teaching of the resurrection. But then he mentioned the strong and often emotional reaction of many Christians who hold to one of the various dispensational views of the Second Coming. For him, given the emotional static, preaching Biblical truth about the Second Coming and the final resurrection was more costly than he was willing to invest. He chose to merely sidestep or downplay his belief in the resurrection. I cannot imagine Paul taking such a posture. In fact, our study passage and the consistent New Testament record contradict such an idea.

Often we miss the rich depth of Scripture's teaching by overlooking the simplest of points. In Paul's words here, two such points stand out. Paul uses the singular form of the word, "resurrection," not "resurrections." Secondly, in the one resurrection of which he speaks, Paul specifically states that both just and unjust shall arise.

Again, the simple and comforting truth of Scripture leads us to view the Lord's final return and resurrection of all humanity in the clearest and simplest of terms. Paul's words will not allow the idea of a secret resurrection of elite believers only. He states that this one resurrection shall witness the raising of both just and unjust. As taught in Scripture, the doctrine of the resurrection can be understood and can comfort little children facing death, as well as seasoned saints. Thank the Lord!

33
Bodily Resurrection: Jesus First

But if the Spirit of him that raised up Jesus from the dead dwell in you, he that raised up Christ from the dead shall also quicken your mortal bodies by his Spirit that dwelleth in you. (Romans 8:11)

Throughout the New Testament, our future bodily resurrection is consistently linked with Jesus' bodily resurrection. God who raised Jesus from the dead shall also raise us. Jesus did not die in spirit, but in body. He told the thief on the cross that they would be together that day in Paradise. His body died on the cross and was raised three days later.

...by his Spirit that dwelleth in you. From new birth to death, the Spirit of God dwells in every child of grace. He doesn't come and go. He permanently resides within us. While man in his unregenerate state (not born again) is totally depraved, to impute total depravity onto a regenerate child of grace blatantly denies the presence, life-creating work, and abiding influence of the indwelling Holy Spirit. This errant idea builds on the false premise that the Holy Spirit does not permanently indwell a born again person, that the new birth makes no real change whatever in a person.

Historically, many who held to fatalistic leanings on predestination also held to a non-permanent residing of the Holy Spirit within and to the no-change-in-new-birth error, sometimes referred to as "Hollow-Logism." The "Hollow log" term refers to a frequent analogy used to describe this error. A rabbit may enter and leave a hollow log at will, never changing the log. So those who embrace this error hold that the Spirit of God may enter and leave a person at will, but He makes no change in the person. This errant view denies that the new birth makes any change in the person at all.

Building on the false premise that God causes everything, folks with this belief are hard pressed to explain sin in the life of a regenerate person. One attempt at this explanation is that, when God temporarily resides within, He irresistibly and wholly controls every word, thought, and deed. Ah, but how do they explain sin in the life of a child of God. Their answer typically begins with "When left to ourselves...." This term obviously implies that the Holy Spirit at times vacates the individual, leaving them no different than previous to their new birth. So one moment you are a regenerated child of the King, and the next moment you may be wholly no different than a child of wrath. This idea contradicts Scripture (Hebrews 13:5 as only one clear example of many). It also contradicts the basic premise of God's new covenant written in the heart and mind (Jeremiah 31:33-34).

At its heart, this belief utterly denies any permanent and residual effect from the new birth. Whatever impact you experience from the Holy Spirit is, in this view, confined to those occasions when the Holy Spirit chooses to briefly visit you, but you can't rely on His abiding indwelling, so you live with a convenient, built-in rationalization for sin in your life. I suggest that this idea is wholly contradicted by Scripture, not to mention that it is also far too convenient for the person who seeks to rationalize his conscious decision to sin. It further contradicts the obvious fact that the best efforts of a believer are often, if not always, to some extent mixed with sin. If their righteous acts are wholly controlled by the Holy Spirit, you'd expect no sin whatever in their minds or actions when so controlled. They offer no real explanation for the presence of sin, even in their supposed times when wholly and irresistibly moved by the Spirit.

In our study verse, Paul takes us directly and powerfully to the truth that we need to know. The present indwelling Holy Spirit guarantees that we shall be raised "...up from the dead" just as Jesus was raised "...up from the dead." As used in this verse, "quicken" refers to the process of restoring to life that which was dead. And what is it that died but shall be raised up? Paul answers the question, "...your mortal body."

He does not refer to a "spirit body" or to a symbolic body, but to "...your mortal body." Given the corollary between Jesus' resurrection and ours, there can be no doubt that He possessed a real "mortal body," though without sin. Neither at death or in the resurrection does God fabricate and give us a substitute or replacement body. He shall raise that same mortal body that died, though He shall raise it immortal. The resurrection shall not merely restore us to the life that we experienced here. Instead, "...we shall be changed..." (1 Corinthians 15:51).

> The Spirit is both the instrumental cause of the resurrection-act and the permanent substratum of the resurrection-life.[1](2)

Whether we ponder the resurrection event at the Second Coming or the abiding life the elect shall enjoy with the Lord for eternity, the Holy Spirit is the key. Simply put, our continuing life after the resurrection shall not rely on food, oxygen, physiological processes, and the other necessities of our present physical life. The Holy Spirit shall raise us to a life that transcends anything that we can presently comprehend. Further, God, not our private pursuits, shall occupy us in heaven. Paul elsewhere sums up the same principle.

> *...that God may be all in all.* (1 Corinthians 15:28b)

When we think of heaven and being there, do we think of what or how we shall be, of whether we shall know loved ones as we knew them in this life, or other questions related to our personal experience? If we follow the lead of Scripture, should we not rather focus on our Lord and Savior and how we shall praise Him than on how much of our earthly life and relationships shall carry over? For the many loving and affirming relationships that may have blessed us in this life, relationships that we might naturally desire to continue in heaven, we must also consider the less-than-affirming or ideal relationships that we experienced with children of grace in this life who were not agreed with our beliefs or who simply did not

---

[1] Gerhardus Vos, *The Pauline Eschatology*, p. 169.
[2] Tom Constable, *Tom Constable's Expository Notes on the Bible* (Galaxie Software, 2003), Ro 8:11.

mesh with our personality. Think about that brother or sister who yelled at you or who accused you of unworthy motives that likely you had not entertained at all. If earth's relationships carry over intact to heaven, how will these relationships mesh with your experience? Honestly, we know little from Scripture that even indirectly addresses these questions, but Scripture abounds with evidence that we shall enjoy fully our relationship with our Lord and Savior.

The new life to which we shall be raised shall be so different from our present life that we surely have little perception of its details. We presently know only what Scripture reveals, and that emphasis consistently enlightens our praise to our Lord. I gravely doubt that praise in heaven shall remotely resemble our times of worship in church. Don't lose any sleep. Heaven shall not be one eternal uninterrupted season of singing, praying, and preaching—or listening to preaching. Whatever form our worship of God shall take in heaven is worthy of our God and Savior. If the form of worship that He has ordained for glory pleases Him, there can be no question. We shall also find presently unimaginable joy in the experience.

Scripture consistently links the truth of a literal bodily resurrection with the ethics of how we live in the here and now. The physical body in which we now live retains its old, fallen, and sinful nature. However, in the context of this passage, Paul exhorts us to consciously strive to subdue that nature and to cultivate the character of our new spiritual nature, bestowed by the Holy Spirit in our new birth. In short, what the Holy Spirit did for our immaterial being in the new birth, He shall do for our physical body in the resurrection. The Spirit doesn't come and go in us. He resides in us, permanently so. We may either obey His influence or not, though disobedience shall be accompanied by conviction, conflict, and chastening.

Paul does not teach the pagan idea that all individuality ceases, and the individual is wholly re-absorbed back into deity. On the mount of transfiguration, the disciples saw Moses and Elijah, not two non-descript spirit figures. They saw and recognized the two saints from the past. At the least, this point indicates that our individuality shall continue after death and the resurrection. We see a similar fact in the lesson of the rich man and Lazarus. Both the rich man and Lazarus existed as individuals after their death (Luke 16:19-31). Paul rather teaches that God shall be the focal point of all heaven's activities. Often believers who think of heaven so focus on what they shall think, know, or do, that they miss this central truth of heaven. "Thou art worthy..." (Revelation 5:9).

> This verse teaches clearly that the believer still has a sinful human nature within him even though he has died with Christ. God does not eradicate the believer's flesh at conversion. Therefore we must not *"live [walk]* according to" it. Progressive sanctification is not something the Christian may take or leave. God commanded us to pursue it (cf. 2 Pet. 1:3–11).[3]

This point is crucial to our right understanding of our Christian conduct. The Holy Spirit does not orchestrate or puppeteer our advance in godliness. He commands it, but we must consciously exert the effort to grow in grace and in knowledge of God's truth. The believer who falsely embraces the idea that God irresistibly ordained and causes his perseverance in the faith inevitably becomes either lax in his pursuit of godliness, or he shall become unbalanced and legalistic, often prideful that his attainments and knowledge in the faith, divinely orchestrated as he believes, is vastly superior to others who do not hold to his ideas. Satan loves few ideas as fondly as to convince a believer that God has put him on auto-pilot for godliness.

Paul further teaches us that the fact of the indwelling Spirit undeniably leads to certain conclusions, the chief truth being our future bodily resurrection. If the Holy Spirit dwells in you now, rest assured, fully so, that He shall raise you to glory with your Lord Jesus.

---

[3] Tom Constable, *Tom Constable's Expository Notes on the Bible* (Galaxie Software, 2003), Ro 8:12.

34
Resurrection Ethics

Therefore, brethren, we are debtors, not to the flesh, to live after the flesh.
For if ye live after the flesh, ye shall die: but if ye through the Spirit do
mortify the deeds of the body, ye shall live. For as many as are led by the
Spirit of God, they are the sons of God. (Romans 8:12–14)

Paul's "therefore" takes us directly back to his teaching on the resurrection in verse 11. The Bible often teaches the doctrine of the resurrection, but it never teaches this doctrine as either speculative and imaginative, the sadly common teaching of our day, or as a detached "pie in the sky bye and bye" dream. Speculation? Yes, indeed. For example, a few years back I heard a popular radio preacher who mentioned the Isaiah passage about the lion lying down with the lamb; he speculated that he would have his own pet lion in heaven.

A fundamental premise of sound Biblical interpretation is that you build your beliefs on the literal passages of the Bible that teach the topic, and you use the symbolic passages as support texts. It seems at times that much of modern teaching on the doctrine of final things has reversed this principle, building its ideas on a speculative interpretation of the symbolic passages and effectively ignoring the literal passages altogether.

Why teach on the Second Coming and our literal bodily resurrection? In 1 Thessalonians, Paul urges the Thessalonians to comfort each other with this teaching, especially as they faced the death of loved ones. In the passage before us, Paul teaches that our present Christian conduct must build on our belief in the fact of our future resurrection and eternity with the Lord. Filling out the New Testament model with John's teaching, especially in 1 John, we must include our conduct toward other believers, not merely our personal moral conduct.

If a man say, I love God, and hateth his brother, he is a liar: for he that loveth not his brother whom he hath seen, how can he love God whom he hath not seen? (1John 4:20)

In our study passage, Paul's opening analogy compares our obligation to live out the moral character of the Lord Jesus Christ to a debt. A contextual reading of the lesson leads us to conclude that the resurrection of Jesus, fully ensuring our own resurrection in His image, obligates us to a specific lifestyle.

I have a good friend whose lifelong studies and humor make him quite popular as a "CD-preacher," one whose sermons people seek out and obtain on CDs to listen to them. Over the years I have occasionally heard people comment, "I average listening to ten sermons a week from Elder 'P,'" the man in question. Every time I hear comments such as this, I want to ask the person: "You keep track of how many sermons you listen to in a week. How many sermons do you practice in the same week?"

Often the professional sermon-listeners sorely need to become sermon-practicers. Listening to a sound Biblical sermon is an excellent habit, but failure to learn from it and put it into practice reduces an otherwise model habit to near meaningless value. My counsel to these folks would also add another point. You can easily think of sermons heard on electronic media as a form of entertainment, a good form for sure, but the actual spiritual exhortation that you personally need the Lord most often sends to you through the church that you attend and through the pastor who knows your life and who preaches to you face to face.

Paying one's financial debts requires more than words. It requires writing a check and giving it to your creditor. How we act toward our brothers and sisters reveals whether we respect them as our spiritual creditors or not. We would not at all approve of a person who claims to be a believer in God, but who works to avoid paying his debts. How faithful are we to pay our spiritual debts toward our brothers and sisters in Christ? If someone asked them about our spiritual "credit rating," would they agree that we pay our debts?

Often when I participate in the washing of the saints' feet, I make the point. Jesus practiced this act and commanded us to follow His example. If we do so, we do a good thing, but He instituted the practice for a reason. It is not an end in itself. It was intended to teach us a lifestyle of submission and service to our brothers and sisters in the faith, of paying our spiritual debts. If we engage in the practice and then contradict the object lesson before our feet get dry, what is the purpose or value? And if we so contradict the ethical intent of this lesson, can we honestly claim that we pay our debt to the Lord or to His people?

As I ponder the New Testament's teaching on godly, Christ-centered, other-serving Christian conduct, I can find no stronger Biblical motive than the realization of resurrection reality, the point of our study passage. In 1 Corinthians 6:14, Paul uses the literal resurrection of our bodies to motivate the Corinthians to maintain sexual purity in their lives. If God cared enough to purpose the resurrection of your body to praise His matchless grace for eternity, should you not care enough about that body to use it for His praise now, and to avoid using it in ways that dishonor Him?

...not to the flesh, to live after the flesh. Much of our human culture builds on the corrupt idea that we owe our primary debt to our carnal nature and its sinful appetite. "It is my life; I'll live it as I please." Or, "God wants me to be happy, and I can't be happy doing what the Bible teaches me to do, so God is okay with me being happy and not doing what Scripture teaches." Yes, as a pastor, I've heard these words. Paul clears the air on this twisted issue. You do not owe your flesh or its sinful appetites anything. The debt that you owe is not to that "creditor." You owe your use of your body the conduct that sanctifies that body as an honorable temple of service to God and to His people. And do not neglect; Scripture teaches clearly on the subject of happiness, but it always associates godly and true, lasting happiness with obeying God's commandments in Scripture, not living contradictory to them.

For if ye live after the flesh, ye shall die: but if ye through the Spirit do mortify the deeds of the body, ye shall live. Paul has not shifted his focus from how God commands us to live our life of discipleship over to how we get to heaven when we die. He is not writing to unbelievers, but to Christians, children of God who have been born again, children of the King. His sobering point reminds us that there are consequences to what we do. We can't do as we wish and avoid the consequences of our actions. If, despite believing in Jesus and the resurrection, you choose to ignore the moral and spiritual commandments of the Lord in Scripture and the gospel, you must face the frightening reality that a very real spiritual element in you shall die. You do not lose your new birth or your eternal inheritance. However, the fact that Paul associates this loss with death should gravely remind us that the consequences for such sinful conduct are grave indeed.

When you face the stress of your career and the uncertainty of your financial future, do you prefer to face it with God's kind grace at your side or alone without His sheltering providence? When you finally go to your doctor with those nagging symptoms, and you sit in his office waiting to hear the results of the medical tests, are you comfortable sitting there alone, or would you prefer to have the Lord's sustaining grace with you to face the news? A believer in Christ should never devalue the importance of fellowship with the Lord through life's trials.

Scripture simplifies our life choices. In this key passage, Paul follows the consistent pattern of Scripture. We face only two options. We may choose to "live after the flesh," and we shall surely live through the "living death" that Paul warns in this verse. Or we may choose to "through the Spirit mortify the deeds of the body," and we shall experience the "living life" that Paul teaches here.

We could rightly say that Paul presents us with a matter of "life or death." We choose the path of life after the flesh, and we realize the living death of broken fellowship with the Lord and the death that is associated with that broken fellowship. Or we choose the path of killing, "mortifying," the deeds of the body, and the Lord promises that the blessings of a life in fellowship with Him shall be ours.

The power that enables us to live the lifestyle of fellowship with the Lord is not ours based on our human intellect or even our human values. We live this lifestyle "through the Spirit." But Paul in no way suggests that the Spirit makes the decision for us or that He, auto-pilot style, does the doing for us. He is present to aid and to empower our godly choices, but He does not force or manipulate us apart from our conscious moral/spiritual choices.

Paul didn't write that the Holy Spirit makes the choice to mortify the deeds of the body. He instructs—he commands—us to make two decisions and to act on both. He commands us to mortify the deeds of the body, and he commands us to live our life according to the Spirit. The Holy Spirit provides His presence, wisdom, and aid when we choose to mortify the deeds of the body and to live according to His commandments. We can't do either the negative or the positive apart from His aid, but He commands us to make those choices and to act on them, knowing that we need Him and His assisting and directing power to accomplish either task.

You and I are the actors in this conduct, but we engage both activities, mortifying the deeds and associated appetites of the body and filling our lives with love for God and love for His people, "through the Spirit" (Back to 1 John 4:20). You and I face these two choices every moment of our life. And we, not the Holy Spirit, must make the choice, either to live after the flesh and face the consequences, or to mortify the deeds of the body. When we choose to mortify the deeds of the body, the Holy Spirit provides His aid, and we need it.

For as many as are led by the Spirit of God, they are the sons of God. The Holy Spirit leads us in this conduct; He doesn't make the decisions for us. Nor does He move us as mindless robots in His hand. He leads us to choose the right way and to mortify the deeds of the body. Do we follow His leading, or do we choose to ignore Him and His leading? Scripture never leaves us free from consequences to choose our way. Scripture commands us to follow the Holy Spirit's leading. And when you do follow His leading in your life's choices, He assures you that you are His child.

In this assurance that you are a child of God, no preacher holds control over your assurance. The Holy Spirit Himself personally leads and assures you. Ah, and should you choose to cultivate the deeds of the body, you die to that assurance. He will not assure you if you walk in the flesh. You do not lose your eternal life, but you truly die to His assurance that you are the Lords (2 Peter 1:8-9).

35
Heirs with Christ

The Spirit itself beareth witness with our spirit, that we are the children of God: And if children, then heirs; heirs of God, and joint-heirs with Christ; if so be that we suffer with him, that we may be also glorified together. For I reckon that the sufferings of this present time are not worthy to be compared with the glory which shall be revealed in us. (Romans 8:16–18)

The amazing transformation that God in grace effects in the new birth appears in Scripture with implications far beyond our ability fully to comprehend. How can you and I, mere mortals, specks of dust bustling around on a tiny globe in one small corner of the universe, think that the God who created the whole universe would care so deeply for us and would choose to lift us from our sinful pit to the status of His own family? Scripture makes the point, but, apart from Scripture's affirmation, we would have more questions than answers about such a thing?

Paul, in our study passage, however, bases his point on something other than Scripture. To be indelibly clear, the Holy Spirit never—ever—speaks out of two sides of His mouth. He never contradicts what He has revealed in Scripture through His moving the men who wrote the Scriptures. Whatever He truly testifies to anyone will always harmonize with what He has already revealed in Scripture. His "witness," His testimony to us—to "our spirit"— affirms what we find in Scripture.

A few times I have encountered people who, when challenged for their beliefs and found themselves hard pressed to defend those views from Scripture, would resort to "God revealed to me...." The fact that they could not clearly support the idea from Scripture, especially when Scripture contradicts their belief, discredits their claim of a divine revelation. Paul's teaching in our study verses and their contextual setting lies at the foundation of a sound and enduring Biblical faith.

Atheists and generally unbelievers will ridicule the idea that God in any way gives any personal testimony or conviction to a person. Our study passage obviously refutes that deistic[1] notion.   The fundamental premise of Paul's lesson stands on the stated fact; the Holy Spirit, the Spirit of God, actively bears witness to His people, affirming to them that they are His. As we observe the unbeliever's rejection of all divine interaction and testimony to the individual believer, we also observe the opposite extreme idea that God literally tells or even irresistibly causes you precisely to do and say whatever you do every time you face a decision or have a thought. The passage tells us what the Spirit witnesses to us. And, in this point, He bears witness. We may believe that witness, or we may not believe it.

If we receive the witness of men, the witness of God is greater: for this is the witness of God which he hath testified of his Son. He that believeth on the Son of God hath the witness in himself: he that believeth not God hath made him a liar; because he believeth not the record that God gave of his Son. And this is the record, that God hath given to us eternal life, and this life is in his Son. (1 John 5:9-11)

People who say they believe in God often readily believe other people, but they are reluctant to show similar belief in God and what God in Scripture teaches. If they fail to believe His testimony in Scripture, they will likely also refuse to believe His personal testimony to them. Scripture indicates that the Holy Spirit also teaches the child of God many other things to aid them in their pilgrimage. As Jesus interacted with the disciples and taught them during His time with them, in John, chapters 14-16, He taught them

---

[1] Historically, the deistic belief holds that God created the universe, set it all in motion, and then effectively withdrew, firmly thereafter holding only an observer's position. He supposedly looks on, but He in no way intervenes or influences any part of that creation.

that the Holy Spirit whom He would send in His name after He left would also teach them. In Titus 2:11-15, Paul refers to the same grace of God that saves as also teaching us many specific and substantial things that we need to know as we live life for our God and in service to His people. Many other Scriptures affirm this truth. God neither puppeteers the universe or stands back as a passive observer. Biblical truth affirms His active and selective role in teaching and directing His children in wise and kind grace.

The substance of the Spirit's witness to us does not stop simply with the thought that we are children of God. We see problematic families all around us. In fact, do we see any families that are not in some way problematic? Since the Garden of Eden, there has been no human relationship and therefore no family that is void of problems. God's provision for His family that our passage describes is our only hope of ever rising about the problem of sin. By teaching us that we are His children and by actively exercising His loving fatherly care over us, richly described in the context of this lesson, God manifests daily to us the truth of our family relationship with Him. And the lesson describes God raising us in the end from death itself to live with Him in His loving glory for eternity.

And if children, then heirs; heirs of God, and joint-heirs with Christ. You occasionally read or hear about parents disowning or disinheriting one of their children. Paul teaches us that God never disinherits even one of His children. If He bestows the relationship of "child" on you, the final inheritance is certain. Not because of anything in you, but because of God's heart and purpose, He shall no more disinherit one of His children than He would disinherit Jesus.

The idea of being a "joint-heir" with Christ does not mean that God bestows upon all of His children every honor and every privilege that Jesus enjoys. He commands even the angels to worship Jesus. Rest assured; He never commands angels or any other being to worship you or me. That we are "joint-heirs" with Christ means that we are members of the family of God. And God, through Jesus, passes every blessing that He willed for His family to us because of this unbreakable bond in His will.

Many years ago we had neighbors, good neighbors, who will serve to illustrate a point from this passage. The husband's parents were quite wealthy and successful business people. Upon their death, they owned approximately a full city block near downtown in a large city, so the value of their real estate alone was immense. However, the son, an only child, had demonstrated over his lifetime that he lacked wise judgment in his use of money. Knowing their son's limitations, the parents left their estate to the son, but they also imposed a condition in their will. The estate was to be administered by a man whom they knew to be a wise and fair man with good business and good money sense. They empowered this man to control what the son could have from the estate. If the son needed or wanted to draw money out of the estate, he was required to outline his case in writing to the administrator of the estate. If the administrator agreed that the requested use of funds was wise and good for the son and his family, he would approve the request and release the funds to the son. If he did not agree, he was empowered to deny the request.

God has provided everything that His children need, both for time and for eternity, in His Son. He has indelibly executed His will for His family's eternal security. It cannot be altered or compromised. However, He has also provided access for His family to the riches of their estate in this life to the extent to which they request and use these riches wisely. When we ask "in His name" and "according to His will," He freely and lovingly grants our request. When we ask or seek those riches foolishly, He wisely and lovingly denies our request. Notice the careful wording of this verse.

But my God shall supply all your need according to his riches in glory by Christ Jesus. (Philippians 4:19)

Who determines the "need" of your request? Who judges whether our request qualifies as a "need" or as a foolish or childish desire that might prove more a curse to us than a blessing?

Ye lust, and have not: ye kill, and desire to have, and cannot obtain: ye fight and war, yet ye have not, because ye ask not. Ye ask, and receive not, because ye ask amiss, that ye may consume it upon your lusts. (James 4:2-3)

Sometimes believers, particularly strong believers in grace, foolishly debate whether prayer in any way changes anything. What? Do they ever read their Bibles for answers to such questions? Did the importunate widow's repeated petitions to the unjust judge change anything? Of course it did, and Jesus uses this fact to affirm the purpose of the lesson.

And he spake a parable unto them to this end, that men ought always to pray, and not to faint. (Luke 18:1)

Does the parent give bread to the hungry child who asks for food (Luke 11:11, see context)? Does the fervent prayer of a righteous man avail anything, or is it a mere façade that changes nothing (James 5:16)? Given the abundance of Scriptures that affirm this truth, only a blinded fatalist would think that God never responds with literal answers to the prayers of His children, answers that alter their lives and the circumstances in their lives no less than the hungry child fills his stomach with food from his father, or the prayer of a righteous man for the healing of a repentant and confessing brother or sister, or God personally avenging His elect "...which cry day and night unto him, though he bear long with them" (Luke 18:7-8).

Although our ultimate inheritance, including the literal resurrection and glorification of our bodies, remains yet future, Scripture affirms that God has richly provided access to those things that we presently need from our inheritance until the final and full execution of God's "family" will.

For I reckon that the sufferings of this present time are not worthy to be compared with the glory which shall be revealed in us. Sometimes the Lord sends rich blessings, food when we are hungry, healing and forgiveness when we sin, or righteous judgment when we pray faithfully for it. Other times, He may simply remind us in the midst of our present sufferings of His future glory that He has faithfully and surely reserved for us. However deep the present pain of life may be, that glory so exceeds it as to be incomparable! Praise the Lord!

36
The "Creature" & His Hope

For I reckon that the sufferings of this present time are not worthy to be compared with the glory which shall be revealed in us. For the earnest expectation of the creature waiteth for the manifestation of the sons of God. For the creature was made subject to vanity, not willingly, but by reason of him who hath subjected the same in hope, Because the creature itself also shall be delivered from the bondage of corruption into the glorious liberty of the children of God. For we know that the whole creation groaneth and travaileth in pain together until now. And not only they, but ourselves also, which have the firstfruits of the Spirit, even we ourselves groan within ourselves, waiting for the adoption, to wit, the redemption of our body. (Romans 8:18–23)

If you read the commentaries on this passage, variation abounds. Many of them make their case that the "creature" or the "whole creation" in the passage refers literally to the whole created universe. There can be no doubt that Adam's sin impacted the natural world in which he lived. Genesis 3 explains some of those changes as they directly impacted Adam and Eve outside the garden. But does our study passage refer to the brokenness of the natural world as it teaches us about the Second Coming and our literal bodily resurrection?

Occasionally very sincere believers confuse their interpretation of a passage with what the passage actually teaches in its context. Scripture never contradicts itself or teaches error, but well-meaning interpretations often overflow with contradictions when weighed against Scripture's teachings, rightly divided, not privately interpreted (2 Peter 1:20-21[1]). A thorough study of Scripture,

---

[1] While these verses refer to the human authors, the same principle applies. The Holy Spirit, the true "Author" of Scripture gave Scripture with His intent and interpretation, disapproving private interpretation in the human author whom He

carefully stripped of all the preconceptions and personal baggage
that we are liable to take to Scripture as we study it, will reveal and
refute our bad interpretations. I suggest that our present passage
simply says too much and says it too plainly to match well with the
whole created universe view. Here are a few of many reasons why
the passage does not support that view.

1. Paul specifically is dealing with "...the glory which shall be
   revealed in us" in this context. He personalizes the impact of
   the resurrection to the family of God. In the context leading
   up to this passage, Paul does not in any way deal with the
   natural universe. He carefully focuses his teaching on the
   impact of God's grace on His children.
2. Paul personifies the "creature" as having an "earnest
   expectation" and as "waiting for the manifestation of the
   sons of God." Rocks and asteroids have no intelligent,
   spiritual "earnest expectation." Nor do they consciously wait
   for God's manifest glory in His resurrected and glorified
   children. Whatever the creature, it possesses a conscious
   mind that is aware of something far better in the future that
   God has prepared for His children than anything this present
   world can offer. It consciously waits for that day when the
   Lord shall manifest His family, "...the sons of God."
3. The creature of which Paul writes in some form has a will that
   is out of step with the present "vanity" of this sin-cursed,
   fallen and broken world.
4. This creature presently lives under the subjection of "hope," it
   joyfully expects a future deliverance from the present vanity
   and decay of this present world. Hope involves a conscious
   weighing of evidence and concluding from that evidence a
   strong expectation of a specific and good outcome, not
   something that natural elements alone can do.
5. This creature's hope is well placed. The creature "...shall be
   delivered...into the glorious liberty of the children of God."
   Think. If this creature shall experience the liberty and glory

of the "children of God," it seems far more reasonable to conclude that this "creature" is, in fact, a term that refers to "the children of God."

6. Paul equates the present groaning of the "whole creation" with his experience, "...even we ourselves groan within ourselves." And what is the outcome of Paul's (and the "we ourselves" with him) hope, the object or realization of his hope? He makes the point clearly, "the adoption, to wit, the redemption of our body." While it is possible that God's natural creation may in some way be transformed after its meltdown (2 Peter 3:10-13), nothing in Scripture personalizes whatever may happen to the natural world as Paul here personalizes the creature's deliverance of which he writes.

7. Paul personalizes the final outcome of the transformation of the "creature" of which he writes, "the redemption of our body." This term is far too specific a reference to the physical bodily resurrection of the children of God to match a generalized description of everything in nature.

By reading this passage in its context and applying it to the "...children of God" and by accepting the transformation of the "whole creation" as a reference to the family of God and "...the redemption of our body," the lesson flows smoothly with its context, in fact, enhancing and enriching the points that Paul makes regarding his and our hope for the Lord's return at the Second Coming.

Because the creature itself also shall be delivered from the bondage of corruption into the glorious liberty of the children of God. If the final manifestation of the "creature" is the "glorious liberty of the children of God," should we not conclude that Paul's teaching in the passage deals with God's purpose to resurrect and glorify the bodies of His children at the Second Coming?

For we know that the whole creation groaneth and travaileth in pain together until now. First notice the often overlooked word, "together." As this whole creation groans and experiences the intense burden of childbearing, "travaileth," it is not alone. **We are not alone.** As Jesus stood before Lazarus' tomb, he groaned and wept (John 11:35-38). This final deliverance is not a dream or an empty wish. It is a final reality that the Lord Himself shall bring upon His return. Most often in our King James Bible, this word "travail" refers to the birthing process by which a child is born into the world. However, the Holy Spirit occasionally uses the word to teach powerful lessons in the spiritual world.

1. *He shall see of the travail of his soul, and shall be satisfied: by his knowledge shall my righteous servant justify many; for he shall bear their iniquities* (Isaiah 53:11). This verse appears in the context of Isaiah's prophecy of Jesus' suffering and dying for our sins. In the very moment in which Jesus' body died, His "soul" was travailing in the work of securing the life of His beloved children. What a comfort! What a Savior!

2. Our present passage uses the word in the midst of its discussion of pain, groaning, and hope for deliverance. The passage is not dealing with natural childbirth, but with God's ultimate and glorious purpose to keep His children in the glory that He has prepared for them while they live through this present pilgrimage. The process that God reveals in Scripture to resurrect His children and to complete His eternal purpose of glory in them is as logical and as inevitable as the process of childbirth. There is only one difference. In the world of natural childbirth, occasionally things can go wrong, and the baby does not live. However, our study passage, along with the consistent teaching of Scripture, reminds us that no such miscarriage shall occur in the Lord's family. The hope that excited the child of grace through this life shall come to fulfillment. All of those whom the Lord loves and chose in His Son before He created the first molecule of this natural universe shall be "...*delivered from the bondage of corruption into the glorious liberty of the children of God.*"

This passage is rich with metaphors that excite and instruct us. In addition to the thoughts already examined, Paul adds to the richness with yet another metaphor of deliverance. Throughout the lesson, he has contrasted present bondage and groaning with future deliverance. He finally enriches that deliverance with "the glorious *liberty* of the children of God." In degree far beyond our present sense of imprisonment and limitation to serve God as we should and to serve His children as He commands us, we shall then experience the full, the "glorious" liberty of deliverance and glory. In fact, as Paul focuses this lesson in its conclusion with this thought, he also started the lesson with it.

For I reckon that the sufferings of this present time are not worthy to be compared with the glory which shall be revealed in us.

Rather than heaven being a precise compensation for the sufferings that we presently endure, an idea often advanced by folks about heaven, Paul writes that the glory that we shall experience is so much greater than any suffering that we face in this "present time" that we cannot compare one with the other.

This passage reveals one of the prime distinctions between belief in salvation (eternal and final salvation from sin and all of its consequences) by our works and final eternal deliverance by God and by His grace alone. If heaven is to be compensatory for our trials and sufferings, the equation should be equal; to use Paul's word, the two should "compare" equally with each other. The truth of Scripture, that our eternal final deliverance from sin is all of God and His grace alone, leads us to Paul's conclusion in this lesson. Instead of being compensatory and comparable, the glory that we shall experience is incomparable with our present sufferings, because that glory was secured for us by the Lord Jesus Christ and His sufferings for us, not through our purchasing it by our works.

37
Saved by Hope: Focusing on Unseen Reality

For we are saved by hope: but hope that is seen is not hope: for what a man seeth, why doth he yet hope for? But if we hope for that we see not, then do we with patience wait for it. (Romans 8:24–25)

Paul ends this extensive teaching on the Second Coming and our bodily resurrection, "...the redemption of our body," fittingly with these verses on hope. Our modern pedestrian idea of "hope" is something akin to wishful thinking, an escape from reality into a wishful fantasy world where we imagine what we'd like with no expectation whatever of realizing it. The casual Bible student who has little or no exposure to the historical meaning of hope will take this fantasy idea of "hope" to the Bible and wholly miss Scripture's rich teaching on the subject.

The *Shorter Oxford English Dictionary* defines "hope" as "expectation of something desired." The idea of wishful thinking is thus absent. Unless you have a solid expectation of the object, you have no hope. Yes, you have a desire, but a desire with no expectation is not true hope. When we read of "hope" in Scripture, the truth of its teaching always urges us to focus on the expectation and on the thing joyfully expected.

Paul removes this "wishful dream" idea in our study passage. When he writes "For we are saved by hope," he associates hope with his teaching on the Second Coming and our resurrection that he just taught. We might interpret "We are saved by hope" in various ways, but the context will clarify and direct us to the right way. While it is true and beyond doubt that "...Christ in you, the hope of glory" (Colossians 1:27) is the cause and source of our final salvation, the salvation that relates to the Second Coming and our bodily resurrection, Paul's emphasis on the unseen quality of our present hope deals with our present mindset that joyfully anticipates and expects that final glory. The truth of the Second Coming and our resurrection, when rightly believed and kept in our minds, is life changing.

> *By which also ye are saved, if ye keep in memory what I preached unto you, unless ye have believed in vain.* (1 Corinthians 15:2)

Neither in 1 Corinthians 15:2 nor in Romans 8:24 did Paul intend to teach that our final deliverance from sin and death are uncertain and contingent on how strongly and rightly we believe and hope. Both verses remind us of the present "saving" effect our belief and hope have on how we live and face the trials of our present life.

We may give up on anything good and godly and allow ourselves to become consumed with the present groaning for deliverance, but this path will eventually surrender to the groaning and forget the reason for it. Do not miss Paul's analogy of "travail" in this context. The groaning of the creature is in some way similar to the groans of a woman in the midst of child birth. If she for a moment forgets the reason for her groaning, the pain overwhelms her. However, if she steadfastly remembers with each new contraction that a child, her child, is on its way into the world, and she must push all the harder to see that new life, she will look past the pain to the new life that is coming.

Despite the long duration of many of life's pains and trials, often so intense that they produce audible groans, Paul directs us to never forget the fact that our present pain is temporary, that something beyond our ability to reach by ourselves, and something far exceeding the impact of our present pain awaits us in glory when we shall realize the deliverance of the "sons of God." Keeping that truth fresh and alive in our minds today saves us from overwhelming despair at the present pain.

Paul's use of hope in this context properly bridges our thoughts into truths that he will give us through the remainder of the chapter. As our pains drive us to our knees in prayer, the Spirit intercedes in our seasons of weakness with groans that we cannot know. We might focus on the stuttered weakness of our words in prayer, but the saving of hope reminds us of the Spirit's interceding groans. While we groan under our present trials, the Holy Spirit joins our groans, but He never forgets our final and certain deliverance. We may find relief and deliverance—another word for "saved"—when we remind ourselves in our "groaning moments" of the Holy Spirit's groans for us before the Father.

Folks who fail to grasp Scripture's broad teaching on the topic of "salvation" will likely become confused by lessons such as this one. Their confusion grows when they must deal with such passages as 1 Timothy 4:16. Does Jesus save, or does the preacher save both himself and his hearers?

Confusion regarding this Bible topic will lead to one of two extreme and errant beliefs. 1) God micromanages everything that occurs, even to the point of complicity in our sins for a mystical greater good.[1] 2) Or it will lead to belief in one or another forms of salvation by works, either blatant salvation by works as in the teachings of Arminius, or "side door" salvation by works, as with so many contemporary teachers who use the terms of salvation by grace, but they inevitably teach a view of grace that falls short unless accompanied and implemented by human contribution, as in MacArthur's "Lordship Salvation."

The Biblical principles of salvation divide into multiple aspects or types of salvation or deliverance. When we encounter the word in any of its various forms in Scripture, good study and right division require us to ask questions of the context in which the word appears. "Saved from what?" "Saved to what?" "Saved by what?" "Saved now?" "Saved in the past?" Or "Saved in the future?" In fact Scripture uses the word "saved" in many different ways.

We may wisely break Scripture's use of the word into two major categories: 1) temporal deliverances that relate to our discipleship,

---

[1] As an example of this errant belief, I recently stumbled across a website of a man who holds to this belief. In one of his lessons, the man stated that, at times, God prevents sin, as when he prevented Abimelech from committing adultery with Sarah, but at other times "God purposes sin" and thus the sin, in this case adultery, occurs. The obvious implication; if you or I commit adultery, it is because God "Purposed" it. Paul answers this thinking in clear terms. We should stand with Paul (Romans 3:8).

our service to God and to His people in the here and now, or 2) eternal deliverance from the eternal consequences of our sins. Occasionally fatalists who teach that God orchestrates every person in every act will heatedly oppose this division of Scripture's use of the word. Since they believe that God manipulates our good works as sovereignly and as irresistibly as He produces the new birth, in principle, they reject or wrest every passage in the Bible where the word "save" is used as a directive or commandment to an individual.

A favorite logical fallacy used by those who lean in this direction creates a "straw man" and ridicules it instead of honestly dealing with the Scriptures that use the word in this way. The straw man says that all of God's works, including the new birth and the final resurrection take place in time, so all Bible salvation is in this way of thinking "temporal." Obviously, this is not the way that Scripture uses the word in the passages that command believers to save themselves and others by walking in faith, obeying God, and teaching others to do likewise.

In these passages, Scripture often uses the word as a directive, a command to action by the believer in time when the consequences of the action are temporal. Our obedience to the gospel, our teaching others the truth of the gospel, being baptized, and all the godly works of faith commanded in Scripture deal with our discipleship here in time. We do not believe that Scripture teaches that we earn our place in heaven by what we do. Thus, despite being emphatically commanded, not gently suggested, the ultimate consequences of our action or our failure in these exhortations of Scripture, are temporal, not eternal. They result in the Lord's severe chastening, not in our eternal separation from Him and from His love, Paul's final point in Romans 8 (Romans 8:38-39). Thus Scripture uses the word "save" in these passages in terms of a temporal, as contrasted with eternal, salvation or deliverance.

Likewise, when Scripture teaches us about God's exclusive work that redeems us from the legal—and the eternal—debt of our sins, extracting us from the condemnation of sin and death and translating us into the kingdom and family of God's dear Son, it always attributes all of the action, the truly "saving" action, to God alone.

Why? Because it is dealing with the eternal consequences of our sins, consequences that God alone can eradicate by His merciful grace.

The Biblical principle that distinguishes the use of "saving" to God alone or that uses the word as a directive to faith and action by us always relates to the consequences involved, not to the irrelevant and superficial question of when the action occurs. The logical fallacy of the straw man is quite obvious in this argument. The straw man fallacy ignores the real issue and tries to divert the other person's mind to the irrelevant question of when something occurred instead of dealing with the consequences involved, which is Scripture's discerning use of the word in two very different, opposite, ways, one involving God alone doing for us what we utterly lacked both the ability and the desire to do, and the other involving God directing and aiding us in believing Him and His truth and acting in faith and with His assistance in our discipleship.

When Paul teaches that we are saved by hope, he is not in any way contradicting his faithful teaching that God alone can and does save us from the eternally damning consequences of our sins. He has just completed a detailed and edifying lesson on the reality of our future resurrection, the adoption/redemption of our body into the family and presence of God at the Second Coming. If we keep that truth in mind, despite the present trials and vanities that we face in life, that truth will strengthen our faith, give us hope in what we might otherwise view as a hopeless situation, and thus save us from the despair of hopelessness that would overwhelm us.

Scripture teaches the truth of a literal bodily resurrection at the Second Coming, but we have not yet experienced that resurrection. Nor have we seen resurrected people walking around in our world. The scoffers who reject the truth of the Second Coming mockingly remind believers that cemeteries are growing daily, that thousands of years have gone by, and still we see no indication of an imminent resurrection. "Where is the promise of his coming" (2 Peter 3:4)? Believers who fail to dedicate their lives to a growing, fruitful faith are liable to fall prey to this depressing error and forget God's saving grace (2 Peter 1:9). False teachers may overthrow the faith of weak believers by false ideas regarding the Second Coming and resurrection, but they cannot overthrow God's merciful grace that refuses to let go of even one of His beloved children of grace (2 Timothy 2:16-19).

Paul's teaching drives to the heartbeat of the gospel's good news. Shall we believe it and experience the joyful deliverance of hope right now, or shall we believe the scoffers and the false teachers and become overwhelmed and lost in the depressing false teachings that abound in this sinful world? The more we keep God's glorious "resurrection truth" fresh and alive in our minds the more we shall experience the reality of being "...saved by hope" as we trek through a hostile world, looking for that better country.

But if we hope for that we see not, then do we with patience wait for it. We do not see the resurrection in our present field of vision. If we surrender to the scoffers who mock the doctrine of a literal resurrection of the body and the literal Second Coming of Christ, we lose any expectation of that day and the events that Scripture assigns to that day. Instead of being saved by hope, this abandonment of our faith leads us directly into the dark and depressing world of hopelessness. Folks who fall into this trap of the great deceiver often manifest an angry void of patience. In fact, they often live in a state of constant anger. They are not happy people. If they have abandoned such a central truth of Scripture, how can they have any other attitude?

Whom having not seen, ye love; in whom, though now ye see him not, yet believing, ye rejoice with joy unspeakable and full of glory. (1 Peter 1:8)

If we fall to the lowest common denominator of "seeing is believing," and choose to believe only what we can see or touch with our natural eyes and hands, we not only deny the Second Coming and our bodily resurrection, but we also deny the very Person of the Lord Jesus Christ. However, if, despite not seeing Him, we love Him, believe in Him and believe Him, we "...rejoice with joy unspeakable and full of glory." You see, what we believe directly shapes our frame of mind.

When you see a believer who lives in nearly constant anger and irritated agitation at his brothers and sisters in Christ, you may not know the details, but you may rest assured that you are dealing with a brother or sister who live with a deeply flawed faith and a wrested belief system. These traits are not the fruit of a sound and firmly believed Bible truth.

Over some sixty years, I have observed more than a few strong believers, including preachers, who slipped from their productive and active life into the shrinking world of their older years, dominated by the spirit of bitterness and anger. At first, I was puzzled by the observation. It seems that growing into this final era of one's life causes some people to grow more gracious, kindly thoughtful of others, and mellow at the trials of life, while others grow increasingly bitter and angry. Knowing some of these people fairly well, I have observed a consistent pattern behind these opposite attitudes and behaviors. True to Scripture's teachings, those who keep their hearts and lives focused on serving God by serving His people—all the while looking with joyful anticipation to their hope in Christ—manifested traits of grace and calm peace at life's never-ending trials. These dear saints exemplify before our eyes the joyful and Biblical reality of being "...saved by hope." Those who turned inward and became more focused on self and on the self-obsessed idea of creating and leaving their legacy became the angry bitter folk.

As I ponder this passage, the questions loom in my mind. Which class of people will I imitate? What kind of believe will I become? Which class will become your steady companions? God has not decreed you to one or the other. He has pointed us to self-denying faith and a life that immerses its work in serving others, not in lording our will over them. He has richly described the blessings of obedience in Scripture, and He has frighteningly reminded us of the price we shall pay for choosing our own way and interests above His.

Which path shall we choose? That choice shall shape our attitude in the closing chapter of our life. If we seek the path of joyful peace, of experiencing what it means to be "...saved by hope," we must choose the way of service, not the way of self.

38
All Things Work Together for Good?

*And we know that all things work together for good to them that love God,
to them who are the called according to his purpose. For whom he did
foreknow, he also did predestinate to be conformed to the image of his Son,
that he might be the firstborn among many brethren. Moreover whom he
did predestinate, them he also called: and whom he called, them he also
justified: and whom he justified, them he also glorified. What shall we then
say to these things? If God be for us, who can be against us? He that
spared not his own Son, but delivered him up for us all, how shall he not
with him also freely give us all things? Who shall lay any thing to the
charge of God's elect? It is God that justifieth. Who is he that
condemneth? It is Christ that died, yea rather, that is risen again, who is
even at the right hand of God, who also maketh intercession for us.*
(Romans 8:28–34)

Almost every verse in Romans 8 begins with a connective word;
"For...", "That...", "Because...", "So...", "But...", etc. If we
blindly ignored the context of these thirty-nine verses, even these
simple words would challenge our thoughts and demand that we
view the chapter as a whole fabric, not thirty-nine independent and
unrelated ideas.

The opening thought of the chapter affirms that those whom God
has placed in His Son have no condemnation. It ends with the
proclamation that those whom God has enfolded in His love shall
never be separated from His love. And the verses that make up the
chapter take us from that first thought to the last. They explain why
and how both divine miracles occur.

Despite this obvious and firm union of connected truth, many
people read verse 28 as if it exists in a vacuum, in no way linked to
its context. From beginning to end, Romans 8 deals with God and
with His work in and for His people. It therefore contradicts the

context of the whole chapter to ignore this point and focus in this one verse on all the things that men and devils do, attempting to sanctify the work of men and devils as if they were God in action. How does Paul characterize human actions throughout the chapter? Consider.

1. Verse 6, "...to be carnally minded is death."
2. Verse 8, "...they that are in the flesh cannot please God."
3. Verse 13, "...if ye live after the flesh, ye shall die."

In none of these verses do we read any suggestion that sinful carnal minds who live after the flesh in some way mysteriously work together with God to further or to accomplish His will. Quite the opposite, as in all other Scriptures, this chapter consistently affirms that sinful actions produce bad results. Period.

> *Be ye not unequally yoked together with unbelievers: for what fellowship hath righteousness with unrighteousness? and what communion hath light with darkness? And what concord hath Christ with Belial? or what part hath he that believeth with an infidel? And what agreement hath the temple of God with idols? for ye are the temple of the living God; as God hath said, I will dwell in them, and walk in them; and I will be their God, and they shall be my people.* (2 Corinthians 6:14-16)

In these verses, Paul emphatically affirms what Scripture consistently teaches: God and Satan, righteousness and unrighteousness, light and darkness, the temple of God and idols never work together. The errant interpretation of Romans 8:28 that claims every act of wicked men and demons mysteriously work together with God or anything that He does, much less that they work for good to God's people, blatantly contradicts 2 Corinthians 6:14-16, along with many similar passages throughout the Bible.

When people interpret any passage so that it contradicts other Scriptures, the problem lies in their bad interpretation, not in Scripture itself. If we understand the moral foundations of God in

Scripture and read Scripture's consistent teaching from Genesis to Revelation, we fully appreciate this diametrical contradiction that exists between God and Satan and between everything that God does versus everything that Satan or sinful men do.

The first error committed by those who attempt to force Romans 8:28 to teach that Paul is referring to every act that ever occurs as mysteriously working together, much less for good, is that they isolate the verse from the context of Romans 8 and impose their private interpretation onto it. The second error they commit is that they interpret this one verse in a way that glaringly contradicts what Scripture consistently teaches elsewhere. I have used only one such passage from the same inspired human author, but similar contradictory passages could be offered throughout the Bible. The third and perhaps most problematic error committed by those who impose a universal view onto the "all things" of Romans 8:28 is that they, directly or indirectly, charge God with complicity in the sin and depravity that exists in this world.

Paul directly dealt with that moral problem in Romans 3:5-8, charging that those who so thought and taught slandered the truth of the gospel that he preached and that they wholly misrepresented his teachings. I believe Paul's writings, both in Romans 3 and in Romans 8, and I choose to follow his teachings in both contexts so as to find harmony in his inspired writing, not contradiction, especially moral contradiction against God.

Often advocates of this errant view of "all things" in Romans 8:28, will play the straw man logical fallacy with "Well, don't you believe that God can sometimes use the acts of wicked men for His purpose?" The question doesn't deserve the honor of an answer, for it dishonestly misrepresents what its interrogator believes. The point that Paul makes in Romans 8:28 is not that some things sometimes work together for good. Whatever the Holy Spirit's intent in Paul's words, He used "all things," not "some things sometimes." I suppose these folks must think that their own personal dishonesty in misrepresenting their own beliefs by their fallacious "some things" in some way works together for good. I suggest that any idea that conveniently justifies open dishonesty is not honoring to God, is not taught by Scripture, and never works together for good, good being defined and established by God, not by morally compromised and logically challenged sinful minds.

The challenge before us is to question the context in which Paul wrote this verse to find a contextual answer to the question "What are these all things?" and to understand how and why they all (not some things some of the time) work together for good to them that love God, who are called by Him according to His purpose.

The focus of the whole chapter, Romans 8, is on God and what He does to accomplish the dual-objective that Paul affirms, no condemnation to no separation, and all that God must accomplish to secure both objectives. If we start with the contextual fact that Paul consistently in this chapter praises God for what He does and condemns human sin in whatever form it takes, we will be far more inclined to seek an explanation of this verse and Paul's reference to "all things" that relates to God and what He does, not to wicked men and what they do. Nor will we seek to mystify God's work that Paul has declared simply and with edification to the struggling and suffering saint by indirectly making demons and wicked men and all of their actions—not just some of them, as these folks illogically state—by magnifying wicked men and what they do as part of what God is doing to accomplish His stated dual objective, no condemnation to no separation. Human sin in this context is the problem, not the solution. God will have His glory in overcoming this sin and suffering problem, despite the "things" that wicked men and demons do, not because of them or through them.

If we consider the literary framework of this chapter and of Paul's writing in general, we will note that Paul contextually defines and explains the terms that he uses. Left to its literary meaning alone and ignoring the context in which the words appear, "all things" is general and vague beyond any logical definition. However, if we read the greater context of Romans 8, we shall discover many logical, consistent, and even literary indicators that tightly focus these "all things" by the literary setting in which the words appear.

The lesson immediately prior to verse 28 deals with our prayers and the assuring knowledge that the Holy Spirit takes our stuttering, faltering words and pleas in prayer through His sanctifying grace before presenting them to the Father. Not only so, but Jesus adds His own intercession to the Spirit's help (v. 27).

Verse 28 begins with "For," a connective word that relates the true point of the lesson to the work of the Spirit and of Jesus to the Father. Something in this verse adds strong assurance to the prior point. If we view the "all things" of which Paul writes here in terms of what God, Father, Son, and Spirit do on behalf of His children, we grasp the point that this verse adds powerful assurance to our faltering prayers.

Verse 29 also begins with another "For." Why and how do "...all things work together" as Paul states? Because...the five monumental acts of God specified in verses 29-30 all work together. God works these actions personally. "Things" have no intelligence, much less a moral compass. But God always works faithfully to His moral character, and He always works consistently with His moral character and with His eternal purpose. There is no literary or moral tension whatever if we allow the theme to flow through these verses in logical and connected sequence.

In verse 31, Paul raises the question, "What shall we then say to these things?" Do not ignore his inspired conclusion, "IF God be for us, who can be against us?" Inherently, intuitively, there is nothing in the wicked acts of depraved men and demons that convinces us that God is for us. However, if we ponder the five things that Paul names, five things that encompass God's timeless provisions for His chosen people, we "inherently and intuitively" grasp Paul's conclusion. No accident: the Greek word translated "know" in Romans 8:28 is a word that refers to intuitive or reflective knowledge, yet another affirmation of the Holy Spirit's focused intent in these words.

In verse 32, Paul answers any question that might remain about his intent in the "all things" of verse 28.

*He that spared not his own Son, but delivered him up for us all, how shall he not with him also freely give us **all things**?* (Emphasis added)

Whether we study the words "all things" in verse 28 and in verse 32 in Greek, King James English, or contemporary English, they are exactly the same. In the greater context, but emphatically and undeniably in verse 32, the Holy Spirit directed Paul to include a clear definition of what He intended by "all things" in verse 28.

What wicked men and demons do in no way contributes to either of God's stated purposes in Romans 8, no condemnation and no separation. What wicked men and demons do cannot be artificially sanctified by false teachers or by naïve Christians to contribute in any way to either of these inspired and stated divine purposes. Further, nothing that wicked men and demons do ever intuitively and reflectively enlightens our minds to the overwhelming assurance of God's work in and for us, work that covers every necessary step from no condemnation to no separation. Nothing about the depraved and wicked acts of men and demons convinces us to conclude, "If God be for us, who can be against us?" But if we reflect on the five divine actions of verses 29-30, we cannot logically reach any other conclusion.

But the strongest possible point appears in verse 32. In the context of Romans 8, a chapter that begins with God's declaration of no condemnation to all of His, all who are "in Christ Jesus," and ends with the triumphant declaration that nothing real or imagined can possibly separate us from the love of God which is in Christ Jesus our Lord, we must resolve our focus on what verse 39 emphasizes. The final success, the final resolution of God's stated purpose and objective is accomplished in "Christ Jesus our Lord."

Verse 32 answers the question about "all things" in verse 28 in words chosen by the Holy Spirit, not in amoral philosophical speculations: 1) through God's not sparing His own Son; 2) through God delivering His own Son up for us all; 3) God through Him freely gives us "all things." Paul removes all question or doubt from verse 28 in this verse.

Unless advocates of the amoral "all things" view that attempts to sanctify the sinful acts of depraved men and demons so as to morph them into a divine and mysteriously caused action can provide convincing Biblical witness that Jesus' death necessarily, irresistibly, and inevitably *caused* all of these wicked acts, their claim that verse 28 refers to such acts fails and must be rejected. Paul affirms that the ultimate outcome of God's not sparing His Son, of delivering His Son up for us all results in God "...with him..." freely giving us "*all things*."

Does this lesson belong in a thesis that deals with the Second Coming and our bodily resurrection? Indeed it does. Take note that the final accomplishment listed in Paul's five divine actions in verses 29-30 is "...them he also glorified." God's work that makes His final and triumphal return and our personal bodily resurrection a certainty has been fully performed. He does not delay His return because He has failed to complete some necessary or desired step. He delays only because the last of those whom He loved and for whom He "spared not His own Son" are yet to be born. Nothing else delays His coming. Nothing!

All the good things that appear in the whole of Romans 8 God gives to us because of His not-spared Son, and He "freely" gives them to us because of His Son. And all of those things, the things that God has purposed through His not-spared Son, because they are His work, not the work of depraved men and demons, He personally ensures to work together and to work together for the good of those who love Him, those whom He has called according to His purpose.

What is His ultimate purpose? Those whom He has loved in His Son He shall never allow to be separated from that love. Whatever awaits us in heaven shall be wholly and gloriously in harmony with God's love for us. Praise God!

Scripture at times gives us brief glimpses into eternal glory. We could bear no more and survive such glory. But we may live our life and face its trials and sufferings with grace if we keep in mind God's supreme love and His undefeatable purpose to keep every one of those whom He loved "...from of old" (Jeremiah 31:3) securely in His love. That, my friends, is God's lesson to us in Romans 8. God help us never to lose sight of that truth, especially by the siren song of deceit that seeks to sanctify the work of depraved men and demons, as if they in some way contributed to God's ultimate "good" and final glory.

39
Till He Come

For as often as ye eat this bread, and drink this cup, ye do shew the Lord's death till he come. (1 Corinthians 11:26)

Much of the typical discussion regarding Communion examines the elements used in the observance. Do you use wine, or is grape juice or even a cheap imitation grape soda acceptable? Do you use "unleavened" bread, or is a loaf of Wonder® Bread just as fitting? I suggest that the symbolism consistently associated with Communion in the New Testament requires that the elements used are important to teach the lesson intended by the service. In the New Testament, those elements are consistently described as wine; yes real wine, and unleavened bread, bread made with no yeast.

Occasionally the frequency of the observance is questioned. Here there is no specific Scripture to indicate that a church should observe Communion on any specific frequency. It is my view that "breaking of bread," as in Acts 2:46, refers to Communion. It could refer to a simple meal, but the context of the passage, I believe, favors Communion. "...with such an one no not to eat" (1 Corinthians 5:11) likewise seems in context to refer to Communion, not to a common meal. Clearly, Paul's "as oft as ye..." in our study context does not demand a certain frequency for Communion. We should observe it sufficiently often to keep the truth of its symbols and the lessons they teach clearly imbedded in our minds.

Although we follow the original pattern in Scripture, Communion and washing the saints' feet at the same time, we should keep the two observances distinct in our minds. One observance focuses exclusively on Jesus and His death for our sins. The other action focuses just as emphatically on our Biblical obligation to serve each other. A person who believes that Jesus' death plus anything that he does is necessary for eternal salvation, beginning in his personal experience of the new birth, can't fully take the elements of Communion "worthily," rightly "discerning the Lord's body" plus nothing else. And a person whose heart and attitude are aimed at his brother's or sister's throat or back (Scripture uses analogies that dramatically expose the act, "backbiting" and "gnashing on him with their teeth") cannot rightly practice washing the saints' feet. If we are to rightly discern the Lord's body in Communion, we must enter the service believing wholly in what He has done for us to impart the new birth to us and to preserve us to His eternal glory. If we are to rightly engage in washing the saints' feet, as Jesus described and commanded it in John 13, we must enter into the service with a profound and pervasive sense of our own unworthiness, and equally deep love and respect for our brothers and sisters in the church, and a lifestyle that consistently labors to serve them, not lord ourselves and our ways over them. The two observances do not make up Communion. They make up two distinct services, Communion and washing the saints' feet.

Second Peter 1:20 in context refers to the giving of Scripture through the holy men whom the Lord chose to write His words in His Book. The Bible is His Book, written by some thirty to forty or so men over more than fifteen centuries. Not once did He allow those men to write their own "private interpretations" of the way they thought things should be. If God so clearly forbad private interpretations in the men who wrote His Book, we should enter into our study of His Book with an equally strong conviction that He will no more accept our private interpretation than He did theirs. More often than one might imagine, a believer will confuse what Scripture actually teaches with what he believes it teaches, his own "private interpretation," and will impute into his own ideas and private interpretations equal weight as the words of Scripture, something of a personal version of Roman Catholic "ex cathedra," the pope's alleged infallibility in what he "speaks" or says in his official teachings.

This presumption of infallibility contradicts both lessons, of Communion and of washing the saints' feet. Both are to be observed in the setting of a community of believers, not as private individual believers. Every appearance of these two events in the New Testament was a public and community observance.

While the New Testament teaches the priesthood of every believer, it also teaches an essential community of believers. One believer alone should never trust his personal interpretations and opinions above all other believers. Scripture teaches that the Lord has endowed His church (not one elite, at least in his own eyes, believer) to be His vehicle for the maintenance, preservation, and spreading of His truth (1 Timothy 3:15). No individual believer, be he preacher, deacon, or member, should become so self-consumed as to think that he and his ideas are God's official and exclusive insight into His truth. In this quest for authoritative truth, can a church be wrong? Indeed it may. However, the fact that flawed and frail humans may err does not negate the emphatic statement of this passage.

In this broken, flawed, sin-cursed world in which we live, the Lord gave His people the very best vehicle possible to keep them informed and directed to Him and to His truth. That vehicle is not the self-proclaimed prophet or would-be spiritual despot. *It is the Lord's church*. Never do we read in the New Testament that any individual believer is ever elevated by the Lord to be His "pillar and ground of the truth." I've known a few folks who attempted to play that role, and, no surprise, every such incident always resulted in chaos, spiritual schism, and degeneration, never in edification and the spiritual growth of the church.

In His church, the Lord has established the safest possible vehicle for His people to know and to maintain their faith in Him and in His truth. While individual believers, however sincere and well-meaning, are liable to err in their beliefs and conduct, a respectful union of like-minded believers who wholeheartedly give themselves to the Lord and to each other, often graciously corrects and refines the stumbles of individual believers and collectively encourages each other in the right way (1 Corinthians 4:6; 16:15; 2 Corinthians 8:5 and context; Galatians 6:1-5). This truth is powerfully emphasized in the New Testament's use of "communion," a word that describes sharing. When a believer adopts any idea or attitude that promotes his private faith, not humbly participating in the common faith of the church, the Lord's declared "pillar and ground of the truth," he loses the spirit of Communion that the Lord teaches in this His stated role for His church.

That Communion is intended by Scripture to be a church ordinance, not simply a common act of fellowship among individual Christians, appears in several references to the service. In 1 Corinthians 5, one of the New Testament's most despised and rejected whole chapters, Paul directly associates church membership, church discipline, and Communion together. "...with such an one no not to eat" in context refers to verses 5-8 and observance of Communion, not to sitting down with an erring believer for a common meal.

In the context of our study passage, 1 Corinthians 11, several similar points are made: 1) verse 18, "...when ye come together in the church..."; 2) verse 20, "When ye come together therefore into one place..."; 3) verses 27-28, eating and drinking, taking the physical elements of the Communion, "unworthily," refers to our belief about Jesus and what He did, not to any kind of self-assessment that we are so righteous as to deserve Communion; 4) throughout the lesson, Paul uses the second person pronoun plural. In the King James vernacular of the English language, in perfect harmony with the distinction made in first century Greek language's different words to reveal singular and plural second person pronouns. All of these references refer us to the collective body of the Corinthian Church, not to individual believers at Corinth.

The weight of this lesson on the Second Coming should be obvious, "...till he come." Someone whose beliefs do not include a solid belief in the Second Coming cannot enter into Communion and participate with honest conviction, for he does not believe the Lord will return. Likewise, a believer who, like the folks in the Corinthian Church, denies the resurrection (cf. chapter 15) could not take Communion rightly, for they do not believe that He shall return.

Often in Scripture, God gives us mounds of information in the simple points. We need not be a theologian to understand Scripture. "...till he come." How powerful these three simple words! Think about Paul's teaching here. If someone accepts the historical fact of a man named Jesus who lived in Judah in the first century, but does not also believe that He was God manifest in the flesh or that, though He died at the hands of wicked men, He also literally arose from the dead and now lives, why take Communion to remember or to honor that Jesus? Communion, as taught in the New Testament, only makes logical sense for those who believe that He is God Incarnate, God manifest in human flesh, who died *and* arose from the dead, ascended back to heaven, and now sits on heaven's throne with the Father (Revelation 3:21).

We show His death by taking the two items of Communion separately. Blood separated from the body depicts a dead body. We show His death in Communion because we believe that He lives. He only briefly occupied Joseph's tomb, but Scripture's powerful testimony teaches us that He arose as literally as He died, that He appeared to the disciples over a period of approximately forty days, and that He ascended in that literal resurrected body back into heaven in victorious glory. Our Communion shows our belief in this truth. Though we do not know when He shall return, we live in the constant and joyful belief that He shall surely do so. Until He does come back, we are to regularly, sincerely, and faithfully continue this precious act of service and worship, "…till he come."

"…till he come" also underscores our firm belief that He shall return, that His promises of return, resurrection, and eternal glory for His beloved children, is real. It gives us reason to joyfully celebrate this truth until that glorious day dawns.

A right mindset about Communion and feet washing should overflow so as to permeate our every act of worship toward Him and service toward each other in our daily conduct. No less in life than in the associated celebration of these two events, our worship of God in Scripture strongly associates with our respect and service to each other. Jesus made that point in the lesson that He taught after washing the disciples' feet (John 13), and 1 John repeatedly emphasizes the same truth. I seek to show His death till He comes. May I serve you now?

40
"First of All" –
The Gospel's Top Priority

Moreover, brethren, I declare unto you the gospel which I preached unto you, which also ye have received, and wherein ye stand; By which also ye are saved, if ye keep in memory what I preached unto you, unless ye have believed in vain. For I delivered unto you first of all that which I also received, how that Christ died for our sins according to the scriptures; And that he was buried, and that he rose again the third day according to the scriptures: And that he was seen of Cephas, then of the twelve: After that, he was seen of above five hundred brethren at once; of whom the greater part remain unto this present, but some are fallen asleep. After that, he was seen of James; then of all the apostles. And last of all he was seen of me also, as of one born out of due time. For I am the least of the apostles, that am not meet to be called an apostle, because I persecuted the church of God. But by the grace of God I am what I am: and his grace which was bestowed upon me was not in vain; but I laboured more abundantly than they all: yet not I, but the grace of God which was with me. Therefore whether it were I or they, so we preach, and so ye believed. (1 Corinthians 15:1–11)

Listen to a dozen different preachers, and you'll likely think that a dozen different ideas are the most important segment of the gospel. Not only do modern non-Christians struggle with priorities, but Christians, even preachers, do as well. Paul strips away the veneer and takes us directly to the heart of the gospel in this chapter, including its most important and most foundational truth, "...first of all...."

Although at the time of Paul's writing 1 Corinthians, the Corinthian Church was confused and divided in conduct and in its beliefs, apparently at one time, when he first preached to them, they believed and were united, "...which also ye received." Even in their present disarray and confusion, they worked at standing in it as they should, "...wherein ye stand." They seem to have been staggering profoundly, but Paul kindly honors their effort.

"By which also ye are saved, if ye keep in memory what I preached unto you." Folks who see heaven in the Bible every time they read the word "saved" might have something of a problem with this verse. If you are saved only when you have the gospel prominently in your mind, your eternal destiny stands in frightening instability. You go to church on Sunday morning and hear a good sermon. It is in your mind. Heaven is yours. On Monday morning you walk into your office or place of business and face a surprising and complicated string of problems. You immerse your mind in solving them. You are so involved in those problems that you don't even think about lunch or much of anything else all day long. You definitely didn't keep your faith in memory during the day. Think. Stress is an insidious force to both our mind and our body. At three o'clock in the afternoon, the stress claims its prey. You have a massive heart attack and die. You didn't have your faith in Jesus and the resurrection in your mind at that moment. You were up to your neck trying to resolve your business problems. So, do you go to heaven or not? Are you "saved" or not? You were definitely not keeping Jesus and the resurrection in your mind at the moment of your death. If going to heaven when you die is what Paul intended by being saved in this verse, you just lost out, didn't you?

I suggest that being saved in this verse has nothing to do with going to heaven when you die. If so, heaven may be frighteningly underpopulated. Contemporary Christians need to rethink the Bible's use of "salvation." We would be wise and far more accurate in our understanding of Scripture if, when we see any form of "save" in a verse, we'd ask of the passage, "Saved from what?" "Saved by what or by whom?" "Saved to what or to whom?" "Saved how?" After all, some Bible contexts present salvation as an exclusive act of God alone, while others present it as something that we do in partnership with Him, but distinctly by our faithful action.

While Scripture uses this word across a very broad spectrum, we may logically break it down into two major categories. Given that populist Christianity is so fixated on going to heaven when we die when they read the word, we can distinguish the Bible's use of the word to those occasions when heaven and eternity really are its objective versus when the context is dealing with discipleship and temporal issues in the here and now. I suggest that few verses in the Bible, when interpreted in context, more clearly make the case for this approach than this verse. To force the idea of being saved only as we keep the gospel in our memory into going to heaven when we die borders on the nonsensical. To view the verse as relating to our peace of mind and to our present discipleship is altogether sensible and logical. More important, this idea matches the context in which Paul uses the word in the verse.

Paul follows his "...first of all" point with the leading theme of the gospel, as the New Testament teaches the gospel, "...how that Christ died for our sins according to the scriptures." Christians of every stripe will tell you their belief about Jesus and His death, but they each give you a different "take" on the "how" of His death. We need to go to Scripture for our answer to the "how" question, not to our private interpretations or beliefs.

From perhaps the most mundane perspective, you will often read in newspapers around Easter time the question, "Did the Romans or the Jews kill Jesus?" And the answers will vary according to the author's personal opinion. If we follow Scripture, we will discover two answers. First, based on their wicked motives, both Romans and Jews were charged with the crime. Secondly, and far more to the Biblical point, John 10:17-18 and similar passages remind us that no human on earth was capable of killing Jesus. He voluntarily gave Himself in death to the Father for our sins.

The greater point of the "how" of Jesus' death will take us in a different direction. Yes, He died on His own terms. But this point fails to adequately address the "how" question at all. He had no personal sin, so we can't say that He died for His own sins. Not only did He voluntarily give His life in death, but He also voluntarily came into this world as a man. "For I came down from heaven..." (John 6:38). No other person who ever lived chose his birth circumstance, but Jesus chose both His birth and His death circumstance. So the "how" of His death must lead us to ponder motives and objectives in Himself alone and not in those who hated and rejected Him.

"...for our sins." A primary definition of the Greek word translated "for" in this verse means "over, above, or in behalf of." I think of the mythical "Sword of Damocles." In the myth, the king, while apparently living in luxury actually lived under a large sword that hung directly over his head, suspended only by a horse hair. It could drop at any moment, and he would die. Not only did Jesus live under the weight of our sins, they actually fell on Him, and He took their legal and damning weight off of His people and onto Himself. He suffered at the hands of divine justice what we deserved so that we could realize the full outpouring of God's love and grace. When the sword of justice was suspended and ready to drop, He stood "over" us, between the sword and us, so that He, not we, suffered the death of its blow. This thought takes us far closer to the "how" of Jesus' death than any empty discussion of Roman or Jewish blame.

"...according to the Scriptures." At the time of his writing, Paul specifically refers to the Old Testament Scriptures. With this point in mind, I started this series in the Old Testament and spent significant time there before moving to the New Testament account of the actual event of "Jesus and the resurrection." Some scholars have documented two or three hundred different Old Testament passages that include some element of prophecy regarding Jesus and His coming. Some of them may be a brief reference. Others, Isaiah 53 for example, include a detailed account.

If you focus on the four gospels in the New Testament, specifically on their description of Jesus' activities during that last week in Jerusalem, including His death and resurrection, you will find more references to fulfilled Scripture than in any other portion of the New Testament. The single most powerful witness to Jesus' death (to the "how" of His death) available for our instruction is Scripture itself. Paul will go on to document the many eyewitnesses who saw Jesus in person after His resurrection, including over five hundred people who saw Him at one time, but, for Paul, and for us, if we think rightly, the most powerful witness to the "how" of Jesus' death is Scripture. When Jesus answered the unbelieving Sadducees' trap question about the resurrection (which they denied) He made this point. They erred based on two major flaws in their thinking. They did not know the Scriptures, and they did not know the power of God (Matthew 22:29). With these two flaws, they couldn't know anything about God correctly.

While Jesus' death is essential for our understanding of why He came and what He accomplished for us, we cannot stop at His death. After His death on the cross, He was buried in a borrowed tomb. Then He arose from the dead, no less literally, physically, or bodily than His death. Paul goes to great length to list those who were eyewitnesses of His resurrection. Do not overlook that Paul lists himself as an eyewitness of Jesus' resurrection. A likely reference to his Damascus Road experience, Paul didn't merely have a mental experience, but he also literally saw Jesus so that he, despite being late in his arrival on the scene of believers, could legitimately include himself as yet one more eyewitness of Jesus' life, death, and resurrection.

When a Navy officer wants to call all of his people together for something important, supposedly he uses the command, "All hands on deck." When God prepared His people for the news of Jesus and the resurrection, for those men whom He had chosen to be His personal eyewitnesses of this central fact of the gospel, He issued His own "All hands on deck." He gave Paul an untimely revelation of Himself in resurrection. He sent word to then-absent Peter, "...and Peter" (Mark 16:7), so very soon after Peter had publicly denied even knowing Him.

Paul briefly, but in compelling words, includes in this passage an account of how this knowledge of Jesus and the resurrection impacted his life. Folks, you can't believe in Jesus and the resurrection and not be changed, wondrously so, by the knowledge. Are you and I showing by our personal conduct that we truly believe this truth? Does our life manifest to those around us that we believe Him to be alive and ruling on heaven's throne?

41
Beliefs Have Consequences

Now if Christ be preached that he rose from the dead, how say some among you that there is no resurrection of the dead? But if there be no resurrection of the dead, then is Christ not risen: And if Christ be not risen, then is our preaching vain, and your faith is also vain. Yea, and we are found false witnesses of God; because we have testified of God that he raised up Christ: whom he raised not up, if so be that the dead rise not. For if the dead rise not, then is not Christ raised: And if Christ be not raised, your faith is vain; ye are yet in your sins. Then they also which are fallen asleep in Christ are perished. If in this life only we have hope in Christ, we are of all men most miserable. (1 Corinthians 15:12–19)

In the last study, we noted that Paul refers to the Corinthian Church by the commendable clause, "...wherein ye stand" regarding the resurrection. However, as we examine our present study, we realize that some members of the Church at Corinth had departed from the faith and embraced the errant denial of the resurrection.

How does Paul deal with this schism in the church? Rather than ignore it or, commonplace in contemporary churches, protest, "Oh, but he is such a good brother," Paul exposes and rejects the error no less directly than he rejects the moral error of chapter 5.

The problem with doctrinal error has nothing to do with a person's personality. Often the wildest heretics have the most winsome personalities. Otherwise folks wouldn't give their heresies the time of day. The issue is quite simple. Do they stand in the truth or not? Scripture emphasizes that believers in a local church or in a common fellowship should agree in their faith and spiritual conduct (Romans 12:16; 1 Corinthians 1:10; Philippians 2:2, 3:16, 4:2; Ephesians 4:5, 13-16). Paul, Peter, and John all give us inspired and rather simple, detailed instructions regarding how to reject error or, when it invades the church, repel it. After godly admonition, you avoid the person (Romans 16:17-18; Titus 3:9-11). You do not engage him in endless debate and ungodly wrangling.

Folks who engage in errant beliefs and choose to live in conflict with brothers and sisters who are supposed to share a common faith, tend to add ever-increasing ethical compromise to their error. They seek to gain disciples to their ideas, and they often will work deceitfully to do so. Jesus confronted this sinful conduct (Matthew 23:15). So should we.

Scripture speaks with emphatic clarity about this schismatic attitude and conduct (Proverbs 6:16-19).[1] People who choose to compromise their ethics often put themselves on a moral "slippery slope" on which they sink deeper and deeper into their questionable ideas and conduct, a point that Scripture affirms and warns the godly believer to avoid. Review each of the "same mind" passages listed above. Example: years ago I knew a man who strongly believed and defended the doctrines of grace. Over time he abandoned these doctrines and became, by his own confession, a Gnostic. However, despite his reversal of beliefs, he thought that everyone who had formerly respected him should treat him as if he had not at all changed his beliefs.

...how say some among you that there is no resurrection of the dead? Here we discover that some, possibly only a few, of the Corinthian folks were not in fact standing in that sound truth that Paul had preached to them and that Scripture affirmed. They utterly rejected him and his teachings. Instead of affirming the foundational truth of Jesus and the resurrection, they remained in the church while claiming that there was no resurrection of the dead at all. At this point, Paul begins methodically to expose these errant beliefs to the grim reality of their implications. One cannot embrace an idea and ignore or avoid the logical and inevitable consequences of that error. So Paul begins to reason. If in fact there is no resurrection, what are the consequences that these people must face?

---

[1] Scripture reserves the idea of God hating people to a careful few, but it includes this person in the list.

1. *Jesus did not rise from the dead.* He is the power and cause of the resurrection for the child of grace. If there is no resurrection, you can't avoid facing that every tenet of the gospel that proclaims and builds on His resurrection is false. If your gospel is false, why do you bother to claim it and to embrace it at all?
2. *Our preaching is vain, empty and meaningless.* Why preach a fantasy and claim it to be true?
3. *Your faith is vain.* What part of Biblical truth stands independent of Jesus and His resurrection? How about none of it? None whatever. Every aspect of your faith is empty if Jesus didn't rise from the dead.
4. *Paul and every other gospel preacher is a false witness.* We all proclaim that God raised Jesus from the dead, the centerpiece of our proclamation. If He did not arise, we are false witnesses.
5. *Your faith is vain.* Paul repeats the previous point. The Corinthians needed this emphasis. They simply could not claim to be godly, faithful believers in Christ while denying the most foundational truth of His Person and work.
6. *You are yet in your sins.* Talk about consequences. If Jesus didn't arise from the dead, you still have a sin problem with no solution whatever. How do you expect to resolve that problem without Jesus? You can't, so deal with the reality that it imposes on you.
7. *Loved ones who have died have perished.* If Jesus didn't arise from the dead, we have no evidence and no hope of any life after death. To borrow the cliché, you are like your pet dog Rover, "dead all over."
8. The capstone of error. *You are the most miserable of people alive.* If you claim to be a Christian and to hold membership in a Christian church, but you reject this bedrock truth, you effectively claim to believe in Jesus as a man, not as God manifest in the flesh, much less risen victoriously from death, so your belief makes you literally the most miserable person imaginable. To borrow the logical inconsistency of dressing up a dead atheist for his funeral, you are all dressed up with no where to go.

Paul hardly ends his list of consequences with these points, but he gets our attention with them.

...how say some among you...? Paul confronts the inconsistency in the error that these people in the Corinthian Church had embraced and obviously were attempting to spread among the membership to the extent that even Paul at a distance away became aware of their ideas. We do not live in the age of apostles. There is no Paul or John today to confront a church wherever error may erupt. Sadly, there are occasionally "wannabe" apostles who attempt to take such usurped authority to themselves and to work to impose their unorthodox ideas onto any and all people whom they happen to know. It has been my observation that they typically and very carefully choose to work out of the local pastor's awareness among weaker members in the faith whom they may influence to follow them and their ideas. Plant the seed and encourage the weak-in-the-faith member to quietly spread the error when the pastor isn't around. Scripture never approves of deceit (Proverbs 6:16-19 leaves no doubt about God's view of this conduct).

If we accept that no apostles are alive today, we logically must conclude that each local church is a separate entity, accountable to the Lord for her conduct, not to political mob bosses who work behind the scenes to control everyone they know. And each church with her members should work harder at maintaining local harmony in the church than at following anyone outside that church.

Over the years, as I have studied such passages as mentioned above from Romans 16 and Titus 3, I've pondered how precisely to deal with those who work at spreading their error within a fellowship of churches. My conclusion is that both passages give precise instructions to each local church, instructions that each church should follow when confronting and rejecting error, regardless the source of the error that invades their number. One church and her pastor can't control what another church and pastor do, but they are responsible, responsible to God, for what they do. Within the church, they should practice these verses simply and consistently. Often folks who invest in promoting error do so with much ego and pride. The best way to starve sinful pride is to simply ignore it.

In dealing with the moral issue in 1 Corinthians 5, Paul uses a principle that as fully applies to doctrinal error as to immoral conduct, "...a little leaven leaveneth the whole lump" (1 Corinthians 5:6). In bread dough, you introduce yeast (leaven) to the solution in one area, but very quickly the leaven permeates the whole mass of dough. Paul warns that error imitates leaven. Thus, he never teaches that a church dealing with those in error should merely ignore them and hope they go away or do not cause lasting harm. He does not attack the person. The personality is not an issue. He does attack and reject the error for it is the issue.

If we consider the idea of resurrection (literally, coming back to life and, in the case of Biblical resurrection, being glorified and taken into timeless eternity to consciously know the Lord's presence and to be aware of and to praise God for our personal redemption - Revelation 5:9), the idea transcends the human mind to grasp. On occasion when preaching a funeral and teaching on the resurrection to comfort the family, I have observed the skeptical body language of people from the medical community who were in the audience. I also, however, rejoice to have known a good number of physicians who were devoted believers who rejoiced in this truth. Luke, the inspired New Testament writer, was a physician.

You and I have hope of resurrection on one and only one basis, Jesus and His own resurrection. Our belief of that truth cannot originate from our natural mind. We come to believe in the resurrection from the evidence set forth in Scripture, affirmed by the witness of the Holy Spirit within (Romans 8:19-23). Do not miss that Paul's first and "star" witness to the resurrection at the beginning of this chapter is "...according to the scriptures." Paul repeats this point in verses 3 and 4.

Think about his reasoning. You have multiple eyewitnesses of an event, including over five hundred people who collectively witnessed it. Not only so, but you are also an eyewitness of the event. However, when you set forth your case for others to consider, hoping that they will also believe it, your first witness is the writings of Scripture, not one or even all of these eyewitnesses. They all serve as supporting witnesses to the primary testimony of the written record of Scripture. Scripture is not the only witness, but Paul makes the case that it is his first witness.

After thoroughly rejecting the errant denial of the resurrection within the Corinthian Church, Paul turns the negative factor of their denial into an occasion to preach the positive truth of the resurrection, outlining this truth thoroughly and simply for the Corinthians and for us. While direct and uncompromising in his confrontation of those who held to the errant idea, Paul seeks to gain them, not alienate them. Obviously, they need to repent and to abandon their errant beliefs, and they need to stop advocating their error to others in the church, "…how say some among you…?"

In the end, requiring that people face the consequences of their ideas, good or bad, is an essential strategy in exposing error, exposing it to those in the error so that you give them good reason to abandon it and embrace the truth. Study 1 Corinthians 15 in terms of consequences of belief. First, go through the chapter and list the many consequences of believing in no resurrection. Then go back over the chapter and list the many consequences of believing in the resurrection, beginning with Jesus and His resurrection. If you reasonably compare the two lists of consequences, there is no real contest at all. Think of just one consequence that Paul mentions.

1. If in this life only we have hope in Christ, we are of all men most miserable.
2. Now restate the opposite premise, the truth that Paul preaches. If in this life and in contemplating the life to come, we have hope in Christ, we are of all men most joyful, hopeful, and blessed.

No less real than Job's self-reminder, we should ever encourage a fruitful and believing mind toward this glorious Biblical truth. Job thought of a tree in its dormant season. It looks dry and lifeless. But, when the spring sun begins to warm the soil and the spring showers water it, you begin to see new buds of life and vitality sprout out from the tree's branches. Surely, reasons Job, there is far more hope for us with our loving, merciful God than for a tree in the forest (Job 14).

I choose the inspired and true words of Paul. I believe in Jesus and the resurrection, a very literal, physical, bodily resurrection that shall transform my present frail body into a new form (same body; better form) suitable for praising my God for His merciful love and grace throughout an endless and joyful eternity. How about you, Pilgrim? Will you join me on this joyful path?

42
He Arose! He Lives! Literally.

*But now is Christ risen from the dead, and become the firstfruits of them
that slept. For since by man came death, by man came also the
resurrection of the dead. For as in Adam all die, even so in Christ shall all
be made alive. But every man in his own order: Christ the firstfruits;
afterward they that are Christ's at his coming.* (1 Corinthians 15:20–23)

Given the severity of errantly denying the resurrection among
some in the Corinthian Church, Paul promptly refutes the error
and moves to the positive and documented truth of Jesus'
resurrection. First and foremost, the gospel deals with facts, not
fantasy or imagination. Just as Paul has dealt with the consequences
of denying the resurrection, he now deals with the glorious
consequences of the truth of the resurrection.

Despite contemporary human-centric ideas that a church should
be a "free for all" of debated ideas, often the idea supported by the
smoothest, or loudest, speaker prevailing, Scripture teaches that a
church is to be a body of believers who cohesively believe the same
things (Ephesians 1:3). Whenever you see doctrinal disagreement in
the New Testament, you see major problems, problems that a wise
and godly church should strive to avoid.

...firstfruits of them that slept. "Firstfruits" links the thought with
the firstfruits sacrifice under the Old Testament Law. A farmer
would gather the first ripe shoots from his crop and offer them to the
Lord. God deserves the first priority of our life's effort, not the left-
overs, a sound reminder to us from the Old Testament. The hope
was if God accepts the firstfruit offering, He will bless with a good
harvest. Regardless the final harvest, God deserved the firstfruits.

In the setting of Paul's teaching on the resurrection, the point
powerfully affirms the reality of the final resurrection of the Lord's
beloved family in precisely the same literal way that Jesus arose

from the dead to die no more. And the same assurance comes to us in Jesus' resurrection as to the Old Testament farmer. If God accepted the firstfruits from the dead, the Lord Jesus Christ, He gives us promise that He shall also accept the final harvest, "Behold I and the children which God hath given me..." (Hebrews 2:13).

The point of firstfruits is not one of time, but of importance. Enoch was taken bodily from the earth, as was Elijah. There is indirect indication that Moses may also have been resurrected and taken bodily to heaven; he appeared with Elijah on the mount of transfiguration, and we have the brief reference to the dispute over his body in Jude. We find occasional references to bodily resurrections in the Old Testament, along with a number of resurrections that Jesus performed during His ministry, including Lazarus (John 11). Other than Enoch and Elijah, possibly Moses, the other resurrections were back to a temporary time in this life. But we do have at the least two men whose bodies were taken to heaven prior to the time of Jesus' bodily resurrection and ascension. Despite their arrival in glory prior to Jesus' bodily resurrection and ascension, they could not be the official "firstfruits" of them that slept, for their resurrection was not brought about by their own power or purity. Jesus alone stands out as the exclusive "firstfruits" of resurrection in terms of modeling the final ingathering of all the elect.

For since by man came death, by man came also the resurrection of the dead. Paul here states a foundational truth of the gospel. Whatever God's chosen people lost in Adam, Jesus regained and secured so that it could not again fall into jeopardy. Of course, Jesus gained far more for His elect than we lost in Adam—"...double for all her sins" (Isaiah 40:2). We should never stop with thinking that Jesus merely regained what Adam lost.

A thorough study of Genesis 3 will indicate that "death" had more than one meaning in that context. God warned Adam that he would face the consequences of his sin "...in the day that thou eatest thereof" (Genesis 2:17). As we move into Genesis 3 and read the account of Adam's actual sin, we discover that Adam didn't die a literal or physical death on the day that he ate the forbidden fruit.

He actually died several hundred years later. What did happen on that same day that he ate the forbidden fruit? He died to his innocence with God. He died to his comfortable fellowship with God. Instead of comfortably and joyfully anticipating his afternoon "stroll" with God in the Garden, he now feared God's appearance. For the first time in Scripture, the emotion of fear appears in the record: "I was afraid" (Genesis 3:10). Prior to his eating the forbidden fruit, we see no indication in Scripture that Adam in any way feared his time with God each afternoon in the Garden.

Why was Adam afraid? What changed? While Adam didn't die a physical death on that same day, there can be no doubt that he died that day. It is not accidental that Paul refers to the Lord's reversing our sinful fallen state in Adam with similar words that also appeal to the analogy of life and death. "And you hath he quickened, who were dead in trespasses and sins" (Ephesians 2:1).

It seems right and fitting that the source of the colossal problem of sin should also be the source of the remedy. However, Adam, now dead to God, can't step up to the task. And since we were also dead in trespasses and sins, we couldn't accomplish the work. One and only one man, the Lord Jesus Christ, could and did remove the stain and the death itself of our sins by His work, including His death and resurrection (1 Timothy 2:5; notice the specific reference to "...*the man* Christ Jesus").

Occasionally sincere Christians will engage in friendly debate over the length of time that Jesus was in the grave. Did He die on Friday afternoon and rise early Sunday morning, a portion of three days, sometimes reckoned by the Jews as three days? Since the Jews reckoned each day as indicated in Genesis 1, the day beginning at 6:00 P. M., a full three day and three night duration requires a Wednesday afternoon death and burial near the 6:00 P. M. transition. On Thursday, Friday, and Saturday, He is in the tomb, in death. And then sometime between 6:00 P. M. on Saturday and 6:00 A. M. on Sunday morning, He arises. Whether Jesus was dead for bare portions of three days (the Friday death view) or three full days (the Wednesday death view), He literally died, and He literally arose from the dead.

Paul ignores this question, but he affirms the literal reality of Jesus' death and resurrection. He literally, actually died. His body experienced literal, real death. But the faithful record of Scripture fills out the account. His body also experienced literal, real resurrection from death. "Why seek ye the living among the dead?" (Luke 24:5). Man, Adam, first brought death upon himself and his offspring. Man, Jesus Christ, just as literally brought life, resurrection life, to Himself and to His offspring.

But every man in his own order: Christ the firstfruits; afterward they that are Christ's at his coming. Just as the firstfruits sacrifice distinguished between the first ripe clusters and the final harvest, Paul follows the analogy. And just as the Old Testament farmer hoped for a final blessed harvest as he offered the firstfruit sheaves, Paul affirms that God has guaranteed the final "reesurrection" harvest in Jesus' resurrection. While we inherit the accomplishments of Jesus' death and resurrection, we fall in the order of harvest, not firstfruits.

...afterward they that are Christ's at his coming. Paul's point deals with ownership, with possession: *...they that are Christ's.* When Jesus died, He died to purchase a people, the point made in the Bible doctrine of redemption. Those people were held captive under a legal debt. Jesus paid their debt in full and thereby freed them from that old debt. He didn't merely make a partial payment or offer to pay their debt. He actually and fully paid it. They no longer owe a single penny against that debt.

Occasionally you will hear the idea that Jesus died for the sin debt of all humanity, but He didn't die for their specific sin of unbelief, so, unless you believe, you remain indebted to God and doomed to eternal separation. You only gain freedom from that sentence by your decision to believe. This idea builds on the concept of partial payment. It stops distinctly short of the Biblical teaching of payment in full by Jesus. Paul doesn't so much as imply that resurrection shall bless those that "mostly" or "almost" belong to Christ at His coming. They belong fully to Him. He paid for all their sins, none excepted.

Which is the earnest of our inheritance until the redemption of the purchased possession, unto the praise of his glory. (Ephesians 1:14)

Paul's point is clear. There is a purchased possession, fully purchased. We now enjoy the loving mercy of the earnest of that final inheritance, though the Lord shall not stop until all of that purchased possession is redeemed, a reference to their (our) bodily resurrection at the Second Coming. Based on Paul's words in this passage, we cannot make any numerical distinction between the number of those "purchased" by Jesus and His "redemption" of them at His Second Coming. All of those whom He "purchased" shall be "redeemed" from death and the grave to live with Him in glory for eternity. Hallelujah! What a Savior!

Augustus Toplady wrote a beautiful poem that addresses this Biblical truth.

It Pleased the Lord to Bruise Him
August Toplady

From whence this fear and unbelief?
Did not the Father put to grief
His spotless Son for me?
And will the righteous judge of men,
Condemn me for that debt of sin,
Which Lord was charg'd on thee?

Complete atonement thou hast made,
And to the utmost farthing paid,
Whate'er thy people ow'd:
Nor can his wrath on me take place,
If shelter'd in thy righteousness,
And ransomed by thy blood.

If thou hast my discharge procur'd,
And in the sinner's room endur'd,

The whole of wrath divine:
Payment he cannot twice demand,
First at my bleeding surety's hand,
And then again at mine.

If thou for me hast purchas'd faith
By thy obedience unto death,
He must the grace bestow:
Would Israel's God a price receive,
And not the purchas'd blessing give?
His justice answers, No!

Turn then, my soul, unto thy rest;
The merits of thy great High Priest,
Have bought thy liberty:
Trust to his efficacious blood,
Nor fear thy banishment from God,
Since Jesus died for thee.

43
Redemption's Final Scene

*Then cometh the end, when he shall have delivered up the kingdom to God,
even the Father; when he shall have put down all rule and all authority
and power. For he must reign, till he hath put all enemies under his feet.
The last enemy that shall be destroyed is death. For he hath put all things
under his feet. But when he saith, all things are put under him, it is
manifest that he is excepted, which did put all things under him. And when
all things shall be subdued unto him, then shall the Son also himself be
subject unto him that put all things under him, that God may be all in all.*
(1 Corinthians 15:24–28)

Then cometh the end.... When folks leave Scripture and attempt
to describe the final chapter of God's work, volumes of
muddled and confusing complexity result. Try making sense of a
discussion between folks who hold to the various views of
dispensationalism. Will the "rapture" occur before, during, or after
the "Great Tribulation"? You might as well try to make sense out of
a discussion about how many angels can fit on the point of a needle.
When God describes His final redemption chapter in Scripture, He
simplifies the revelation. The most obvious difference between the
complexity of human theories and God's revelation stands out in this
passage. Human ideas focus (no surprise) on humans. God's
revelation emphasizes God, just as it should.

Multiple passages reveal that the Father assigned the role of
active dominion to Jesus (Matthew 11:27; 28:18; John 3:35; as
examples). This lesson tells us that Jesus returns to the Father what
the Father assigned to Him, and He returns it with His seal of
"mission accomplished." Sometimes folks tend to mystify this
passage, but it is no more mystical than those many passages that
reveal the Father's commitment of present rule to His Son.

The idea is one of function, not of any change in God's essence or being. God doesn't change. How many passages remind us? But the dynamic of the Son's present dominion over creation, including the Father's chosen spiritual "creation" (2 Corinthians 5:17), is in fact "dynamic" and active. In this present superintendence over His creation, both natural and spiritual, Jesus actively interacts with it, and especially with His chosen people and their needs, but in all of this interaction, He never alters His essential nature. He brings that nature to bear on His interaction, always to the benefit of His beloved people.

God's essential unchangeableness always appears in Scripture as a supreme blessing to His people (Malachi 3:6). Imagine a being all-powerful but void of a fixed moral character. All-powerful fickle gives no comfort!

Occasionally folks who believe in an excessive, fatalistic view of God's sovereignty senselessly wrestle with the idea of answered prayer. If God is unchangeable, how can He answer prayer—prayer that changes things in our lives—and remain unchangeable? The question is a classical example of logical fallacy thinking. It shifts the focus from God to God's creation and tries to impose change in God's creation back onto God. God remains the same while actively, graciously, and dynamically interacting with His people and His creation for the aid of His beloved children. Does God answering prayer according to His loving grace and mercy in any way alter His love and mercy? Not at all. In fact, answering prayer in this way is essential to the traits of His love and mercy. He would not fully manifest or employ those traits if He did not so use them.

Too much fatalism needlessly complicates what Scripture simply declares for the comfort and peace of the Lord's beloved children. Fatalism is a trait that belongs to pagan false gods, not to the one true and living God whom we serve, the God whom Scripture reveals to us. Pagan gods are often carved of stone and are impersonal and not at all interactive in any way with their surroundings. Why degrade the God of the Bible into one more impersonal and non-interactive piece of stone? If Scripture categorically declares that God hears and answers the prayers of His people, what is the confusion or the debate? He does just what Scripture declares that He does, and His doing so in no way compromises Him or His attributes.

...*he must reign till*.... Notice the obvious point in these words. Jesus reigns. He reigns right now. His reign is not presently suspended, awaiting rapture or anything else. He reigns! And that present reign shall continue till every enemy, every being or thing in existence that opposes Him, has been defeated.

That God reigns does not imply that God therefore actively causes and/or orchestrates every event that occurs. It means that there is none above Him, none to whom He must answer, and none who can supersede Him in what He does choose to do in His dominion.

Consider a simple example. I grew up on a small farm where my family grew cows, pigs, and other farm animals. My father was the ruler over his farm. He chose which portions of the farm to fence off for the cows, which portion to fence off for the pigs, and the chickens. Dad provided within these areas everything that the animals needed for their wellbeing. If one of his cows chose to eat green grass at 9:35 A. M. in the morning, Dad didn't step in and force the cow to do something else. And if another cow chose to go down to the brook and get a drink of water at exactly that same time, Dad didn't interfere. However, when one of our cows decided to break out of the fenced pasture and start eating the growing corn plants, Dad did interfere and put the cow back into her assigned place.

Scripture teaches a similar role, though obviously far more complex, in God's governance of His universe. "Hitherto shalt thou come, but no further..." (Job 38:11); "...the **bounds** of their habitations" (Acts 17:26). When James reminds us to think of our plans for the future with "if the Lord will..." the point is the same.

Typically, fatalists practice the logical fallacy of excluded middle or, in the older terminology, the horns of the dilemma. According to this flawed and illogical thinking, you must either believe that God actively causes everything that occurs, or you must believe that He causes nothing, making you "a virtual deist." Scripture refutes both errant ideas. God doesn't cause everything that occurs.

For he performeth the thing that is appointed for me: and many such things are with him (Job 23:14). In this one verse, God refutes the fatalist who claims that God causes everything that occurs, along with the fatalist's illogical fallacy that anyone who disagrees with him is a "virtual deist." There are certain "things" that the Lord has graciously appointed for each of His beloved children. In those "things," the Lord faithfully performs what He has appointed. If God caused all things that occur, "many such things" would be insufficient to state the case; the language should have been "all things...." And the passage refutes the fatalist's false charge of "virtual deist" against his detractors by "...many such things are with him." He did not write "...a few such things," but "many."

For all that is in the world, the lust of the flesh, and the lust of the eyes, and the pride of life, is not of the Father, but is of the world (1 John 2:16). John categorically refutes that everything in the world, specifically sin and sinful things, originated with God.

Scripture ignores both the fatalist and his false charge, firmly occupying the ignored middle ground in the fatalist's logical fallacy. God is intimately involved in the lives of His children. When we face trials or needs beyond our ability, He is present to comfort, to guide, and to strengthen us in our weakness.

Based on Scripture's consistent teaching, God governs His universe as its Moral Governor, not as its cosmic puppeteer. When God created Adam, He gave Adam a moral commandment, including a warning of consequences should Adam chose to ignore His moral commandment and eat the forbidden fruit. As He prepared His people for their life outside of Egypt, He gave Moses a code of Ten Commandments to govern and to enlighten their conduct. In Scripture, God gives His Law, His commandments, and He "commands" His people to obey. He always informs us with knowledge of both blessings in obedience and judgments or consequences in disobedience. We choose the blessing or the judgment when we choose to either obey or disobey.

Fatalists have a problem with their idea that God causes all things, so they occasionally try to also claim they deny that He causes sin. Simply, He can't cause all things and not cause sin. When challenged to explain sin in the life of a child of God, they typically plead that "when left to ourselves, we can only sin..." claiming that God occasionally "leaves us to ourselves" to teach us a greater lesson.

In this claim, the fatalist violates multiple Biblical truths. First, Scripture repeatedly affirms that the Lord does not leave us to ourselves, but that He is always present, "...never leave thee...." Secondly, Scripture affirms that God in the new birth alters our being so that we now possess His Law in our hearts and minds, and that we now possess the ability to believe and to obey Him, abilities that we did not formerly possess. In effect, the fatalist denies any change whatever in the new birth. Thirdly, the fatalist's false idea that God either causes or allows our sin to accomplish a greater good is directly contradicted by Paul in Romans 3:1-8. Paul repeatedly affirms that imputing the orchestration notion of a greater good imposes direct complicity onto God for sin, leaving God in the seat of accused, and not in the seat of righteous Judge. Paul assesses this idea as a slander against his teaching, not as a right explanation of his teaching.

Scripture affirms that God is the Moral Governor of His universe, and that He always governs His universe according to His revealed and stated moral Law. His moral governance also teaches that He holds man accountable for his conduct, so the notion that man merely acts out what God causes, puppeteer-like, contradicts Scripture's holding man personally accountable to God and responsible himself for his sins.

...then shall the Son also himself be subject unto him that put all things under him, that God may be all in all. This expression often causes much discussion. The first step to eliminate the confusion is to take note of what the passage states, and what it does not state.

I earlier cited some passages that indicate that the Father has assigned present dominion to the Son. When the Father so assigned this dominion to the Son, neither the Father nor the Son were in any way personally or essentially altered. God remained God, unchanged and unchangeable. So why do we ignore this point and impose a dilemma onto this passage that the passage doesn't require? If neither Father nor Son were altered when the Father made the assignment to the Son, why think that either Father or Son will be altered when the Son returns what was assigned to Him back to the Father?

The point of the passage deals with a specific function that the Father assigned to the Son, and now the Son returns to the Father. The idea of "function" deals with what God does, not with His personal and essential Being. He functions as loving, and sometimes chastening Father to His children. He functions as Judge against the wicked. These various functions in no way alter who God is. They deal with what He does. And this is the point of the passage before us.

The careful and deliberate use of "Son" in this verse leads our thinking. Even though Scripture uses the term in a way that far exceeds the Incarnation, it uses the term to identify a certain function or work. When Scripture refers to Him in His deity, it uses the term "Word." When Scripture uses "Son" to refer to Jesus' deity, you will find "...of God" associated with "Son." A simple observation that this verse in no way indicates that the "Word" shall be subject to the Father should resolve our self-imposed dilemma.

God, expressed in Scripture as God or Father, Word, and Holy Spirit, remains unchanged and unchangeable after the "Son" returns the dominion assigned to Him to the Father. The function of Son, the assignment of redemption and atonement being fully completed, and the purchased possession being fully restored to the Father's loving embrace, the function is fulfilled. That function then is subjected. God (God, Word, and Holy Spirit), all in all, victorious, praised for endless eternity, and immutable in His Being, is then fully seen as God!

Consider 1 Timothy 2:5: "For there is one God, and one mediator between God and men, the man Christ Jesus." Since the role of Mediator has been fully completed successfully at the Second Coming and the bodily resurrection to glory of all the elect is accomplished, that function unique to Mediator, to "...*the man* Christ Jesus," is accomplished. Therefore, that function shall cease in full harmony with and declared to be so by His success, God shall be "...all in all."

It is significant that this final punctuating note of completion does not occur until after the resurrection. In fact, Scripture associates "redemption" with the resurrection (Hosea 13:14; 1 Corinthians 15:55-56; Ephesians 1:14). God's work of redemption remains unfinished until He has fully claimed the bodies of His beloved children that He purchased when He paid the price of our redemption. When He raises our bodies and glorifies them in the likeness of His beloved Son, only then shall redemption be completed. Redemption's price was fully paid in Jesus' death. It will be completed when God fully claims and takes possession of the last vestige of His "...purchased possession." He paid for this possession, and He shall not punctuate the final chapter of redemption till He claims what He purchased and takes it to Himself in eternal glory. What a Savior!

44
Baptized for Whom?

*Else what shall they do which are baptized for the dead, if the dead rise not
at all? why are they then baptized for the dead?* (1 Corinthians 15:29)

For whom are we baptized? Who is the centerpiece of this entire
chapter? What does baptism depict? Whether we accept the
opening verses of Romans 6 as referring to water baptism or
something else, the analogy of baptism prevails. And what does Paul
associate baptism with in this lesson? The answer is Jesus' death,
burial, and resurrection.

In water baptism, necessarily full bodily immersion in water[1], we
depict our personal belief in Jesus' death, burial, and resurrection
from the dead, and we profess our faith in Him and in His work as
the complete and exclusive remedy for our sins. So in a very real
sense, Paul teaches that water baptism relates specifically to Jesus'
death, burial, and resurrection.

Thus, if someone in a New Testament church does not believe in
the resurrection, he has lost all reason for his being baptized. If you
do not believe in the resurrection, you do not believe in Jesus'
resurrection. And if you do not believe in His resurrection, you have
no basis whatever for allowing anyone to baptize you in water.
Your unbelief in the resurrection leaves you with no logical reason
to submit yourself to water baptism. It is this point that Paul is
making in the context of the verse and in the flow of the greater
lesson of 1 Corinthians 15.

Some commentaries suggest that the idea of surrogate baptism
was believed and practiced by a few people in the Corinthian
Church. Nothing in the verse in any way suggests this idea. Paul

---

[1] The most reliable New Testament Greek dictionaries, even those compiled by
men who practiced sprinkling, consistently define the Greek word translated
"baptize" in the New Testament as immersion.

refers to "they" who are baptized for the dead. Other commentaries refer to a small pagan religion in the Greek peninsula who did practice surrogate baptism and hold that Paul was refuting their practice. I suggest that neither interpretation holds strong support in this verse. Paul would hardly bother to raise or refute every pagan idea that existed in his day.

He wrote the Corinthian letter with a pastor's heart (or, more correctly, an apostle's heart). Every error that Paul raises and refutes or rebukes throughout the letter was a practice that was being entertained by at least some people in the Corinthian Church. I suggest that Paul's reference to "they" has to do with a broad practice that, if believed and practiced, must rely on Jesus' death, burial and resurrection, or it has no Biblical support at all for its observance. Presumably everyone in the Corinthian Church had been baptized. If some of them now rejected the resurrection, they had no factual or truth basis for that baptism. Why did they submit to a rite that built its very existence on something that they did not believe? They reduced themselves to hypocrites who did something that they did not personally believe in. They could not answer Paul's "Why?" question at all.

Two aberrant ideas need brief mention. One group of professing Christians claims that the verse teaches surrogate baptism, meaning that they believe you, a living believer, can actually be baptized as a surrogate for dead relatives who died not baptized, and your baptism imputes the merits of your baptism to them, as if they had been baptized. When we examine this verse in its broad context of Paul's fifty-plus verses on the resurrection, we find no support and no reference to surrogate baptism at all. To isolate this verse from its context and impose this meaning onto it ignores and in fact contradicts its contextual setting and meaning. Would Paul devote over fifty verses focused on the centrality of Jesus' resurrection as the exclusive basis for our resurrection to glory and then devote a single verse to believer's surrogate baptism? The idea has no logical or contextual support. It must ignore context and view this one verse as if it stands alone and not in a broad contextual flow.

The second errant idea is more indirect, but I mention it only because it suggests that what you or I do can be imputed to another person as merit for their eternal salvation. I refer to the Roman Catholic idea of purgatory. According to this teaching, you may do something, typically write a check to the church for a tidy sum of money, and thereby effectively "buy" your dead loved-one out of an imaginary intermediate state of punishment. The idea of purgatory didn't exist, even within Roman Catholic doctrine, prior to Augustine, roughly four centuries too late to be a New Testament doctrine.

Further, both ideas patently rely on the doctrine of human works for eternal salvation. In fact, both ideas rely on the idea that one human being is capable of acting as a personal mediator and substitute for another person's sins. In effect, both ideas promote a mortal human to the role of Savior that Jesus alone holds in Scripture. In effect, a human is elevated to the same level as Jesus and is credited with substitute work on behalf of another that puts away that other person's sins. Paul emphatically writes words that refute and contradict both ideas at their foundation.

For there is one God, and one mediator between God and men, the man Christ Jesus. (1 Timothy 2:5)

How many gods does Paul acknowledge? One? Yes, only one. How many mediators does Paul acknowledge? One? Yes, one and only one. No mortal, regardless of time or place born, regardless of ancestry, and regardless of personal conduct, can supplant, replace, or even assist "the man Christ Jesus" as the one and only one mediator between God and men.

No, Mary fails that test. In fact, in her song of praise to God before Jesus' birth, she stated her joy in "...God my Savior." Mary was not a savior. She needed a Savior, and she knew who her Savior was (Luke 1:47). Take note. Mary did not think of herself as an intermediary between God and men. She thought of herself as a mortal sinner who had been supremely blessed with a Savior whom she praised for her present blessing. Both ideas utterly lack Biblical support and must therefore be rejected. Further, both ideas contradict Paul's teaching that Jesus alone is the one mediator between God and men. He quite sufficiently fills that role so that there is no need whatever for any other.

...if the dead rise not at all. Rather than thinking of these words as an exclusive look into the future and doing something to ensure the resurrection of others, Paul points backward to the one and only historical resurrection that had already occurred. If the dead rise not at all, then Jesus did not rise. Forget about anyone's future resurrection. The idea is false and hopeless if Jesus didn't already rise from the dead. Paul's emphasis throughout this chapter builds on Jesus and His personal resurrection.

Review Paul's eight consequences that the Corinthians must face if Jesus didn't arise from the dead. What is the state of your faith and our preaching if Jesus didn't arise? To ignore this foundation and impose the novel idea of using the term to refer to people who are now dead and to a believer being baptized as a surrogate on behalf of that person utterly ignores and contradicts Paul's teaching in the whole chapter. If we reject that Jesus arose, everything about our faith is a farce and leaves us "...of all men most miserable." And, following Paul's reasoning, if Jesus didn't arise from the dead, why does any believer accept the idea of water baptism as a public statement of their faith in Jesus and His resurrection?

This verse imposes a powerful example onto our thinking. We've examined the negative and errant idea. Think about the implications of Paul's words in this verse on your life. Do you believe in Jesus and in His resurrection? Do you believe that He alone is the one true mediator with God for you? Have you been baptized? If not, why? On what logical basis do you believe in Jesus and the resurrection, but decline to show by your personal act that you so believe? If you believe that His ultimate sacrifice was for you and that His ultimate victory was equally for you, should you not manifest that belief by a personal act that shows your belief in Him and in His resurrection?

The casual attitude of believers in our day contradicts the example of first century believers. "Here is water. What doth hinder...?" The danger of persecution did not dampen their faith, but pride and the alluring notion of living with one foot in the kingdom of God and one foot in the world effectively hinders contemporary believers. Admittedly, the confusing array of contradictory teachings, all claiming to teach the truth of Scripture, plays a sad role in this neglect.

First century believers had one Christian truth that stood in vivid contrast with a wide array of pagan ideas that taught the mirror opposite worldview to Jesus. Our culture contains an almost endless array of diverse groups and ideas that claim the Bible and Jesus, leaving the inquiring believer confused and bewildered about which set of ideas and Biblical interpretations to believe. In our culture, the lines of demarcation have been confusingly blurred. One day the popular politician of the day will openly speak words of rejection and criticism against any form of conservative, Bible-based Christian faith, and the next day, faced with the latest crisis or catastrophe, that same politician will sing "God bless America" and ask his constituents to pray for our country. While this hypocritical rhetoric seems to play well with superficial citizens, I have to wonder. What does God think of such empty faith?

We need constantly to return to Scripture to keep the Biblical view of faith and of our obedience, including our baptism, fresh in our minds and clear in our purpose. Obedience that focuses on anyone or anything other than our Lord fails the Biblical test of the righteousness of faith.

William Gadsby's Hymnal, 1.709
(Published 1838)

The Lord that made both heaven and earth,
And was himself made man,
Lay in the womb, before his birth,
Contracted to a span.

Behold, from what beginnings small
Our great salvation rose;
The strength of God is owned by all;
But who his weakness knows?

Let not the strong the weak despise;
Their faith, though small, is true;
Though low they seem in others' eyes,
Their Saviour seemed so too.

Nor meanly of the tempted think;
For O what tongue can tell
How low the Lord of life must sink,
Before he vanquished hell?

As in the days of flesh he grew
In wisdom, stature, grace,
So in the soul that born anew,
He keeps a gradual pace.

No less almighty at his birth,
Than on his throne supreme;
His shoulders held up heaven and earth,
When Mary held up him.

- Thomas Hart

45
What Jeopardy?

And why stand we in jeopardy every hour? I protest by your rejoicing which I have in Christ Jesus our Lord, I die daily. If after the manner of men I have fought with beasts at Ephesus, what advantageth it me, if the dead rise not? let us eat and drink; for to morrow we die. Be not deceived: evil communications corrupt good manners. Awake to righteousness, and sin not; for some have not the knowledge of God: I speak this to your shame. (1 Corinthians 15:30–34)

These verses provide a lively example of context defining and explaining a verse. Our study verses raise the question of imminent jeopardy that threatened the Corinthians, contextually related to what immediately preceded these verses. If we interpret verse 29 as surrogate baptism, we are obligated to probe the potential jeopardy of the action. Surrogate baptism was supposedly practiced by one pagan religion in the Greek peninsula with no objection in the pagan or civil community. In fact, no logical jeopardy could reasonably fall upon anyone who refused to be baptized for another person who previously died. Most of those who read this piece, and the writer, do not believe in surrogate baptism. Have you or I encountered any kind of jeopardy recently because we do not believe in or practice surrogate baptism? None whatever.

The point of our study verses clearly associates some form of jeopardy with the right interpretation of verse 29. Paul even gives a personal example, his fight "...with beasts at Ephesus," likely being thrown in the arena with wild animals, something the Lord obviously delivered him from. Paul broadens the question. For their belief in Jesus as God's one and only Son and Savior, including His death and resurrection, Paul and other first century Christians faced constant "jeopardy" for their rejection of the endless array of pagan religions and false deities. It was the Christian belief in one and only one God and in Jesus and His resurrection that jeopardized these believers, and their belief in Him and in His resurrection was the basis for their baptism.

I die daily. In this comment, Paul reminds us of an often ignored reality of a true Biblical faith in the Lord Jesus Christ. Our faith is not all about us. It should be all about Him! When Jesus defined following Him, His primary criteria included two behaviors: 1) denying self; and 2) taking up one's personal cross. We must do both before we can truly follow Him.

To take up one's cross in first century Roman culture referred to the Roman practice of crucifixion as a primary means of capital punishment. The convicted criminal was traditionally required to carry the cross piece of his cross to the place of final crucifixion. We see the Romans imposing this odious task onto Jesus. Obviously, a professing believer does not literally die by crucifixion. However, the symbolism is undeniable. Self must die if we are to ever realize the power of God in our lives.

We do not practice self-denial and cross-bearing by promoting ourselves and denigrating anyone who dares to question or disagree with what we think. The Biblical attitude in correcting another believer is not brow-beating or insulting the other person. It rather requires us to approach the erring believer *"...in the spirit of meekness, considering thyself, lest thou also be tempted"* (Galatians 6:1-6). Only to the extent that self "dies" can we reach out to others in this godly spirit and help them if they indeed are in error.

The spirit of meekness and self-consideration means that we approach those with whom we disagree with the mindset that we might be the one who is wrong, so they might correct us rather than we correcting them. We reason with them; we do not browbeat or verbally abuse them. Christian dialogue is not an uncivilized contest whose winner is determined by who speaks the loudest or who is the most overbearing, more a pagan "might makes right" attitude than a Biblical attitude that functions on the foundation of words well seasoned with grace (Colossians 4:3-6).[1]

---

[1] In this lesson, Paul asks the Colossians to pray for him that he may be able to speak as he "...ought to speak." And he shortly follows this point with an

Much of contemporary Christianity strains to contradict or to ignore this fundamental premise of New Testament Christian conduct. While belief in the Biblical doctrines of grace sets a sound basis for "grace-speak and grace act," all too often even those who strongly profess to believe in Biblical grace ignore its ethical (moral) obligations to their personal behavior and interactions with other believers. And then they wonder why their words and actions do not evoke respect and imitation in the people around them.

The power of the gospel only appears when we practice the gospel in thought, word, and deed, not when we ignore its ethics toward others. We can find a "me-first" person anywhere, any day of the week. And most folks who have a reasonable sense of Biblical character are looking for someone different, more akin to self-denial and cross-bearing than to self-centeredness and a stronger penchant for imposing crosses on others than on bearing our own cross.

Both in Jesus' discipleship criteria and in this passage, the death process is marked as "daily," not as an occasional or a once in a lifetime event (Luke 9:23). Until dying to self becomes a habit in us, we have not attained the true "habit" of New Testament Christianity in practice.

Once many years ago I had preached on the habit of self-denial. After the service, I happened to overhear some of the folks talking about the sermon. One person mentioned this specific point and then proudly told about an occasion several years earlier when he denied his wishes in a mundane issue in the church and went along with others rather than insisting on his preference. One such act does not earn "bragging rights." One such act does not establish a lifelong habit, and this dying daily demands just such a constant habit of thinking and acting.

I fear that all too many contemporary professing Christians embrace a similar attitude. As a pastor, I have often heard people respond to various New Testament commanded behaviors with

---

exhortation to the Colossians to strive to ensure that they speak words accompanied by grace, grace toward the brother or sister with whom they speak. In this context, grace is not a trait that we practice toward ourselves, but rather something that we are commanded to practice toward others when we engage them in dialogue.

"Well, this is just the way I am, and you can either take me the way I am or forget it," when the way the person is does not remotely resemble the Biblical behavior. This self-serving attitude has become so commonplace that many pastors quietly whisper the effective outcome of the dominant attitude, "It is easier to ask forgiveness after the fact than to ask permission beforehand." The attitude seems to prevail; do whatever you wish to do, regardless of what Scripture teaches. If no one is upset or challenges you, you "get away with it." If anyone reacts or becomes upset, then pretend humility and ask their forgiveness. This attitude proudly ignores and contradicts the Biblical teaching that we here study, especially Biblical repentance and life changing reform.

The idea of dying *daily* confronts a reality that we need to regard seriously. Even if you and I today face down our self-indulgent carnality and keep it in check today, we'll awake with it revived and ready to do battle with us tomorrow. The dying process, the self-denial and bearing one's cross must occur constantly, not once in a lifetime or once every year or two.

And what does this in-your-face discipleship issue have to do with baptism "for the dead," for the Jesus who died, but who now lives? Based on Paul's framing the lesson, it apparently has everything to do with baptism. If we acknowledge our commitment to the Lord Jesus as Scripture requires, self-promotion must be "killed." In fact, it must be killed over and over again, daily.

I protest by your rejoicing which I have in Christ Jesus our Lord.... Paul did not commit a word stumble here. He wrote his point with careful precision. While each of us must accept personal responsibility for our choices and conduct, the true Christian lifestyle demands a comprehensive community relationship. When the Corinthians rejoiced, Paul rejoiced. When they suffered for their faith, Paul suffered with them. In neither situation did Paul stand on the sidelines and observe the Corinthians. He was intimately and personally involved and intertwined with them in their faith.

Recently our church has suffered several difficulties. One of our members lost his mother and father-in-law in one week. He works with a man whose young adult son was killed in a biking accident.

Another person suffered in remembrance that her mother passed away a year ago, and she struggled with the reminder of grief. A young mother is soon to deliver her second child; we should hold her and her family up in prayer for deliverance and kind, wise grace as they raise their children. Several of our folks all contracted the latest raging respiratory virus at the same time. As I pondered our many difficulties, I felt a compelling and abiding need to pray for these folks and to ask the church to jointly pray for them as well. This is part of the Biblical sense of community that characterizes a godly New Testament culture in a church.

We must not forget that the faithful Church of Ephesus, one of the few churches to whom Paul wrote a recorded New Testament letter with no rebukes included, though sound and strong in her doctrinal posture, faced the Lord's solemn warning just a few short years later because she had left her "first love," the Lord Himself. We may attain near impeccable doctrinal soundness, but if we fail to show a Biblical attitude toward our brothers and sisters, showing them the love and grace that the Lord showed to us, we are no different from that Ephesian Church.

In his first letter, John repeatedly makes the point. Our attitude toward our brothers and sisters cannot be contradictory to our attitude toward the Lord. We can't claim to love the Lord while showing spite and disregard or even contempt toward our brothers and sisters in Christ.

Paul's point is powerful and convicting. Though we live in a culture that does not condone outright persecution of Christians, our culture is rapidly growing hostile toward anyone who takes the Bible at all literally and faithfully holds to traditional Christian values. The jeopardy a believer faces for living out his baptism commitment to the Lord Jesus Christ, especially His death and resurrection which makes Him our living God and Savior, not our remote philosophy, may be closer to our lives than we think. If that jeopardy falls upon us, will we face it, or will we compromise our faith? That, my friends, drives us to the heart of Paul's question.

46
Christian Ethics Based on the Resurrection

If after the manner of men I have fought with beasts at Ephesus, what advantageth it me, if the dead rise not? let us eat and drink; for to morrow we die. Be not deceived: evil communications corrupt good manners. Awake to righteousness, and sin not; for some have not the knowledge of God: I speak this to your shame. (1 Corinthians 15:32–34)

When Paul made the point, "If in this life only..." in 1 Corinthians 15:29, he affirmed that our belief in the resurrection, specifically in Jesus' resurrection, is a crucial foundation for our Christian ethic in its entirety. Biblical belief in the resurrection is not simply about "pie in the sky bye and bye," but it forms the energizing power of our whole Christian outlook and conduct. Repeatedly in 1 Corinthians 15, Paul underscores this point, as in our study verses.

As Paul emphasizes the present impact of belief in the resurrection on the way he lived, he also underscored the truth of a literal, bodily resurrection, not some kind of mystical Gnostic "spiritual resurrection." Paul's spirit faced no danger from beasts at Ephesus. While our Christian ethic begins within, it must express itself through our actions, actions that integrally involve the physical body. If the dead do not rise, why would Paul be willing to expose himself, specifically his physical body, to the mortal danger of wild beasts in the arena? As a Roman citizen, he could readily have avoided the arena, as he later avoided an unjust trial when he appealed to Caesar (Acts 25:11). If there is no literal, physical, bodily resurrection, by all means protect your physical body. In fact, if there is no literal bodily resurrection, why not indulge the physical body? Eat and drink for tomorrow you die.

Be not deceived: evil communications corrupt good manners. The simplest and most literal interpretation of this statement challenges us with a truth that we often ignore. Inevitably, we pick up attitudes and habits from the people with whom we associate. Spend much time with an "ill-mannered" person, and you will slowly desensitize yourself to that person's bad habits, picking them up yourself. You can see this principle at work in families, in the work place, and in churches. Let me give just one example.

The internet gives Christian people multiple opportunities to enrich themselves by accessing recorded sermons from preachers across a broad scope of geography and time. We can download a sermon from a powerful preacher, past or present, and hear him preach in his own voice, far more communicative than reading a transcription of the same sermon. I have relished hearing several sermons by Martin Lloyd-Jones, the famous British preacher who inspired his London congregation during the fierce German bombings of World War II.

The same internet that blesses holds equal potential for harm. We may just as easily download and listen to sermons from self-serving preachers who are frighteningly adept at smooth talk, deceiving their hearers into believing the worst of errors. Paul warns us that the deceiver skillfully knows how to cover his error with convincing words and attitudes (Romans 16:17-18). Amazingly, the naïve listener will pick up words, phrases, and attitudes from the deceitful teacher, and those ideas will slowly erode both sound faith and gracious, godly conduct, "good manners." A discerning person may often know who someone has been listening to by taking note of that person's attitude and words, especially little catch phrases that the unfaithful teacher uses repeatedly. These catch phrases are carefully framed to sound really good, but, upon examination, they appeal to our emotions and our good intentions far more than to Biblical soundness.

We cannot avoid this link between the communications to which we expose our minds and the manners, attitudes and actions, that we practice. Jesus warned against this problem even more sternly than Paul. He taught the disciples to take care not only what they hear (meaning that you simply avoid hearing some men whose teachings

"...corrupt good manners"), but also to take heed how they hear (be mindful and obedient hearers of good things, not forgetful hearers).[1]

Awake to righteousness, and sin not; for some have not the knowledge of God. Paul's words follow in logical sequence to the points made. The naïve or undiscerning hearer cannot awake to righteousness, for he/she has accepted ideas as true that contradict God's righteousness. What we believe as true has a powerful impact on our attitudes and conduct. By the basic meaning of the word, belief means that we accept as true, as fact, certain things, and that we act on our acceptance of what we have accepted as true. Thus our whole idea of belief builds on our presumption of knowledge.

Belief and ignorance are antithetical. Anyone who thinks of himself as a believer so thinks based on what he believes to know. He truly views that information as factual, and he sincerely holds it to be true. However, our sense of knowledge itself can be deceitful. What if we accept something as true that is false? Scripture deals with knowledge fully as much as with belief. Given that the two principles are corollaries, this must be the case.

1. *And if any man think that he knoweth any thing, he knoweth nothing yet as he ought to know* (1 Corinthians 8:2). Paul wrote these words in the context of correcting the confusion in the Church at Corinth regarding meat offered to idols. Given the tension between knowing and not knowing, it is no surprise that Paul chose two different Greek words for "know" in this verse. The first word emphasizes seeing, perhaps one's personal belief that he sees this idea clearly. The second word emphasizes a full or thorough knowledge. Think. As soon as anyone thinks that he has a subject really mastered, he ceases trying to learn more about it. He thinks he already knows everything. In matters spiritual, this attitude reveals a self-centered smugness that deceives the person with pride. He refuses to hear what other people think. Why not? He thinks he already knows more than they or anyone else. Paul's point is clear and powerful. As soon as we cover our ideas and beliefs in the wardrobe of pride and

---

[1] Luke 8:18 – the "how"; Mark 4:24 – the "what"

smugness that we have mastered the idea, we factually fall into unbelief and ignorance. The word translated "disciple" in the New Testament primarily means a "learner" or a "student." This word simplifies Paul's point. As soon as we think we have graduated, we cease to learn, and therefore we cease to be a true disciple, a learner or student of Jesus and of the gospel. And Paul's point becomes obvious. In fact, as we think ourselves to be experts, masters of the subject, we reduce ourselves to hopeless ignorance of it.

2. *Ever learning, and never able to come to the knowledge of the truth* (2 Timothy 3:7). We need to consider this verse in light of the full chapter in which it appears. Paul begins the chapter with a warning about perilous times and perilous people who exploit the times and people for their personal gain. In Christian circles, these folks know all the right words and feigned attitudes to appear humble and righteous, but watch them over time. Notice, as well, Paul's contrast in the chapter. Beginning with verse 10 ("But thou hast fully known..."), he draws a sharp contrast between these people and his faithful and godly example of self-denial and service to others. Often folks in this category of ever learning--never knowing the truth memorize a lot of Scriptures and appear to know much. They confuse the reliable truth of Scripture with their personal interpretation of Scripture, so that their interpretation becomes, to them, equal to Scripture itself. In this attitude, they magnify their mind and private interpretation to the elevated and authoritative posture of Scripture itself. In fact, this is a major reason they shall never come to rightly know the truth. After setting forth his personal example, Paul concludes the lesson with one of Scripture's most powerful appeals to Scripture itself as our source of knowledge, not to our individual private interpretation, but to Scripture itself.

Knowledge of God in this context likely refers to the knowledge of God that we gain when we wholly rely on Scripture, not Scripture plus our private interpretations, our inflated confidence in our private interpretation, or any other secondary and fickle source of information, for our knowledge of truth and of the God of truth. Paul's exhortation, "Awake to righteousness and sin not..." is directly linked to this lack of right knowledge of God. When folks lose their way and their reliance on Scripture alone, they typically rely increasingly on one rationalization after another to justify their pretense of knowledge.

I recall a friend telling me about a Bible discussion he had years ago with a man on a given text and topic. During the conversation, the man specifically stated that at times we must ignore the actual text of Scripture to arrive at its meaning. How can we ignore the language of Scripture and thereby arrive at its truth? Bizarre indeed. In this case, the man magnified his private ideas and rationalized interpretation above the actual content of Scripture.

I speak this to your shame. Paul is not dealing with unregenerate sinners, but with confused believers who do not know the truth. If Paul's words shamed the Corinthians, there were some folks in the Corinthian Church who had this problem. Occasionally folks who have a narrow view of God's grace will use thoughts such as this in Scripture to give supposed support for their idea that only people who believe as they believe and act as they think a believer should act are "really born again." If anyone wrests the passage in this way, they need to read Paul's inspired description of the Corinthians in the opening verses of the book. Where in that description do we find any grounds whatever for his letter being addressed to unregenerate people? It isn't there at all.

In instructive contrast to the pride-filled and confused ideas of those whom Paul here shames, let us take good heed to Paul's words, *"Awake to righteousness and sin not."* As long as we live in this world, we need the constant correction and instruction of Scripture. We need to ever learn and come to right knowledge. If we follow Scripture's clear and consistent teaching, we learn that service to others, not promotion of ourselves and our ideas, should occupy every moment and every ounce of energy that we have. Pastors often hear members in various settings ponder or question what their "job" is, what they should be doing to serve the Lord. They need to open their eyes and look around. Is there a believer anywhere in your personal "world" who is struggling with a problem, who may be discouraged or weighed down with a heavy burden? That person and his burden is your divine job assignment. What can you do to give them encouragement and help in their life? Do it and keep on doing it. You just might thereby accomplish both a personal awakening to righteousness and a personal avoidance of sin in your life.

47
How are the Dead Raised Up?

But some man will say, How are the dead raised up? and with what body do they come? Thou fool, that which thou sowest is not quickened, except it die: And that which thou sowest, thou sowest not that body that shall be, but bare grain, it may chance of wheat, or of some other grain: But God giveth it a body as it hath pleased him, and to every seed his own body. All flesh is not the same flesh: but there is one kind of flesh of men, another flesh of beasts, another of fishes, and another of birds. There are also celestial bodies, and bodies terrestrial: but the glory of the celestial is one, and the glory of the terrestrial is another. There is one glory of the sun, and another glory of the moon, and another glory of the stars: for one star differeth from another star in glory. (1 Corinthians 15:35–41)

When someone asks a question, I often not only listen to the question, but I also try to understand why he asked the question. Did he ask for information? For clarification of his thoughts? Or to use my answer to engage in a debate that he would use to promote his idea? The question that Paul here answers from "some man" reveals unbelief in the resurrection. If we miss that point in the question, we can't possibly miss it in Paul's answer. New Testament writers seldom refer to any one as a fool, but Paul uses the term to address this man and his unbelieving question.

A common belief of our day regarding the resurrection holds that at death God fabricates a "heavenly" body that our soul inhabits. Does the soul inhabit this fabricated body permanently or only until the Second Coming? Opinions are not clear or consistent among those who believe this idea. I have observed that a number of those who hold this idea wholly reject the idea of a literal resurrection of the body in which we lived during this life. Advocates of the idea will cite the passage before us or a few other passages, and impose a wrested (twisted out of joint and out of context) interpretation onto it.

If we isolated these verses from their context, we might think these people have some ground for their belief. However, when we examine the context, in this case the verses following, we learn that Paul emphasized that the same body that is "sown" in death is "raised" in power. Paul's consistent reference to "it" in verses 42-44 utterly rejects the idea of a fabricated body. That same body that is sown and that returns to the earth after death is the body that God shall raise. If you were to examine the full DNA of the body that died and the body that shall be raised, you'd discover that they would be the same, not different. The scientific basis is obviously anachronistic, but it does make the point that Paul makes. Otherwise Paul's use of "it" to refer both to the corrupt body that is sown in death and to the body that is raised incorruptible and in power would be meaningless. Whatever Paul intended by the "it" that is sown in death is the same thing that he intended by the "it" that is raised in power.

With our finite minds, we cannot fully understand how a literal resurrection is possible, but then that same finite mind cannot understand how God could create the universe out of nothing (Hebrews 11:3). Faith, not human intellect, must work for us to believe either truth. When Jesus refuted the Sadducees who did not believe at all in the resurrection or in life after death, He pointed out that their unbelief was caused by two major flaws in their thinking. They did not know the power of God, and they did not know the Scriptures. I suggest that rejection of a literal bodily resurrection in our time is anchored in the same two factors.

No surprise, throughout First Corinthians 15, Paul follows Jesus' method of proving the resurrection by appealing to the power of God and to Scripture. As you read this chapter, take special notice of Paul's references to "according to the scriptures" or "as it is written" or similar words. In our study verses, he reminds us of God's power, so Paul wisely and rightly followed Jesus' example to prove the truth of the resurrection.

Rather than teaching the idea of a fabricated body in these verses, given the contextual emphasis on that same "it" that is sown being the very same "it" that God raises, what do we make of these verses? I suggest that Paul is addressing the same issue that caused both the ancient Sadducees and modern unbelievers in the resurrection to reject it, their ignorance of the power of God and the teaching of Scripture. From a tiny seed that a farmer plants in his field to the sun and the heavenly bodies that God planted in space, all of creation bears witness to the power of God, power quite sufficient to raise the dead and so change that dead body that He raised as to be wholly at home and rejoicing in God for eternity.

In assessing the character of those in the Corinthian Church who prompted Paul's intense analysis, A. T. Robertson, *Word Pictures in the New Testament*, observes that these people likely took on an air of prideful acuteness in their unbelieving questions. However, as Robertson points out, one's personal claim of intelligence does not make one intelligent. Jesus didn't tell the Sadducees that they lacked intelligence, but that they lacked knowledge of the power of God and of the Scriptures.

Paul reminds us that God who shall raise the dead is the same God who created the whole material universe. If He can form something out of nothing, He has the power to raise the dead. And if in that creation He can form such incredible miracles of function and harmony, from the miracle of sub-microscopic diversity to massive heavenly bodies separated by "light years" of distance, why should we question, "How are the dead raised up?" If God created various parts of His creation to manifest different degrees of glory, He shall have no problem raising a body that died in corruption to the glory of incorruption. God didn't create a "cookie cutter" mass production one among many universe. He created one and only one unique universe that uniquely declares His glory (Psalm 19:1).

Occasionally professing and well-meaning Christians will abandon Scripture and indulge their minds in fanciful philosophical conjecture. One such venture that I've observed over the years has to do with creation, especially as this creation fell under the curse of sin. Supposedly, prior to creation, God "imagined" every possible universe that He could create and every possible outcome that He could bring about, and then He chose to create this universe. I've asked for even one Scripture to support this idea of cosmic imagination, but I've never received one. God is not man. He need not imagine endless potentials before choosing one.

> *But he is in one mind, and who can turn him? and what his soul desireth, even that he doeth.* (Job 23:13)

At its heart, this idea of God imagining multiple universes encroaches on the Biblical truth of God's immutability. I find nothing in Scripture, not a drop of Biblical ink, regarding God imagining multiple universes, but I find an abundance of testimony in Scripture regarding God's immutability. When we examine the opening verse of the Bible, we do not read about God stroking His cosmic beard, pondering what He might do, even imagining each possible option, and then deciding to create this universe instead of another. "In the beginning God...." In this verse, as in all other Biblical passages, God is decisive and immutable. For God to pursue this imaginative concept, we must embrace the idea that God didn't know what He intended to do, and that over time He pondered His options and their outcomes. At the least, the idea reduces God to a rather indecisive being. This is not the image of God that we find revealed in Scripture.

God's natural creation declares His glory (Psalm 19:1-6). Likewise, His spiritual creation declares His glory, and shall do so through endless eternity (Ephesians 3:20-21).

If we accept the teaching of Scripture, God's one and only limitation has to do with His moral character. He cannot lie (Titus 1:2). He cannot deny Himself (2 Timothy 2:13). When Paul faced a group that was divided on this question of the resurrection, some believing and some denying, he framed his question on the premise of God's power.

> *Why should it be thought a think incredible with you, that God should raise the dead?* (Acts 26:8)

During Jesus' public ministry, the proud, self-righteous Pharisees stand out as His most fierce critics. When we move to Acts and see the apostles and early preachers consistently preaching Jesus and the resurrection, the Sadducees join the fierce opposition. The weight and the source of opposition to what these men taught bears convincing evidence to the truth that they proclaimed, the same truth that we should preach today, fully knowing that those who do not believe that truth shall likewise oppose.

A simple final point. Psalm 19:1 reminds us that the natural creation declares God's glory. The glory of which Paul writes in our study passage is no less a reference to the Lord's glory than Psalm 19:1. Sadly, the corruptions of thinking in contemporary ideas about the Second Coming often focus far more on man than on God. You frequently hear or read about ideas that give more glory to man than to God. A popular advocate of this idea a few years ago in a radio sermon cited the passage about the lion lying down with the lamb and asserted that he would have his personal pet lion in heaven. Others in this camp of thought strive to earn jewels to decorate their personal crown of glory in heaven. According to Scripture's record, the redeemed saints in heaven will not promote their personal crown. Quite the opposite, whatever crown they may have shall be cast at the feet of their Lord and Redeemer, and they shall praise Him alone for their redemption.

Thou art worthy, O Lord, to receive glory and honour and power: for thou hast created all things, and for thy pleasure they are and were created. (Revelation 4:10-11)

The idea or earning stars in a personal crown of glory by good works utterly corrupts the Biblical model of obedience out of love for the Lord and devotion to His glory.

48
Only One "It"

So also is the resurrection of the dead. It is sown in corruption; it is raised in incorruption: It is sown in dishonour; it is raised in glory: it is sown in weakness; it is raised in power: It is sown a natural body; it is raised a spiritual body. There is a natural body, and there is a spiritual body. And so it is written, The first man Adam was made a living soul; the last Adam was made a quickening spirit. Howbeit that was not first which is spiritual, but that which is natural; and afterward that which is spiritual. The first man is of the earth, earthy: the second man is the Lord from heaven. As is the earthy, such are they also that are earthy: and as is the heavenly, such are they also that are heavenly. And as we have borne the image of the earthy, we shall also bear the image of the heavenly. (1 Corinthians 15:42–49)

In most extended Bible themes, you can find a few brief verses that capture the essential idea in simple terms. In Biblical interpretation studies, the term "the perspicuity of Scripture" is often used to refer to this idea. The more important an idea is the more frequently **and clearly** it appears in Scripture. We've studied several verses in our examination of 1 Corinthians 15 that required some careful and thorough examination. In the verses before us, we see the resurrection set forth as simply as possible for human words and minds. If we follow the simplest grammatical and contextual rules, we must conclude that Paul was referring to one and only one "it" in these verses. The same "it" that is "sown" is the "it" that is raised. Let's start at the beginning.

So also is the resurrection of the dead. The word translated "dead" in this sentence is quite consistent in its New Testament meaning. Consider.

1. The English spelling of the Greek word translated "dead" is *nekrós*. Several years ago as Sandra's mother was approaching death, we knew that she was slipping quickly, but we did not have any sense of the situation beyond our observations. Then we met the hospice nurse in the hallway and talked with her. She told Sandra that the process of "necrosis" had started and that her passing was imminent. The word she used is derived from this Greek word. It quite specifically refers to death, in Scripture either to the death of the body or to dead bodies.

2. *Woe unto you, scribes and Pharisees, hypocrites! for ye are like unto whited sepulchres, which indeed appear beautiful outward, but are within full of **dead** men's bones, and of all uncleanness* (Matthew 23:27; emphasis on the word translated from this Greek word).

3. *For as the body without the spirit is dead, so faith without works is dead also* (James 2:26). In this verse both appearances of "dead" are translated from this word.

There can be no reasonable argument made that this word refers to anything other than a literal human body that has died. Further, the word translated "resurrection" in this verse and context literally means to "stand up again," just as Lazarus stood up alive after Jesus raised him, restored life to his dead body. The word is further qualified by "to restore to life again." Simply stated, Paul is not teaching any form of Gnostic or other mystical idea that denies the literal resurrection of the same body in which we live today, which shall die at some time in the future. Further, praise the Lord, He shall raise that very same body and change it so that it shall never again sin, be sick, suffer pain, or die, but it shall be wholly glorified so as to live eternally and praise God for redemption.

It is sown in corruption; it is raised in incorruption. At death, the body is in some way or another buried in the ground, as a seed that a farmer sows in the field and covers with a light covering of soil. But that same body that is planted in its grave shall be raised by the power of God according to the Scriptures (to borrow the precise reasoning that Jesus used against the Sadducees). When He raises it, its form shall not be a return to the form in which it lived, weak, frail, subject to disease, suffering, sin, and death. All of these traits remind us of the word that Paul used to describe our body in death, "corruption." In vivid contrast, the Lord shall raise that same "it" that died in corruption, but when it appears in resurrection, it shall have undergone a miraculous transformation. It shall then be "incorrupt" and "incorruptible." It shall be immune from all the tentacles of corruption that characterized it in this life.

It is sown in dishonour; it is raised in glory. Notice the two contrasting words that Paul uses to identify the two opposite states of the body. When it dies, it is marked by dishonor. In itself and its sinful condition and its death, there is no honor. The person who lived in that body may be honored by family, friends, and even by godly people, but their honor cannot alter what happened in its end. The person died, marking the dishonor of the fallen body by sin. But when the Lord raises that body, all of its former dishonor will have vanished. It no longer exists! The body comes out of death in glory.

The word translated "glory" in this verse specifically refers to glory to the Lord. We sing a delightful hymn, "Praise God from whom all blessings flow." Notice the title of that hymn, "Doxology." The Greek word translated "glory" in this verse is *doxa* from which we derive our English word "doxology." The same body that died in dishonor shall be raised in a form that uniquely and wholly is fitted to praise God for eternity.

Consider just one reflection from Scripture of the redeemed in glory. "*And they sung a new song, saying, Thou art worthy to take the book, and to open the seals thereof: for thou wast slain, and hast redeemed us to God by thy blood out of every kindred, and tongue, and people, and nation*" (Revelation 5:9). They shall not be raised to glorify themselves or to parade their own crowns of glory, but rather to praise their God and Savior for their redemption.

... it is sown in weakness; it is raised in power. One of the greatest examples of weakness imaginable for our physical body is death itself. As we age, various parts or systems of our body slowly

deteriorate. They grow weaker than they were in our youth. Eventually one of those parts or systems will break, producing sudden death, or the whole body will slowly weaken till it can no longer support our life. Whether we die suddenly or slowly, death proclaims that weakness. Ah, but God shall raise that body that was characterized by weakness in great power. Our resurrection body state shall not be subject to deterioration or weakness. We shall not be subject to death or system failures in our resurrected body. We see and assess power based on what a person does. Scripture never gives us a detailed view of what heaven shall be after the resurrection, or before it for that matter, but Scripture does give us glimpses into that world of praise and glory to God. Nothing in Scripture's teaching gives any indication of weakness in that world of glory.

Today we struggle against our physical and spiritual weakness. Paul described his own such struggle.

> *I find then a law, that, when I would do good, evil is present with me.* (Romans 7:21)

Paul uses the term "law" to describe a principle that explains his present struggle, indeed, his present weakness. When he desired to do good, his performance of that good was hindered by the presence of evil within.

In this context, Paul indicates that he often does what he does not desire to do and does not approve, and he often fails to do what he deeply desires to do. These words describe the struggle of every regenerate (born again) child of grace. We live with weakness that shall surely end in death unless the Lord returns prior to our death. But Scripture's message reminds us. When our body rises at the Second Coming, all such weakness shall be truly "left behind," and we shall arise in God's power to fully praise Him for eternity.

It is sown a natural body; it is raised a spiritual body. Here Paul refers to the dominant principle that animates the physical body. We may have reason to think of this point more fully in later verses. We presently possess a natural body that is animated by our present nature. And since we presently possess both our old sinful nature and our new spiritual nature, we live in the conflict mentioned above. Both of these "natures" struggle to drive our use of our body, our conduct. At death, the spirit returns to the Lord who gave it. It does not cease to exist. Nor does it slip into an unconscious state of "soul sleep." After their deaths, both Lazarus and the rich man appear in Jesus' teaching as conscious and active (Luke 16:20-31). Our spiritual "nature" shall continue with the Lord, not die with the body.

When the resurrection occurs, our body shall be raised, no longer struggling with conflict and weakness. We shall have no fallen, sinful nature in heaven. Our spiritual nature shall fully govern our physical body so that we shall praise the Lord for endless eternity and without the conflict and weakness that not antagonizes us.

And as we have borne the image of the earthy, we shall also bear the image of the heavenly. In these verses Paul refers to the "first Adam" and the "last Adam." The first "Adam" is the first man whom the Lord created from dust, the man we see in Genesis. The "last Adam" is the Lord Jesus Christ. Both Adam and Jesus appear in Scripture as representative heads of their offspring. Despite being born of God and possessing that spiritual nature, we presently, in our physical body, continue to bear the image of that first Adam, including sin. In the resurrection, we shall drop that broken sinful image, and we shall then, in our resurrection body, bear the image of our Lord Jesus Christ.

The words of an old hymn delightfully capture Scripture's teaching regarding our glorious existence in glory with the Lord.

His own soft hand shall wipe the tear
From sorrow's weeping eye.
And pains and groans and griefs and fears
And death itself shall die.

Index of Scriptures Examined

Chapter 1: Acts 17:18ff

Ch. 2: 2 Thessalonians 2:5-12

Ch. 3: Job 19:23-27

Ch. 4: Genesis 25:8-9

Ch. 5: Psalm 16:10

Ch. 6: Isaiah 25:8

Ch. 7: Isaiah 26:19

Ch. 8: 2 Peter 3:11-12

Ch. 9: Psalm 49:15

Ch. 10: John 11:41-43

Ch. 11: Matthew 22:23-33

Ch. 12: Luke 23:39-43

Ch. 13: Luke 24:36-43

Ch. 14: John 5:28-29

Ch. 15: Acts 24:14-15

Ch. 16: Matthew 25:31-46

Ch. 17: Matthew 25:46

Ch. 18: John 6:37-39

Ch. 19: John 11:4-15

Ch. 20: John 11:20-27

Ch. 21: John 11:39-44

Ch. 22: John 11:44-48

Ch. 23: John 11:47-54

Ch. 24: John 14:1-4

Chapter 25: John 14:1-4

Ch. 26: John 20:19-20, 27

Ch. 27: Acts 1:6-11

Ch. 28: Acts 1:6-11

Ch. 29: Acts 2:22-24

Ch. 30: Acts 2:29-32

Ch. 31: Acts 13:29-33

Ch. 32: Acts 24:14-15

Ch. 33: Romans 8:11

Ch. 34: Romans 8:12-14

Ch. 35: Romans 8:16-18

Ch. 36: Romans 8:18-23

Ch. 37: Romans 8:24-25

Ch. 38: Romans 8:28-34

Ch. 39: 1 Corinthians 11:26

Ch. 40: 1 Corinthians 15:1-11

Ch. 41: 1 Corinthians 15:12-19

Ch. 42: 1 Corinthians 15:20-23

Ch. 43: 1 Corinthians 15:24-28

Ch. 44: 1 Corinthians 15:29

Ch. 45: 1 Corinthians 15:30-34

Ch. 46: 1 Corinthians 15:32-34

Ch. 47: 1 Corinthians 15:35-41

Ch. 48: 1 Corinthians 15:42-49

www.ingramcontent.com/pod-product-compliance
Lightning Source LLC
Chambersburg PA
CBHW031237090426
42742CB00007B/235